Python® Programming for the Absolute Beginner, Third Edition

Michael Dawson

Course Technology PTR
A part of Cengage Learning

Australia • Brazil • Canada • Mexico • Singapore • United Kingdom • United States

Python® Programming for the Absolute Beginner, **Third Edition**
Michael Dawson

Publisher and General Manager, Course Technology PTR: Stacy L. Hiquet

Associate Director of Marketing: Sarah Panella

Manager of Editorial Services: Heather Talbot

Marketing Manager: Mark Hughes

Acquisitions Editor: Mitzi Koontz

Project Editor: Jenny Davidson

Technical Reviewer: Robert Hoag

Interior Layout Tech: Value Chain International

Cover Designer: Mike Tanamachi

Indexer: BIM Indexing & Proofreading Services

Proofreader: Heather Urschel

For product information and technology assistance, contact us at **Cengage Customer & Sales Support, 1-800-354-9706 or support.cengage.com.**

For permission to use material from this text or product, submit all requests online at **www.copyright.com.**

Python is a registered trademark of the Python Software Foundation.

All other trademarks are the property of their respective owners.

All images © Cengage Learning unless otherwise noted.

Library of Congress Control Number: 2009933304

ISBN-13: 978-1-4354-5500-9
ISBN-10: 1-4354-5500-2

Cengage
200 Pier 4 Boulevard
Boston, MA 02210
USA

Cengage is a leading provider of customized learning solutions with employees residing in nearly 40 differe nt countries and sales in more than 125 countries around the world. Find your local representative at: **www.cengage.com.**

To learn more about Cengage platforms and services, register or access your online learning solution, or purchase materials for your course, visit **www.cengage.com.**

To my parents, who have read everything I've ever written.

ACKNOWLEDGMENTS

Writing a book is like giving birth—and I have the stretch marks of the brain to prove it. So I want to thank all the people who helped me bring my little bundle of joy into this world.

Thanks to Jenny Davidson for pulling double duty as both project editor and copyeditor. I appreciated your hard word and attention to detail.

Thanks to Robert Hoag for his technical editing skills. (Thanks for your non-technical suggestions and good humor too.)

I also want to thank Pete Shinners, original author of Pygame, and all the folks who contributed to LiveWires. Because of all of you, writing multimedia programs (especially games!) is now within reach of a new Python programmer.

Last, but certainly not least, I want to thank Matt for his audio expertise, Chris for his musical talents, and Dave for wearing a chef's hat.

ABOUT THE AUTHOR

Michael Dawson has worked as both a programmer and a computer game designer and producer. In addition to real-world game industry experience, Mike earned his bachelor's degree in Computer Science from the University of Southern California. Currently, he teaches game programming in the Game Production Department of the Los Angeles Film School. Mike has also taught game programming to students through UCLA Extension and The Digital Media Academy at Stanford. He's the author of three other books: *Beginning C++ through Game Programming*, *Guide to Programming with Python*, and *C++ Projects: Programming with Text-Based Games*. You can visit his website at www.programgames.com to learn more or to get support for any of his books.

TABLE OF CONTENTS

Chapter 4   FOR LOOPS, STRINGS, AND TUPLES: THE WORD JUMBLE GAME.. 87

Chapter 5   LISTS AND DICTIONARIES: THE HANGMAN GAME 121

Chapter 7   FILES AND EXCEPTIONS: THE TRIVIA CHALLENGE GAME 189

Chapter 9   OBJECT-ORIENTED PROGRAMMING: THE BLACKJACK GAME 247

Chapter 10   GUI Development: The Mad Lib Program **285**

Chapter 12 SOUND, ANIMATION, AND PROGRAM DEVELOPMENT: THE ASTROCRASH GAME 361

INTRODUCTION

Staring back at me on the screen was an image I recognized: a face—my face. Grainy and pixelated, it was still me. I watched with detached curiosity as my expression twisted and contorted beyond human limits until finally, an alien embryo burst from my head. A voice behind me said, "You wanna see it again?"

No, this wasn't some horrible dream, it was my job. I worked at a company producing and designing computer games. I also got to "star" in our first release, an adventure game where the player clicks me around the screen. And if the player fails to solve the game in time... well, I think you know how that turns out. I've also worked as a programmer for a major Internet services company, traveling to sites around the country. And while those two lines of work may seem quite different, the basic skills necessary to succeed in each started to take shape while I wrote simple games on my home computer as a kid.

The goal of this book is to teach you the Python programming language, learning to program the same way I did: by creating simple games. There's something more exciting about learning to program by writing software that's fun. And even though the examples are entertaining, you'll still see some serious programming. I cover all of the fundamental topics you'd expect from an introductory text and then some. In addition, I point out concepts and techniques that you can apply to more mainstream projects.

If you're new to programming, you've made the right choice. Python is the perfect beginners' language. It has a clear and simple syntax that will get you writing useful programs in short order. Python even has an interactive mode, which offers immediate feedback, allowing you to test out new ideas almost instantly.

If you've done some programming before, you've still made the right choice. Python has all the power and flexibility you'd expect from a modern, object-oriented programming language. But even with all of its power, you may be surprised how quickly you can build programs. In fact, ideas translate so quickly to the computer, Python has been called "programming at the speed of thought."

Like any good book, this one starts at the beginning. The first thing I cover is installing Python under Windows. Then, I move through concepts, one step at a time, by writing small programs to demonstrate each step. By the end of the book, I'll have covered such fancy-sounding topics as data structures, file handling, exceptions, object-oriented design, and GUI and multimedia programming. I also hope to show you how to design as well as program. You'll learn how to organize your work, break problems down into manageable chunks, and refine your code. You'll be challenged at times, but never overwhelmed. Most of all, you'll have fun while learning. And in the process, you'll create some small, but cool computer games.

All of the code for the programs presented in this book, along with necessary supporting files, can be downloaded from the companion website (www.courseptr.com/downloads). The website also includes installers for the software you'll need to run the programs. You can find a more detailed description of what's available on the website in Appendix A, "The Companion Website."

Throughout the journey, I'll offer a few signposts to highlight important concepts.

 These are good ideas that experienced programmers like to pass on.

 There are a few areas where it's easy to make a mistake. I'll point them out.

 These will suggest techniques and shortcuts that will make your life as a programmer easier.

IN THE REAL WORLD

As you examine the games in this book, I'll show you how the concepts are used for purposes beyond game development.

CHALLENGES

At the end of each chapter, I'll suggest some programs that you can write with the skills you've learned.

C H A P T E R

GETTING STARTED: THE GAME OVER PROGRAM

Programming basically is getting your computer to do stuff. This is not the most technical definition, but it's a pretty accurate one. By learning Python, you'll be able to create a program, whether it's a simple game, a small utility, or a business product with a full-featured graphical user interface (GUI). It'll be all yours, something you made, and it will do just what you told it to. Programming is part science, part art, and one great adventure. This chapter starts you on your Python programming journey. In it, you'll learn:

- What Python is and what's so great about it
- How to install Python on your computer
- How to print text to the screen
- What comments are and how to use them
- How to use Python's integrated development environment to write, edit, run, and save your programs

EXAMINING THE GAME OVER PROGRAM

The chapter project, Game Over, displays the two most infamous words in computer gaming: "Game Over." Figure 1.1 shows the program in action.

FIGURE 1.1

The all-too familiar words from a computer game.

Figure 1.1 shows what's called a *console window,* a window that can display only text. Though not as nice as windows in a Graphical User Interface (GUI), console applications are easier to write and a good place for the beginning programmer to start.

The Game Over program is pretty simple; in fact, it's one of the simplest Python programs you can write. That's the reason it's presented in this chapter. By completing such a modest program, you cover all the setup work required to start programming in Python, such as installing the language on your system. You also work through the entire process of writing, saving, and running a program. Once you finish all of this groundwork, you'll be ready to tackle larger programs with some real meat to them.

IN THE REAL WORLD

The Game Over program is really just a variation of the traditional Hello World program, which displays the words "Hello World" on the screen. The Hello World program is often the first program a beginner writes in order to dip his or her toe in a new language. It's such a common first program that Hello World is an understood term in programming.

INTRODUCING PYTHON

Python is a powerful yet easy-to-use programming language developed by Guido van Rossum, first released in 1991. With Python, you can quickly write a small project. But Python also scales up nicely and can be used for mission-critical, commercial applications.

If you check out any Python documentation, you may notice an alarming number of references to spam, eggs, and the number 42. These references all pay homage to Monty Python, the English comedy troupe that inspired Python's name. Even though Guido van Rossum named Python after the group, the official mascot of the language has become the python snake. (Which is really for the best, since it would be pretty hard to fit six British comedians' faces on a program icon anyway.)

There are a lot of programming languages out there. What's so great about Python? Let me tell you.

Python Is Easy to Use

The major goal of any programming language is to bridge the gap between the programmer's brain and the computer. Most of the popular languages you've probably heard of, like Visual Basic, C#, and Java, are considered *high-level languages,* which means that they're closer to human language than machine language. And they are. But Python, with its clear and simple rules, is even closer to English. Creating Python programs is so straightforward that it's been called "programming at the speed of thought." Python's ease of use translates into productivity for professional programmers. Python programs are shorter and take less time to create than programs in many other popular languages.

Python Is Powerful

Python has all the power you'd expect from a modern programming language. By the end of this book, you'll be able to write programs that employ a GUI, process files, and use a variety of data structures.

Python is powerful enough to attract developers from around the world as well as companies such as Google, IBM, Industrial Light + Magic, Microsoft, NASA, Red Hat, Verizon, Xerox, and Yahoo!. Python is also used as a tool by professional game programmers. Electronic Arts, 2K Games, and the Disney Interactive Media Group all publish games that incorporate Python.

Python Is Object-Oriented

Object-oriented programming (OOP) is a modern approach to solving problems with computers. It embodies an intuitive method of representing information and actions in a program. It's certainly not the only way to write programs, but, for large projects, it's often the best way to go.

Languages like C#, Java, and Python are all object-oriented. But Python does them one better. In C# and Java, OOP is not optional. This makes short programs unnecessarily complex, and it requires a bunch of explanation before a new programmer can do anything significant. Python takes a different approach. In Python, using OOP techniques is optional. You have all of OOP's power at your disposal, but you can use it when you need it. Got a short program that doesn't really require OOP? No problem. Got a large project with a team of programmers that demands OOP? That'll work too. Python gives you power and flexibility.

Python Is a "Glue" Language

Python can be integrated with other languages such as C, C++, and Java. This means that a programmer can take advantage of work already done in another language while using Python. It also means that he or she can leverage the strengths of other languages, such as the extra speed that C or C++ might offer, while still enjoying the ease of development that's a hallmark of Python programming.

Python Runs Everywhere

Python runs on everything from a Palm to a Cray. And if you don't happen to have a super-computer in the den, you can still run Python on Windows, Macintosh, or Linux machines. And that's just the top of the list.

Python programs are *platform independent,* which means that regardless of the operating system you use to create your program, it'll run on any other computer with Python. So if you write a program on your PC, you can e-mail a copy to your friend who runs Linux or to your aunt who has a Mac, and the program will work (as long as your friend and aunt have Python installed on their computers).

Python Has a Strong Community

Most programming languages have a dedicated newsgroup, but Python also has something called the Python Tutor mailing list, a more informal way for beginning programmers to ask those first questions. The list is at http://mail.python.org/mailman/listinfo/tutor. Although the list is called Tutor, anyone, whether novice or expert, can answer questions.

There are other Python communities focused on different areas, but the common element they share is that they tend to be friendly and open. That only makes sense since the language itself is so approachable for beginners.

Python Is Free and Open Source

Python is free. You can install it on your computer and never pay a penny. But Python's license lets you do much more than that. You can copy or modify Python. You can even resell Python if you want (but don't quit your day job just yet). Embracing open-source ideals like this is part of what makes Python so popular and successful.

SETTING UP PYTHON ON WINDOWS

Before you can jump in and write your first Python program, you need to get the language on your computer. But don't worry—I'll walk you through the process of installing Python on a Windows machine.

Installing Python on Windows

To install Python under Windows, follow these steps:

1. Download the Python Windows installer from the companion website (www.courseptr. com/downloads). The file is in the Software folder, inside the Python subfolder; the file name is python-3.1.msi.
2. Run the Python Windows Installer, python-3.1.msi. Figure 1.2 shows the installer in action.
3. Accept the default configuration. Once you're done, you'll have Python 3.1 on your system.

 The companion website for this book can be found at www.courseptr.com/ downloads. It hosts the code for every complete program presented in these pages, along with all necessary supporting files and software installers. You can find a more detailed description of what's available in Appendix A, "The Companion Website."

FIGURE 1.2

Your computer is soon to be home to Python.

SETTING UP PYTHON ON OTHER OPERATING SYSTEMS

Python runs on literally dozens of other operating systems. So, if you're running something other than Windows, be sure to visit the official Python website, http://www.python.org, to download the latest version of the language for your machine. You can check out the Python home page in Figure 1.3.

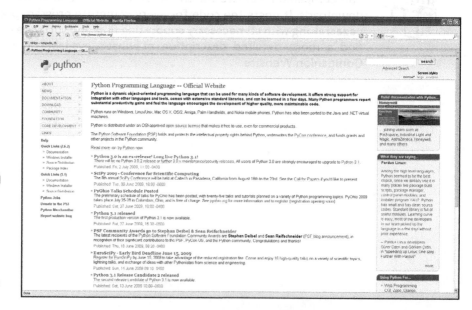

FIGURE 1.3

Visit Python's home page to download the latest version of Python and read loads of information about the language.

TRAP Your computer may have Python preinstalled; however, you must be using Python 3 in order for the programs in this book to work correctly.

Introducing IDLE

Python comes with an integrated development environment called IDLE. A *development environment* is a set of tools that makes writing programs easier. You can think of it as a word processor for your programs. But it's even more than a place to write, save, and edit your work. IDLE provides two modes in which to work: an interactive mode and a script mode.

Programming in Interactive Mode

Finally, it's time to get your hands dirty with some actual Python programming. The quickest way is to start Python in interactive mode. In this mode, you can tell Python what to do and it'll respond immediately.

Writing Your First Program

To begin your interactive session, from the Start menu, choose All Programs, Python 3.1, IDLE (Python GUI). You should see something very similar to Figure 1.4 on your screen.

FIGURE 1.4

Python in an interactive session, awaiting your command.

This window is called the Python Shell. At the command prompt (>>>), type print("Game Over") and then press the Enter key. The interpreter responds by displaying the following on the screen:

```
Game Over
```

Ta da! You've written your first Python program! You're a real programmer (with a little more to learn, but that goes for all of us).

Using the print Function

Take a look at the line you entered, print("Game Over"). Notice how straightforward it is. Without knowing anything about programming, you could have probably guessed what it does. That's Python in a nutshell. It's concise and clear. You'll appreciate this even more as you learn how to do more complex things with the language.

The print() function can display text, surrounded by quotes, that you put inside the pair of parentheses. If you put nothing inside the parentheses, it will print a blank line.

> **TRAP**　Python is case-sensitive and by convention, function names are in lowercase. So, print("Game Over") will work, but Print("Game Over") and PRINT("Game Over") won't.

Learning the Jargon

Now that you're a programmer, you have to throw around those fancy terms that only programmers understand. A *function* is like a mini-program that goes off and performs some specific task. The task of the print() function is to display a value (or sequence of values). You kick off, or *call*, a function by using the function name, followed by a set of parentheses. You did just this in interactive mode when you typed print("Game Over"). Sometimes you can give, or *pass*, a function values to work with. You put these values, called *arguments*, between the parentheses. In the case of your first program, you passed the print() function the argument "Game Over", which the function used to display the message Game Over.

> **HINT**　Functions in Python also *return* or provide information back to the part of the program that called the function. These values are called *return values*. You'll learn more about return values in Chapter 2.

In this particular case, you can be even more specific by saying that the value "Game Over" you passed the print() function is a *string*. This just means that it's a series of characters, like the ones on your keyboard. "String" may seem like an odd name—"text" or "words" might be more clear—but the name comes from the idea that text is a string, or a series, of characters. Technically, "Game Over" is a string *literal* because it is literally the sequence of characters that make up the words.

The line you entered in the interpreter is also considered a *statement*. In English, a statement is a complete thought. In Python, a statement is a complete instruction. It does something. Every program contains a number of statements.

Finally, now that you're a programmer, you can tell someone that you wrote some Python *code*. Code means programming statements. You can also use it as a verb to mean the act of programming. For example, you can say that you were up all night eating Hot Cheetos, drinking Mountain Dew, and *coding* like crazy.

Generating an Error

Computers take everything literally. If you misspell a function name by even just one letter, the computer will have absolutely no idea what you mean. For example, at the interactive prompt, if I type `primt("Game Over")`, the interpreter will respond with something like:

```
Traceback (most recent call last):
  File "<pyshell#0>", line 1, in <module>
    primt("Game Over")
NameError: name 'primt' is not defined
```

Translated to English, the interpreter is saying "Huh?!" The key line in the error message is `NameError: name 'primt' is not defined`. The message states that the interpreter doesn't recognize `primt`. As a human being, you can ignore my typo and understand what I meant. Computers are not so forgiving. Luckily, programming errors, or *bugs*, like this can be easily resolved by fixing the offending typo.

Understanding Syntax Highlighting

You probably noticed that words on the screen are displayed in different colors (not in the book, of course). This color-coding, called *syntax highlighting*, helps you quickly understand what you've typed by visually categorizing it. And there is a method to this coloring madness. Special words that are a part of the Python language, like `print`, are displayed in purple. Strings, like `"Game Over"`, are in green. And the output—what the interpreter displays as a result of what you type—is in blue. As you write larger programs, this color scheme will come in handy by helping you take in your code in one glance and spot errors more easily.

Programming in Script Mode

Using the interactive mode gives you immediate feedback. This is great because you can see the results. But it's not designed to create programs you can save and run later. Luckily, Python's IDLE also offers a script mode, in which you can write, edit, load, and save your programs. It's like a word processor for your code. In fact, you can perform such familiar tasks as find and replace, and cut and paste.

Writing Your First Program (Again)

You can open a script mode window from the interactive window you've been using. Select the File menu, then New Window. A new window will appear that looks just like the one in Figure 1.5.

FIGURE 1.5

Your blank canvas awaits. Python is ready for you to write a program in script mode.

In this new script window, type `print("Game Over")` and press Enter. Nothing happens! That's because you're in script mode. What you're doing is writing a list of statements for the computer to execute later. Once you save your program, you can run it.

Saving and Running Your Program

To save your program, select File, Save As. I gave my copy the name game_over.py. To make it easy to get to later, I saved it on my desktop.

> **HINT**   Make sure to save your programs with the .py extension. This allows various applications, including IDLE, to recognize these files as Python programs.

To run my Game Over program, I simply select Run, Run Module. Then, the interactive window displays the results of my program. Take a look at my desktop in Figure 1.6.

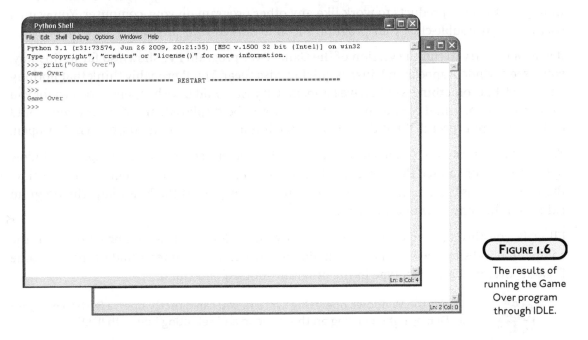

```
Python Shell
File  Edit  Shell  Debug  Options  Windows  Help
Python 3.1 (r31:73574, Jun 26 2009, 20:21:35) [MSC v.1500 32 bit (Intel)] on win32
Type "copyright", "credits" or "license()" for more information.
>>> print("Game Over")
Game Over
>>> ================================ RESTART ================================
>>>
Game Over
>>>
```

FIGURE 1.6

The results of running the Game Over program through IDLE.

You'll notice that the interactive window contains the old text from before. It still has the statement I entered while in interactive mode, print("Game Over"), and the results, the message Game Over. Below all of that, you'll see a restart message, and below that, the results of running the program from script mode: Game Over.

To run your program from IDLE, you need to first save your program.

Interactive mode is great for trying out a small idea quickly. Script mode is perfect for writing programs you can run later. Using both modes together is a great way to code.

Even though I need only script mode to write a program, I always keep an interactive window open. As I write my programs in script mode, I jump over to the interactive window to try out an idea or to be sure I have the usage of a function just right.

The script window is where I craft my final product. The interactive window is like a scratch pad where I can experiment. Using them together helps me to write better programs more quickly.

BACK TO THE GAME OVER PROGRAM

So far, you've run a version of the Game Over program through IDLE. While you're in the process of writing a program, running it through IDLE is a fine way to go. But I'm sure you want your finished products to work like any other program on your computer. You want a user to simply double-click your program's icon to launch your program.

If you were to try to run the version of the Game Over program I've shown so far in this way, you'd see a window appear and, just as quickly, disappear. You'd probably think that nothing happened. But something would have happened. It just would have happened too fast for you to notice. The program would run, Game Over would be displayed, and the program would end, all in a split second. What the program needs is a way to keep its console window open.

This updated version of Game Over, the final chapter project, keeps the program window open so the user can see the message. After displaying Game Over, the program also displays the message Press the enter key to exit. Once a user presses the Enter key, the program exits, and the console window disappears.

I'll walk you through the code one section at a time. You can load the program from the companion website (www.courseptr.com/downloads), in the Chapter 1 folder; the file name is game_over.py. Better yet, type in the program yourself and run it.

 TRICK   Under the Windows operating system, you can directly open a Python program in IDLE by right-clicking on the file icon and selecting Edit with IDLE.

Using Comments

The following are the first two lines of the program:

```
# Game Over
# Demonstrates the print function
```

These lines aren't statements for the computer to execute. In fact, the computer totally ignores them. These notes, called *comments,* are for the humans. Comments explain programming code in English (or any other language for that matter). Comments are invaluable to other programmers and help them to understand your code. But comments are also helpful to you. They remind you of how you accomplished something that may not be clear at first glance.

You create a comment with the number sign symbol, #. Anything after this symbol (except in a string) on the rest of the line is a comment. Comments are ignored by the computer. Notice that comments are colored red in IDLE to make them stand out.

It's a good idea to start all of your programs with a few comments, like I did here. It's helpful to list the title of the program and its purpose. Although I didn't do so here, you should also list the name of the programmer and the date the program was written.

You may be thinking: "Why have comments at all? I wrote the program, so I know what it does." That may be true a month after you write your code, but experienced programmers know that after a few months away from a program, your original intentions may not be as clear. If you want to modify an old program, a few well-placed comments may make your life much easier.

IN THE REAL WORLD

Comments are even more helpful to another programmer who needs to modify a program you wrote. This kind of situation comes up a lot in the world of professional programming. In fact, it's estimated that the majority of a programmer's time and effort go toward maintaining code that already exists. It's not uncommon for a programmer to be charged with the task of modifying a program written by someone else—and there's a chance that the original programmer won't be around to answer any questions. So, good comments are critical.

Using Blank Lines

Technically, the next line in the program is blank. The computer generally ignores blank lines; these, too, are just for the humans reading the code. Blank lines can make programs easier to read. Usually, I keep lines of related code together and separate sections with a blank line. In this program, I separated the comments from the call to the print function with a blank line.

Printing the String

The next line in the program should seem familiar to you:

```
print("Game Over")
```

It's your old friend, the print function. This line, just as it does in interactive mode, displays Game Over.

Waiting for the User

The last line of the program

```
input("\n\nPress the enter key to exit.")
```

displays the prompt, Press the enter key to exit, and waits for the user to press the Enter key. Once the user presses the key, the program ends. This is a nice trick to keep a console window open until the user is done with an application.

Normally, this is about the time I'd explain just what is going on in this line. But I'm going to keep you in suspense. Sorry. You'll have to wait until the next chapter to fully appreciate this one line.

Summary

You covered a lot of ground in this chapter. You learned a bit about Python and its strengths. You installed the language on your computer and gave it a little test drive. You learned to use Python's interactive mode to instantly execute a programming statement. You saw how to use script mode to write, edit, save, and run longer programs. You learned how to display text to the screen and how to wait for the user before closing a program's console window. You laid all the groundwork necessary for your adventure in Python programming.

CHALLENGES

1. Create an error of your very own by entering your favorite ice cream flavor in interactive mode. Then, make up for your misdeed and enter a statement that prints the name of your favorite ice cream.

2. Write and save a program that prints out your name and waits for the user to press the Enter key before the program ends. Then, run the program by double-clicking its icon.

3. Write a program that prints your favorite quote. It should give credit to the person who said it on the next line.

Types, Variables, and Simple I/O: The Useless Trivia Program

Now that you've been introduced to the basics of saving and executing a program, it's time to dig in and create some more. In this chapter, you'll learn about different ways computers can categorize and store data and, more importantly, how to use this data in your programs. You'll even see how to get information from the user so that your programs become interactive. Specifically, you'll learn how to do the following:

- Use triple-quoted strings and escape sequences to gain more control over text
- Make your programs do math
- Store data in the computer's memory
- Use variables to access and manipulate that data
- Get input from users to create interactive programs

Introducing the Useless Trivia Program

Combining the skills presented in this chapter, you'll create the Useless Trivia program shown running in Figure 2.1.

```
C:\Python31\python.exe                                               - □ x
Hi.  What's your name? Steve
How old are you? 28
Okay, last question.  How many pounds do you weigh? 165

If poet ee cummings were to email you, he'd address you as steve
But if ee were mad, he'd call you STEVE

If a small child were trying to get your attention
your name would become:
SteveSteveSteveSteveSteve

You're over 883008000 seconds old.

Did you know that on the moon you would weigh only 27.5 pounds?
On the sun, you'd weigh 4471.5 (but, ah... not for long).

Press the enter key to exit._
```

FIGURE 2.1

Whoa! Steve
might think about
a diet before he
visits the sun.

The program takes three pieces of personal information from the user: name, age, and weight. From these mundane items, the program is able to produce some amusing but trivial facts about the person, such as how much the person would weigh on the moon.

Though this may seem like a simple program (and it is), you'll find that the program is more interesting when you run it because you've had input. You'll care more about the results because they're personally tailored to you. This holds true for all programs, from games to business applications.

USING QUOTES WITH STRINGS

You saw an example of a string, `"Game Over"`, in the previous chapter. But strings can become much longer and more complex. You may want to give a user several paragraphs of instructions. Or you might want to format your text in a very specific manner. Using quotes can help you to create strings to accomplish all of this.

Introducing the Game Over 2.0 Program

Game Over 2.0 improves upon its predecessor program, Game Over, by displaying a more impressive version of the same message, which tells a player that his or her computer game has come to an end. Check out Figure 2.2 to see a sample run.

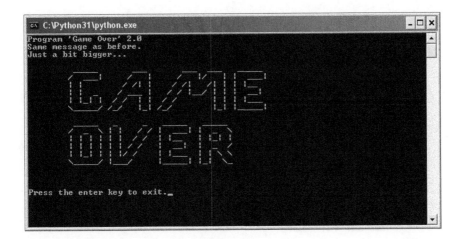

FIGURE 2.2

Now I get it, the
game is over.

The program shows that it's pretty simple to present text in different ways by using quotes. You can find the code for this program on the companion website (www.courseptr.com/downloads) for this book, in the Chapter 2 folder; the file name is game_over2.py.

```python
# Game Over - Version 2
# Demonstrates the use of quotes in strings

print("Program 'Game Over' 2.0")

print("Same", "message", "as before")

print("Just",
      "a bit",
      "bigger")

print("Here", end=" ")
print("it is...")

print(
      """
```

```
      ___        __      __   __  __  ___
     / __|      / |     / |  |/ / | | | __|
    | |        / /| |   / /|  / /| | | | |_
    | | _     / __ |   / / |_/  | | | |  _|
    | |_| |  / /  | | / /       | | | | |__
     \___/  /_/   |_| /_/       |_| |____|

      ___     __  ___      __  ___      __
     / _ \ | |  / /|  __| |  _ \
    | || | | | | / / | |_   | |_| |
    | || | | | | | / /  | _|   | _ /
    | |_| | | | | |/ /   | |__  | | \ \
     \___/ |___/    |___| |_| \_\

     """
   )
```

```
input("\n\nPress the enter key to exit.")
```

Using Quotes Inside Strings

You've seen how to create simple strings by surrounding text with quotes. You can use either a pair of single (' ') or double quotes (" ") to create string values. The computer doesn't care. So, `'Game Over'` represents the same string as `"Game Over"`. But take a look at the first appearance of a string in the program:

```
print "Program 'Game Over' 2.0"
```

This statement uses both kinds of quotes. Check out the sample run in Figure 2.2 again. Only the single quotes show up, because they are part of the string, just like, for example, the letter G. But the double quotes are not part of the string. The double quotes are like bookends, telling the computer where the string begins and ends. So, if you use a pair of double quotes to "bookend" your string, you can use as many single quotes inside the string as you want. And, if you surround your string with a pair of single quotes, you can use as many double quotes inside the string as you like.

Once you've used one kind of quote as bookends for your string, you can't use that type of quote inside your string. This make sense, because once the computer sees the second appearance of the quote that began the string, it thinks the string is over. For example, `"With the words, 'Houston, we have a problem.', Jim Lovell became one of our most famous astronauts."` is a valid string. But, `"With the words, "Houston, we have a problem.", Jim Lovell` became one of our most famous astronauts." isn't valid, because once the computer sees the second double quote, it thinks the string is over. So, the computer sees the string "With the words," followed by the word, *Houston*. And since the computer has no idea what *Houston* is, you'd get a nasty error in your program.

Printing Multiple Values

You can print multiple values with a single call to the print() function—just list multiple argument values, separated by commas. I print multiple values with the line

```
print("Same", "message", "as before")
```

I pass three arguments to the function: "Same", "message", and "as before.", which results in the code displaying Same message as before. Notice that each value is printed with a space as a separator. This is the default behavior of the print() function.

When you have a list of arguments, you can start a new line after any of the comma separators in the list. The next three lines of the program form a single statement that prints the one line of text Just a bit bigger. I start a new line after each comma separator:

```
print ("Just",
       "a bit",
       "bigger")
```

Sometimes it's useful to break up an argument list over multiple lines because it can make your code easier to read.

Specifying a Final String to Print

By default, the print() function prints a newline character as a final value. This means that a subsequent call to print() would display text on the following line. This is generally what you want, but you have the ability specify your own final string to be printed. You could, for example, specify that a space be the final character printed (instead of the newline) when you call the print() function. This would mean a subsequent print() statement would begin printing values right after that space. I take advantage of this functionality in the next two lines of the program:

```
print("Here", end=" ")
print("it is...")
```

The code prints the text "Here it is..." all on one line. That's because, in the first print() statement, I specify a space to be the final string to be printed. So, the statement prints the text "Here " (including a space after the final "e") but no newline character. The next print() statement begins printing the text "it is..." right after the space that follows the final "e" in the "Here" text. I accomplish this by passing a space to the end parameter of the print() function with the code end=" ". You can specify a string to be printed as the final value in your own print() statement, just like I did: with a comma, followed by the parameter name end, followed by an equals sign, followed by the final string to be printed. Being able to specify your own final string to be printed in a print() statement gives you greater flexibility in how you format your output.

 Don't worry if you don't know what a parameter is just yet. You'll learn all about parameters and passing values to them in Chapter 6, in the "Using Parameters and Return Values" section.

Creating Triple-Quoted Strings

Certainly, the coolest part of the program is that it prints out "Game Over" in a big block of text. The following string is responsible:

This is what's called a *triple-quoted string*. It's a string enclosed by a pair of three quotes in a row. Like before, it doesn't matter which kind of quotes you use, as long as you bookend with the same type.

As you can see, triple-quoted strings can span multiple lines. They print on the screen exactly the way you type them.

IN THE REAL WORLD

If you like the letters made from multiple characters in Game Over 2.0, then you'll really like *ASCII Art*. ASCII Art is basically pictures made from just the characters on your keyboard. ASCII, by the way, stands for the American Standard Code for Information Interchange. It's a code that represents 128 standard characters. (This kind of art isn't new, and it didn't start with the computer. In fact, the first recorded typewriter art dates back to 1898.)

USING ESCAPE SEQUENCES WITH STRINGS

Escape sequences allow you to put special characters into your strings. They give you greater control and flexibility over the text you display. The escape sequences you'll work with are made up of two characters: a backslash followed by another character. This may all sound a little mysterious, but once you see a few sequences in action, you'll realize just how easy they are to use.

Introducing the Fancy Credits Program

Besides telling a player that the game is over, a program often displays credits, a list of all the people who worked so hard to make it a reality. Fancy Credits uses escape sequences to achieve some effects it just couldn't without them. Figure 2.3 shows the results.

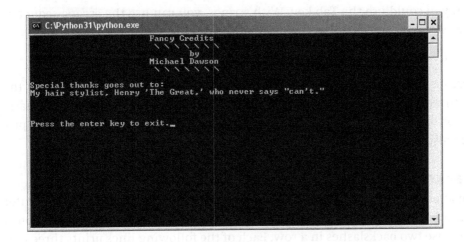

FIGURE 2.3

Please, contain your applause.

The code looks a bit cryptic at first glance, but you'll soon understand it all. You can find the code for this program on the companion website (courseptr.com/downloads) for this book, in the Chapter 2 folder; the file name is fancy_credits.py.

```
# Fancy Credits
# Demonstrates escape sequences

print("\t\t\tFancy Credits")

print("\t\t\t \\ \\ \\ \\ \\ \\ \\")
print("\t\t\t\tby")
print("\t\t\tMichael Dawson")
print("\t\t\t \\ \\ \\ \\ \\ \\ \\")

print("\nSpecial thanks goes out to:")
print("My hair stylist, Henry \'The Great,\' who never says \"can\'t.\"")

# sound the system bell
print("\a")

input("\n\nPress the enter key to exit.")
```

Moving Forward a Tab Stop

Sometimes you'll want to set some text off from the left margin where it normally prints. In a word processor, you could use the Tab key. With strings, you can use the escape sequence for a tab, \t. That's exactly what I did in the following line:

```
print("\t\t\tFancy Credits")
```

I used the tab escape sequence, \t, three times in a row. So, when the program prints the string, it prints three tabs and then Fancy Credits. This makes Fancy Credits look nearly centered in the console window. Tab sequences are good for setting off text, as in this program, but they're also perfect for arranging text into columns.

Printing a Backslash

If you've thought ahead, you may be wondering how you can print a backslash if the computer always interprets a backslash as the beginning of an escape sequence. Well, the solution is pretty simple: just use two backslashes in a row. Each of the following lines prints three tabs followed by seven backslashes (as a result of the seven \\ sequences), separated by spaces:

```
print("\t\t\t \\ \\ \\ \\ \\ \\ \\")
print("\t\t\t \\ \\ \\ \\ \\ \\ \\")
```

Inserting a Newline

One of the most useful sequences at your disposal is the newline sequence. It's represented by \n. By using this sequence, you can insert a newline character into your strings for a blank line where you need it. You can use a newline right at the beginning of a string to separate it from the text last printed. That's what I did in the line:

```
print("\nSpecial thanks goes out to:")
```

The computer sees the \n sequence, prints a blank line, then prints Special thanks goes out to:.

Inserting a Quote

Inserting a quote into a string, even the type of quote you use to bookend it, is simple. Just use the sequence \' for a single quote and \" for a double quote. They mean "put a quote here," and won't be mistaken by the computer as a marker for the end of your string. This is what I used to get both kinds of quotes in one line of text:

```
print("My hair stylist, Henry \'The Great,\' who never says \"can\'t.\"")
```

The pair of double quotes at both ends are the bookends, defining the string. To make the string easier to understand, look at it in parts:

- \'The Great\' prints as 'The Great'
- Each \' sequence is printed as a single quote
- \"can\'t\" prints as "can't"
- Both \" sequences print as double quotes
- The lone \' sequence prints as a single quote

Sounding the System Bell

Upon running this program, you'll notice something different right away. It makes noise! The next statement in the program

```
print("\a")
```

sounds the system bell of your computer. It does this through the escape sequence, \a, which represents the system bell character. Every time you print it, the bell rings. You can print a string with just this sequence, as I have, or you can put it inside a longer string. You can even use the sequence several times to ring the bell more than once.

A few escape sequences only work as advertised if you run your program directly from the operating system and not through IDLE. The escape sequence \a is a good example. Let's say I have a program that simply prints the escape sequence \a. If I run it through IDLE, I get a little square box printed on my screen—not what I wanted. But if I run that same program directly from Windows, by double-clicking the program file icon, my computer's system bell rings just as I intended.

As you can see, escape sequences aren't so bad once you've seen them in action. And they can come in quite handy. Table 2.1 summarizes some useful ones.

TABLE 2.1   SELECTED ESCAPE SEQUENCES

Sequence	Description
\\	Backslash. Prints one backslash.
\'	Single quote. Prints a single quote.
\"	Double quote. Prints a double quote.
\a	Bell. Sounds the system bell.
\n	Newline. Moves cursor to beginning of next line.
\t	Horizontal tab. Moves cursor forward one tab stop.

CONCATENATING AND REPEATING STRINGS

You've seen how you can insert special characters into a string, but there are things you can do with entire strings themselves. You can combine two separate strings into a larger one. And you can even repeat a single string as many times as you like.

Introducing the Silly Strings Program

The Silly Strings program prints several strings to the screen. The results are shown in Figure 2.4.

Though you've already seen strings printed, the way these strings were created is brand-new to you. You can find the code for this program on the companion website (www.courseptr.com/downloads) for this book, in the Chapter 2 folder; the file name is silly_strings.py.

FIGURE 2.4

The strings on the screen appear differently than in the program code.

```
# Silly Strings
# Demonstrates string concatenation and repetition

print("You can concatenate two " + "strings with the '+' operator.")

print("\nThis string " + "may not " + "seem terr" + "ibly impressive. " \
      + "But what " + "you don't know" + " is that\n" + "it's one real" \
      + "l" + "y" + " long string, created from the concatenation " \
      + "of " + "twenty-two\n" + "different strings, broken across " \
      + "six lines." + " Now are you" + " impressed? " + "Okay,\n" \
      + "this " + "one " + "long" + " string is now over!")

print("\nIf you really like a string, you can repeat it.  For example,")
print("who doesn't like pie?  That's right, nobody.  But if you really")
print("like it, you should say it like you mean it:")
print("Pie" * 10)

input("\n\nPress the enter key to exit.")
```

Concatenating Strings

Concatenating strings means joining them together to create a whole new string. A simple example is in the first print statement:

```
print("You can concatenate two " + "strings with the '+' operator.")
```

The + operator joins the two strings, `"You can concatenate two "` and `"strings with the '+'` `operator."`, together to form a new, larger string. It's pretty intuitive. It's like adding the strings together using the same symbol you've always used for adding numbers.

When you join two strings, their exact values are fused together, with no space or separator character inserted between them. So, if you were to join the two strings `"cup"` and `"cake"`, you'd end up with `"cupcake"` and not `"cup cake"`. In most cases, you'll want to insert a space between strings you join, so don't forget to put one in.

The next `print` statement shows that you can concatenate 'til your heart's content:

```
print("\nThis string " + "may not " + "seem terr" + "ibly impressive. " \
    + "But what " + "you don't know" + " is that\n" + "it's one real" \
    + "l" + "y" + " long string, created from the concatenation " \
    + "of " + "twenty-two\n" + "different strings, broken across " \
    + "six lines." + " Now are you" + " impressed? " + "Okay,\n" \
    + "this " + "one " + "long" + " string is now over!")
```

The computer prints one long string that was created by the concatenation of 22 individual strings.

Using the Line Continuation Character

Generally, you write one statement per line. But you don't have to. You can stretch a single statement across multiple lines. All you have to do is use the line-continuation character, \ (which is just a backslash), as I did in the preceding code. Put it anywhere you'd normally use a space (but not inside a string) to continue your statement on the next line. The computer will act as if it sees one long line of code.

The computer doesn't care how long a programming line is, but people do. If a line of your code feels too long, or would be more clear as several lines, use the line-continuation character to split it up.

Repeating Strings

The next new idea presented in the program is illustrated in the following line:

```
print("Pie" * 10)
```

This line creates a new string, `"PiePiePiePiePiePiePiePiePiePie"`, and prints it out. That's the string `"Pie"` repeated 10 times, by the way.

Like the concatenation operator, the repetition operator, `*`, is pretty intuitive. It's the same symbol used for multiplying numbers on a computer, so repeating a string with it makes sense. It's like you're multiplying the string. To repeat a string, just put the string and number of repetitions together with the repetition operator, *.

WORKING WITH NUMBERS

So far, you've been using strings to represent text. That's just one type of value. Computers let you represent information in other ways, too. One of the most basic but most important ways is as numbers. Numbers are used in almost every program. Whether you're writing a space shooter game or home finance package, you need to represent numbers some way. You've got high scores or checking account balances to work with, after all. Fortunately, Python has several different types of numbers to fit all of your game or application programming needs.

Introducing the Word Problems Program

This next program uses those dreaded word problems. You know, the kind that always seems to involve two trains leaving different cities at the same time headed toward each other... bringing back nightmares of junior high algebra as they're about to collide. Well, fear not. You won't have to solve a single word problem, or even do any math at all—the computer will do all the work. The Word Problems program is just an amusing (hopefully) way to explore working with numbers. Check out Figure 2.5 to see a sample run.

FIGURE 2.5

With Python, you can add, subtract, multiply, divide, and keep track of a pregnant hippo's weight.

You can find the code for this program on the companion website (www.courseptr.com/downloads) for this book, in the Chapter 2 folder; the file name is word_problems.py.

```
# Word Problems
# Demonstrates numbers and math

print("If a 2000 pound pregnant hippo gives birth to a 100 pound calf,")
print("but then eats 50 pounds of food, how much does she weigh?")
input("Press the enter key to find out.")
print("2000 - 100 + 50 =", 2000 - 100 + 50)

print("\nIf an adventurer returns from a successful quest and buys each ↵
 ↳ of")
print("6 companions 3 bottles of ale, how many bottles are purchased?")
input("Press the enter key to find out.")
print("6 * 3 =", 6 * 3)

print("\nIf a restaurant check comes to 19 dollars with tip, and you and")
print("your friends split it evenly 4 ways, how much do you each throw ↵
 ↳ in?")
input("Press the enter key to find out.")
print("19 / 4 =", 19 / 4)

print("\nIf a group of 4 pirates finds a chest full of 107 gold coins, ↵
 ↳ and")
print("they divide the booty evenly, how many whole coins does each get?")
input("Press the enter key to find out.")
print("107 // 4 =", 107 // 4)

print("\nIf that same group of 4 pirates evenly divides the chest full")
print("of 107 gold coins, how many coins are left over?")
input("Press the enter key to find out.")
print("107 % 4 =", 107 % 4)

input("\n\nPress the enter key to exit.")
```

Understanding Numeric Types

The program Word Problems uses numbers. That's obvious. But what may not be obvious is that it uses two different types of numbers. Python allows programmers to use several different types of numbers. The two types used in this program, and probably the most common, are *integers* and *floating-point numbers* (or *floats*). Integers are whole numbers—numbers with no fractional part. Or, another way to think about them is that they can be written without a decimal point. The numbers 1, 27, -100, and 0 are all examples of integers. Floats are numbers with a decimal point, like 2.376, -99.1, and 1.0.

Using Mathematical Operators

With mathematical operators, you can turn your computer into an expensive calculator. The operators should look pretty familiar. For example, the code 2000 - 100 + 50 subtracts 100 from 2000 and then adds 50 before printing the result of 1950. Technically, it evaluates the *expression* 2000 - 100 + 50, which evaluates to 1950. An expression is just a sequence of values, joined by operators, that can be simplified to another value. The code 6 * 3 multiplies 6 by 3 and prints the result of 18. And the code 19 / 4 divides 19 by 4 and prints the floating-point result of 4.75.

So far, all of these mathematical operators should be pretty familiar—but check out the next calculation, 107 // 4. Using // as a mathematical operator is probably new to you. Used here, // (two forward slashes) represents *integer division*—division where the result is always an integer (any fractional part is ignored). This is opposed to *true division*, which you just saw with the / operator (where the fractional part of the result is not ignored). So, the result of 107 // 4 is 26.

The next calculation, 107 % 4, might also make you scratch your head. Used here, the symbol % is the *modulus* operator, which produces the remainder of an integer division expression. So 107 % 4 evaluates to 3, the remainder of 107 / 4.

Table 2.2 summarizes some useful mathematical operators.

TABLE 2.2   USEFUL MATHEMATICAL OPERATORS

Operator	Description	Example	Evaluates To
+	Addition	7 + 3	10
-	Subtraction	7 - 3	4
*	Multiplication	7 * 3	21
/	Division (True)	7 / 3	2.3333333333333335
//	Division (Integer)	7 // 3	2
%	Modulus	7 % 3	1

Notice the true division entry in Table 2.2. It says that 7 divided by 3 is 2.3333333333333335. While this is pretty accurate, it's not exact. The results are fine for most purposes, but you should be aware of this when using floats.

> **HINT**
>
> The decimal module provides support for accurate decimal floating-point arithmetic. To learn more, see the Python documentation.

UNDERSTANDING VARIABLES

Through variables, you can store and manipulate information, a fundamental aspect of programming. Python lets you create variables to organize and access this information.

Introducing the Greeter Program

Check out Figure 2.6 to see the results of the Greeter program.

FIGURE 2.6

A shout-out to all the Larry's of the world.

From just the screen shot in Figure 2.6, this program looks like something you could have already written. But within the code lurks the new and powerful concept of variables. You can find the code for this program on the companion website (www.courseptr.com/downloads) for this book, in the Chapter 2 folder; the file name is greeter.py.

```
# Greeter
# Demonstrates the use of a variable

name = "Larry"
```

```
print(name)

print("Hi,", name)

input("\n\nPress the enter key to exit.")
```

Creating Variables

A *variable* provides a way to label and access information. Instead of having to know exactly where in the computer's memory some information is stored, you use a variable to get at it. It's kind of like calling your friend on his cell phone. You don't have to know where in the city your friend is to reach him. You just press a button and you get him. But, before you use a variable, you have to create it, as in the following line:

```
name = "Larry"
```

This line is called an *assignment statement.* It creates a variable called name and assigns it a value so that it references the string "Larry". In general, assignment statements assign a value to a variable. If the variable doesn't already exist, as was the case with name, it's created, then assigned a value.

TRAP   Technically, an assignment statement stores the value on the right side of the equal sign in your computer's memory while the variable on the left side only refers to the value (and doesn't directly store it). Therefore, Python purists would say that a variable "gets" a value instead of saying that a variable is "assigned" a value. However, I use "gets" and "assigned" interchangeably, depending upon which seems clearest.

You'll learn more about the implications of the way variables refer to values (rather than storing them) in Chapter 5, in the section "Understanding Shared References."

Using Variables

Once a variable has been created, it refers to some value. The convenience of a variable is that it can be used just like the value to which it refers. So the line

```
print(name)
```

prints the string "Larry" just like the statement print("Larry") does. And the line

```
print("Hi,", name)
```

prints the string "Hi," followed by a space, followed by "Larry". In this case, I can use name instead of "Larry" with the same results.

Naming Variables

Like the proud parent of your program, you pick the names of your variables. For this program, I chose to call my variable `name`, but I could just as easily have used `person`, `guy`, or `alpha7345690876`, and the program would have run exactly the same. There are only a few rules that you have to follow to create legal variable names. Create an illegal one and Python will let you know about it with an error. The following are the two most important rules:

1. A variable name can contain only numbers, letters, and underscores.
2. A variable name can't start with a number.

In addition to the rules for creating *legal* variable names, the following are some guidelines that more experienced programmers follow for creating *good* variable names—because, once you've programmed for a while, you know the chasm of difference that exists between a legal variable name and a good one. (I'll give you one guideline right now: Don't ever name a variable `alpha7345690876`.)

- **Choose descriptive names.** Variable names should be clear enough so that another programmer could look at the name and have a good idea what it represents. So, for example, use `score` instead of `s`. (One exception to this rule involves variables used for a brief period. Often, programmers give those variables short names, like `x`. But that's fine, because by using `x`, the programmer clearly conveys the variable represents a quick holding place.)

- **Be consistent.** There are different schools of thought about how to write multiword variable names. Is it `high_score` or `highScore`? I use the underscore style. But it's not important which method you use, as long as you're consistent.

- **Follow the traditions of the language.** Some naming conventions are just traditions. For example, in most languages (Python included) variable names start with a lowercase letter. Another tradition is to avoid using an underscore as the first character of your variable names. Names that begin with an underscore have special meaning in Python.

- **Keep the length in check.** This may seem to go against the first guideline: Choose descriptive names. Isn't `personal_checking_account_balance` a great variable name? Maybe not. Long variable names can lead to problems. They can make statements hard to read. Plus, the longer the variable name, the greater the chance of a typo. As a guideline, try to keep your variable names under 15 characters.

TRICK   *Self-documenting* code is written in such a way that it's easy to understand what is happening in the program independent of any comments. Choosing good variable names is an excellent step toward this kind of code.

GETTING USER INPUT

After appreciating all that program Greeter has to offer, you may still be thinking, "So what?" Yes, you could write a program that does exactly what Greeter does without going to the trouble of creating any fancy variables. But to do fundamentally important things, including getting, storing, and manipulating user input, you need variables. Check out the next program, which uses input to give a personalized greeting.

Introducing the Personal Greeter Program

The Personal Greeter program adds a single, but very cool, element to the Greeter program: user input. Instead of working with a predefined value, the computer lets the user enter his or her name and then uses it to say hi. Figure 2.7 shows off the program.

FIGURE 2.7

Now, name is assigned a string based on whatever the user enters, including "Rupert".

Getting user input isn't very hard. As a result, the code doesn't look much different. You can find the code for this program on the companion website (www.courseptr.com/downloads) for this book, in the Chapter 2 folder; the file name is personal_greeter.py.

```
# Personal Greeter
# Demonstrates getting user input

name = input("Hi.  What's your name? ")

print(name)

print("Hi,", name)

input("\n\nPress the enter key to exit.")
```

Using the input() Function

The only line that's changed is the assignment statement:

```
name = input("Hi.  What's your name? ")
```

The left side of the statement is exactly the same as in the Greeter program. name is created and a value is assigned to it, just like before. But this time, the right side of the assignment statement is a call to the function input(). The input() function gets some text from the user. It takes a string argument that it uses to prompt the user for this text. In this case, the argument I passed to input() is the string "Hi. What's your name? ". As you can see from Figure 2.7, input() does indeed use the string to prompt the user. input() waits for the user to enter something. Once the user presses the Enter key, input() *returns* whatever the user typed as a string. That string, the *return value* of the function call, is what name gets. To help visualize how this works, imagine that in the assignment statement, the call to input() is replaced with the string the user typed. Now of course, the code in the program doesn't change, but imagining the return value of a function in place of the call to that function helps drive home how you can use return values.

If you're still not totally clear on function calls, arguments, and return values, here's another way to think about it: using input() is like ordering a pizza. The input() function is like a pizza parlor. You make a call to a pizza parlor to place your order, and you make a call to the input() function to kick it into gear. When you call the pizza parlor, you provide information, like "pepperoni." When you call the input() function, you pass it an argument like, "Hi. What's your name?". After you finish your call to the pizza parlor, the employees get a pepperoni pizza to your door. And after you make your call to input(), the function returns whatever string the user entered.

The rest of the Personal Greeter program works just like the Greeter program. It makes no difference to the computer how name gets its value. So the line

```
print(name)
```

prints the value of name. While the line

```
print("Hi,", name)
```

displays the string "Hi," followed by a space, followed by the value of name.

At this point, you know enough to understand the last line in all of these console programs. The goal of the last line is to wait for the user to press the Enter key:

```
input("\n\nPress the enter key to exit.")
```

It does exactly that through the input() function. Since I don't care what the user enters, so long as he or she presses the Enter key, I don't assign the return value of input() to a variable like before. It may seem weird to get a return value and do nothing with it, but it's my option. If I don't assign the return value to a variable, the computer just ignores it. So once the user presses the Enter key, the call to the input() function ends, the program ends, and the console window closes.

USING STRING METHODS

Python has a rich set of tools for working with strings. One type of these tools is string methods. String methods allow you to create new strings from old ones. You can do everything from the simple, such as create a string that's just an all-capital-letters version of the original, to the complex, such as create a new string that's the result of a series of intricate letter substitutions.

Introducing the Quotation Manipulation Program

According to Mark Twain, "The art of prophecy is very difficult, especially with respect to the future." While it's hard to accurately foretell the future, it's still amusing to read predictions that pundits have made about technology. A good one is, "I think there is a world market for maybe five computers." This was made by then IBM chairman, Thomas Watson, in 1943. The Quotation Manipulation program that I wrote prints this quote several ways using string methods. (Fortunately, I was able to write this program because I happen to own computer #3.) Take a look at the sample run in Figure 2.8.

```
C:\Python31\python.exe

Original quote:
I think there is a world market for maybe five computers.

In uppercase:
I THINK THERE IS A WORLD MARKET FOR MAYBE FIVE COMPUTERS.

In lowercase:
i think there is a world market for maybe five computers.

As a title:
I Think There Is A World Market For Maybe Five Computers.

With a minor replacement:
I think there is a world market for maybe millions of computers.

Original quote is still:
I think there is a world market for maybe five computers.


Press the enter key to exit._
```

FIGURE 2.8

This slightly low guess is printed several ways with the help of string methods.

You can find the code for this program on the book's companion website (www.courseptr.com/downloads), in the Chapter 2 folder; the file name is quotation_manipulation.py.

```
# Quotation Manipulation
# Demonstrates string methods

# quote from IBM Chairman, Thomas Watson, in 1943
quote = "I think there is a world market for maybe five computers."

print("Original quote:")
print(quote)

print("\nIn uppercase:")
print(quote.upper())

print("\nIn lowercase:")
print(quote.lower())

print("\nAs a title:")
print(quote.title())

print("\nWith a minor replacement:")
print(quote.replace("five", "millions of"))

print("\nOriginal quote is still:")
print(quote)

input("\n\nPress the enter key to exit.")
```

Creating New Strings with String Methods

Though there's a new concept at work here, the code is still pretty understandable. Take a look at the line:

```
print(quote.upper())
```

You can probably guess what it does: print a version of quote in all uppercase letters. The line does this through the use of a string method, upper(). A *string method* is like an ability a string has. So, quote has the ability to create a new string, a capitalized version of itself, through its upper() method. When it does this, it returns this new string, and the line becomes equivalent to the following line:

```
print("I THINK THERE IS A WORLD MARKET FOR MAYBE FIVE COMPUTERS.")
```

Now, the line of code is never like this, but you can think of it in this way to help you understand how the method works.

You've probably noticed the parentheses in this method call. It should remind you of functions. Methods are similar to functions. The main difference is that a built-in function, like `input()`, can be called on its own. But a string method has to be called through a particular string. It makes no sense to just type the following:

```
print(upper())
```

You kick off a method, or *invoke* it, by adding a dot, followed by the name of the method, followed by a pair of parentheses, after a string value. The parentheses aren't just for show. As with functions, you can pass arguments inside them. `upper()` doesn't take any arguments, but you'll see an example of a string method that does with `replace()`.

The line

```
print(quote.lower())
```

invokes the `lower()` method of `quote` to create an all-lowercase-letters version of the string, which the method returns. Then, that new, lowercase string is printed.

The line

```
print(quote.title())
```

prints a version of `quote` that's like a title. The `title()` method returns a string where the first letter of each word is capitalized and the rest of the string is in lowercase.

The line

```
print(quote.replace("five", "millions of"))
```

prints a new string, where every occurrence of `"five"` in `quote` is replaced with `"millions of"`.

The method `replace()` needs at least two pieces of information: the old text to be replaced, and the new text that replaces it. You separate the two arguments with a comma. You can add an optional third argument, an integer, that tells the method the maximum number of times to make the replacement.

Finally, the program prints `quote` again, with

```
print("\nOriginal quote is still:")
print(quote)
```

You can see from Figure 2.8 that `quote` hasn't changed. Remember, string methods create a new string. They don't affect the original one. Table 2.3 summarizes the string methods you've just seen, along with a few others.

TABLE 2.3	USEFUL STRING METHODS
Method	**Description**
`upper()`	Returns the uppercase version of the string.
`lower()`	Returns the lowercase version of the string.
`swapcase()`	Returns a new string where the case of each letter is switched. Uppercase becomes lowercase and lowercase becomes uppercase.
`capitalize()`	Returns a new string where the first letter is capitalized and the rest are lowercase.
`title()`	Returns a new string where the first letter of each word is capitalized and all others are lowercase.
`strip()`	Returns a string where all the white space (tabs, spaces, and newlines) at the beginning and end is removed.
`replace(old, new [,max])`	Returns a string where occurrences of the string *old* are replaced with the string *new*. The optional *max* limits the number of replacements.

USING THE RIGHT TYPES

You've used three different types so far: strings, integers, and floating-point numbers. It's important to know not only which data types are available to you, but how to work with them. If you don't, you might end up with programs that produce unintended results.

Introducing the Trust Fund Buddy—Bad Program

The idea for the next program was to create a tool for those souls who play all day, living off a generous trust fund. The program is supposed to calculate a grand total for monthly expenditures based on user input. This grand total is meant to help those living beyond any reasonable means to stay within budget so they don't ever have to think about getting a real job. But, as you may have guessed from the program's title, Trust Fund Buddy—Bad doesn't work as the programmer intended. Figure 2.9 shows a sample run.

FIGURE 2.9

The monthly total should be high, but not that high. Something is wrong.

All right, the program obviously isn't working correctly. It has a bug. But not a bug that causes it to crash. When a program produces unintended results but doesn't crash, it has a *logical error*. Based on what you already know, you might be able to figure out what's happening by looking at the code. You can find the code for this program on the companion website (www.courseptr.com/downloads), in the Chapter 2 folder; the file name is trust_fund_bad.py.

```
# Trust Fund Buddy - Bad
# Demonstrates a logical error

print(
"""

        Trust Fund Buddy


Totals your monthly spending so that your trust fund doesn't run out
(and you're forced to get a real job).

Please enter the requested, monthly costs.  Since you're rich, ignore ↵
↳ pennies and use only dollar amounts.

"""
)

car = input("Lamborghini Tune-Ups: ")
rent = input("Manhattan Apartment: ")
jet = input("Private Jet Rental: ")
```

```
gifts = input("Gifts: ")
food = input("Dining Out: ")
staff = input("Staff (butlers, chef, driver, assistant): ")
guru = input("Personal Guru and Coach: ")
games = input("Computer Games: ")

total = car + rent + jet + gifts + food + staff + guru + games

print("\nGrand Total:", total)

input("\n\nPress the enter key to exit.")
```

It's okay if you don't see the problem right now. I'll give you one more hint, though. Take a look at the output in Figure 2.9 again. Examine the long number that the program prints as the grand total. Then look at all the numbers the user entered. Notice any connection? Okay, whether you do or don't, read on.

Tracking Down Logical Errors

Logical errors can be the toughest bugs to fix. Since the program doesn't crash, you don't get the benefit of an error message to offer a clue. You have to observe the behavior of the program and investigate the code.

In this case, the program's output tells the story. The huge number is clearly not the sum of all the numbers the user entered. But, by looking at the numbers, you can see that the grand total printed is a concatenation of all the numbers. How did that happen? Well, if you remember, the input() function returns a string. So each "number" the user enters is treated like a string. Which means that each variable in the program has a string value associated with it. So, the line

```
total = car + rent + jet + gifts + food + staff + guru + games
```

is not adding numbers. It's concatenating strings!

Now that you know the problem, how do you fix it? Somehow those string values need to be converted to numbers. Then the program will work as intended. If only there was some way to do this. Well, as you may have guessed, there is.

IN THE REAL WORLD

The + symbol works with pairs of strings as well as pairs of integers. Using the same operator for values of different types is called *operator overloading*. Now, "overloading" may sound like a bad thing, but actually it can be a good thing. Doesn't it make sense that strings are joined using the plus sign? You immediately understand what it means. Implemented well, operator overloading can make for clearer and more elegant code.

CONVERTING VALUES

The solution to the Trust Fund Buddy–Bad program is to convert the string values returned by input() to numeric ones. Since the program works with whole dollar amounts, it makes sense to convert each string to an integer before working with it.

Introducing the Trust Fund Buddy–Good Program

The Trust Fund Buddy–Good program fixes the logical bug in Trust Fund Buddy–Bad. Take a look at the output of the new program in Figure 2.10.

```
C:\Python31\python.exe                                    _ □ ×

                      Trust Fund Buddy
Totals your monthly spending so that your trust fund doesn't run out
(and you're forced to get a real job).

Please enter the requested, monthly costs.  Since you're rich, ignore pennies
and use only dollar amounts.

Lamborghini Tune-Ups: 2000
Manhattan Apartment: 10000
Private Jet Rental: 17000
Gifts: 5000
Dining Out: 7500
Staff (butlers, chef, driver, assistant): 12000
Personal Guru and Coach: 6800
Computer Games: 1000

Grand Total: 61300

Press the enter key to exit.
```

FIGURE 2.10

Ah, 61,300 dollars a month is much more reasonable.

Now the program arrives at the correct total. You can find the code for this program on the book's companion website, in the Chapter 2 folder; the file name is trust_fund_good.py.

```
# Trust Fund Buddy - Good
# Demonstrates type conversion

print(
"""
                        Trust Fund Buddy

Totals your monthly spending so that your trust fund doesn't run out
(and you're forced to get a real job).

Please enter the requested, monthly costs.  Since you're rich, ignore ⮑
⮑ pennies and use only dollar amounts.

"""
)

car = input("Lamborghini Tune-Ups: ")
car = int(car)

rent = int(input("Manhattan Apartment: "))
jet = int(input("Private Jet Rental: "))
gifts = int(input("Gifts: "))
food = int(input("Dining Out: "))
staff = int(input("Staff (butlers, chef, driver, assistant): "))
guru = int(input("Personal Guru and Coach: ") )
games = int(input("Computer Games: "))


total = car + rent + jet + gifts + food + staff + guru + games

print("\nGrand Total:", total)

input("\n\nPress the enter key to exit.")
```

Converting Strings to Integers

There are several functions that convert between types. The function to convert a value to an integer is demonstrated in the following lines:

```
car = input("Lamborghini Tune-Ups: ")
```

```
car = int(car)
```

The first line gets input from the user as a string and assigns that value to `car`. The second line does the conversion. The function `int()` takes the string referenced by `car` and returns an integer version of it. Then, `car` gets this new integer value.

The next seven lines get and convert the remaining expenditure categories:

```
rent = int(input("Manhattan Apartment: "))
jet = int(input("Private Jet Rental: "))
gifts = int(input("Gifts: "))
food = int(input("Dining Out: "))
staff = int(input("Staff (butlers, chef, driver, assistant): "))
guru = int(input("Personal Guru and Coach: ") )
games = int(input("Computer Games: "))
```

Notice that the assignments are done in just one line. That's because the two function calls, `input()` and `int()`, are nested. *Nesting* function calls means putting one inside the other. This is perfectly fine as long as the return values of the inner function can be used as argument values by the outer function. Here, the return value of `input()` is a string, and a string is a perfectly acceptable type for `int()` to convert.

In the assignment statement for `rent`, `input()` goes out and asks the user how much the rent was. The user enters some text, and that is returned as a string. Then, the program calls the function `int()` with that string. `int()` returns the integer the string represented. Then, that integer is assigned to `rent`. The other six assignment statements work the same way.

There are other functions that convert values to a specific type. Table 2.4 lists several.

TABLE 2.4   SELECTED TYPE CONVERSION FUNCTIONS

Function	Description	Example	Returns
float(x)	Returns a floating-point value by converting x	float("10.0")	10.0
int(x)	Returns an integer value by converting x	int("10")	10
str(x)	Returns a string value by converting x	str(10)	'10'

Using Augmented Assignment Operators

Augmented assignment operators is a mouthful. But the concept is simple. Let's say you want to know the yearly amount the user spends on food. To calculate and assign the yearly amount, you could use the line

```
food = food * 52
```

This line multiplies the value of food by 52 and then assigns the result back to food. You could accomplish the same thing with the following line:

```
food *= 52
```

*= is an augmented assignment operator. It also multiplies the value of food by 52 and then assigns the result back to food, but it's shorter than the first version. Since assigning a new value to a variable based on its original value is something that happens a lot in programming, these operators provide a nice shortcut to a common task. There are other augmented assignment operators. Table 2.5 summarizes some useful ones.

TABLE 2.5	USEFUL AUGMENT ASSIGNMENT OPERATORS	
Operator	**Example**	**Is Equivalent To**
*=	x *= 5	x = x * 5
/=	x /= 5	x = x / 5
%=	x %= 5	x = x % 5
+=	x += 5	x = x + 5
-=	x -= 5	x = x - 5

BACK TO THE USELESS TRIVIA PROGRAM

You now know everything you need to know to program the project Useless Trivia from the beginning of the chapter. I'll present the program a little differently than the others. Instead of listing the code out in its entirety, I'll go over the program one section at a time. You can find the code for this program on the companion website (www.courseptr.com/downloads), in the Chapter 2 folder; the file name is useless_trivia.py.

Creating the Initial Comments

Although comments don't have any effect while the program runs, they are an important part of every project. As always, I begin with a few:

```
# Useless Trivia
#
# Gets personal information from the user and then
# prints true but useless information about him or her
```

 Experienced programmers also use the initial comments area to describe any modifications they make to code over time. This provides a history of the program right up front. This practice is especially helpful when several programmers have their hands on the same code.

Getting the User Input

Using the input() function, the program gets the user's name, age, and weight:

```
name = input("Hi.  What's your name? ")

age = input("How old are you? ")
age = int(age)

weight = int(input("Okay, last question.  How many pounds do you weigh? "))
```

Remember, input() always returns a string. Since age and weight will be treated as numbers, they must be converted. I broke up this process into two lines for the variable age. First, I assigned the string from input() to a variable. Then, I converted that string to an integer and assigned it back to the variable. For weight, I made the assignment in one line long by nesting the function calls. I made the assignments in two different ways to remind you that you can do either. However, in practice, I'd pick one approach to be consistent.

Printing Lowercase and Uppercase Versions of name

The following lines print a version of name in uppercase and a version in lowercase with the help of string methods:

```
print("\nIf poet ee cummings were to email you, he'd address you as", ↵
 ↳ name.lower())
print("But if ee were mad, he'd call you", name.upper())
```

ee cummings, by the way, was an experimental American poet who didn't use uppercase letters. So, if he were alive and e-mailing you, he'd probably use all lowercase letters in your name. But if he were mad, he'd probably make an exception and "shout" via e-mail by addressing you in uppercase.

Printing name Five Times

The program displays the user's name five times in a row using string repetition:

```
called = name * 5
print("\nIf a small child were trying to get your attention",)
print("your name would become:")
print(called)
```

The variable called is assigned the value of name, repeated five times. Then, a message is printed followed by called.

Calculating seconds

The user's age, in seconds, is calculated and printed in the two following lines:

```
seconds = age * 365 * 24 * 60 * 60
print("\nYou're over", seconds, "seconds old.")
```

Since there are 365 days in a year, 24 hours in a day, 60 minutes in an hour, and 60 seconds in a minute, age is multiplied by the product of 365 * 24 * 60 * 60. This value is assigned to seconds. The next line displays the result.

Calculating moon_weight and sun_weight

The next four lines calculate and display the user's weight on the moon and sun:

```
moon_weight = weight / 6
print("\nDid you know that on the moon you would weigh only",
    moon_weight, "pounds?")

sun_weight = weight * 27.1
print("On the sun, you'd weigh", sun_weight, "(but, ah... not for long).")
```

Since the moon has one-sixth the gravitational pull of the earth, moon_weight is assigned the value of weight divided by 6. And since the gravitational force on the sun is about 27.1 times stronger than it is here on Earth, I multiply weight by 27.1 and assign the result to sun_weight.

Waiting for the User

The last statement waits for the user to press the Enter key:

```
input("\n\nPress the enter key to exit.")
```

SUMMARY

In this chapter, you saw how to create strings with single, double, and triple quotes. You learned how to include special characters in them with escape sequences. You saw how to join and repeat strings. You learned about two different numeric types, integers and floating-point numbers, and how to work with them. You also now know how to convert values between strings and numbers. You learned about variables and saw how to use them to store and retrieve information. Finally, you learned how to get user input to make your programs interactive.

CHALLENGES

1. Create a list of legal and illegal variable names. Describe why each is either legal or illegal. Next, create a list of "good" and "bad" legal variable names. Describe why each is either a good or bad choice for a variable name.

2. Write a program that allows a user to enter his or her two favorite foods. The program should then print out the name of a new food by joining the original food names together.

3. Write a Tipper program where the user enters a restaurant bill total. The program should then display two amounts: a 15 percent tip and a 20 percent tip.

4. Write a Car Salesman program where the user enters the base price of a car. The program should add on a bunch of extra fees such as tax, license, dealer prep, and destination charge. Make tax and license a percent of the base price. The other fees should be set values. Display the actual price of the car once all the extras are applied.

Branching, while Loops, and Program Planning: The Guess My Number Game

So far, the programs you've written have had a simple, sequential flow: each statement is executed once, in order, every time. If you were limited to just this type of programming, it would be very difficult, if not impossible, to write complex applications. But in this chapter, you learn how to selectively execute certain portions of your code and repeat parts of your program. Specifically, you learn to do the following:

- Generate random numbers using `randint()` and `randrange()`
- Use `if` statements to execute code based on a condition
- Use an `else` clause to make a choice based on a condition
- Use `elif` clauses to make a choice based on several conditions
- Use `while` loops to repeat parts of your program
- Plan your programs using pseudocode

INTRODUCING THE GUESS MY NUMBER GAME

The program you'll create in this chapter is the classic number guessing game. For those who missed out on it in their childhood, the game goes like this: the computer chooses a random number between 1 and 100 and the player tries to guess it in as few attempts as possible. Each time the player enters a guess, the computer tells the player whether the guess is too high, too low, or right on the money. Once the player guesses the number, the game is over. Figure 3.1 shows Guess My Number in action.

```
C:\Python31\python.exe                                    _ □ X
            Welcome to 'Guess My Number'!

I'm thinking of a number between 1 and 100.
Try to guess it in as few attempts as possible.

Take a guess: 50
Lower...
Take a guess: 25
Lower...
Take a guess: 15
You guessed it!  The number was 15
And it only took you 3 tries!


Press the enter key to exit.
```

FIGURE 3.1

Got it in only three guesses! Try to beat that.

GENERATING RANDOM NUMBERS

As much as users want consistent, predictable results from programs, sometimes what makes the programs exciting is their unpredictability: the sudden change in a computer opponent's strategy, or an alien creature bursting out from an arbitrary door. Random numbers can supply this element of chance or surprise, and Python provides an easy way to generate those random numbers.

TRAP Python generates random numbers based on a formula, so they are not truly random. This kind of random generation is called *pseudorandom* and is good enough for most applications (just don't try to start an online casino with it). If you really need truly random numbers, visit http://www.fourmilab.ch/hotbits/. The site generates random numbers based on the natural and unpredictable process of radioactive decay.

Introducing the Craps Roller Program

Craps Roller replicates the dice roll of the fast-paced, casino game of craps. But you don't have to know anything about craps to appreciate the program. Craps Roller just simulates the roll of two, six-sided dice. It displays the value of each and their total. To determine the dice values, the program uses functions that generate random numbers. Figure 3.2 shows the program in action.

FIGURE 3.2

Ack! I got a total of 7 on my first roll, which means I lose.

You can find the code for this program on the companion website for this book (www.courseptr.com/downloads), in the Chapter 3 folder; the file name is craps_roller.py.

```
# Craps Roller
# Demonstrates random number generation

import random

# generate random numbers 1 - 6
die1 = random.randint(1, 6)
die2 = random.randrange(6) + 1

total = die1 + die2

print("You rolled a", die1, "and a", die2, "for a total of", total)

input("\n\nPress the enter key to exit.")
```

Importing the random Module

The first line of code in the program introduces the import statement. The statement allows you to import, or load, modules, in this case, the random module:

```
import random
```

Modules are files that contain code meant to be used in other programs. These modules usually group together a collection of programming related to one area. The `random` module contains functions related to generating random numbers and producing random results.

If you think of your program as a construction project, then modules are like special toolkits that you can pull out from the garage when you need them. But instead of going to the shelf and grabbing a powered, circular saw, here I imported the `random` module.

Using the randint() Function

The `random` module contains a function, `randint()`, which produces a random integer. The Craps Roller program accesses `randint()` through the following function call:

```
random.randint(1, 6)
```

You'll notice the program doesn't directly call `randint()`. Instead, the program calls the function with `random.randint()`, accessing the function `randint()` through its module, `random`. In general, you can call a function from an imported module by giving the module name, followed by a period, followed by the function call itself. This method of access is called *dot notation*. Dot notation is like the possessive in English. In English, "Mike's Ferrari" means that it's the Ferrari that belongs to Mike. Using dot notation, `random.randint()` means the function `randint()` that belongs to the module `random`. Dot notation can be used to access different elements of imported modules.

The `randint()` function requires two integer argument values and returns a random integer between those two values, which may include either of the argument values. So, by passing the values 1 and 6 to the function, I'm guaranteed to get back either 1, 2, 3, 4, 5, or 6. Since I'm simulating the roll of a six-sided die, this is perfect.

Using the randrange() Function

The `random` module also contains a function, `randrange()`, which produces a random integer. There are several ways to call `randrange()`, but the simplest is to use a single, positive, integer argument. Called this way, the function returns a random integer from, and including, 0, up to, but not including, that number. So the call to `random.randrange(6)` produces either a 0, 1, 2, 3, 4, or 5. Alright, where's the 6? Well, `randrange()` is picking a random number from a group of six numbers—and the list of numbers starts with 0. So, I just added 1 to the result to get the right value for a `die2`:

```
die2 = random.randrange(6) + 1
```

As a result, `die2` gets either a 1, 2, 3, 4, 5, or 6.

TRAP

I used both the `randint()` and `randrange()` functions in the Craps Roller program so that I could show off two different functions for generating random numbers. In general, you'll want to pick the function that best fits your needs.

USING THE IF STATEMENT

Branching is a fundamental part of computer programming. It basically means making a decision to take one path or another. Through the `if` statement, your programs can branch to a section of code or just skip it, all based on how you've set things up.

Introducing the Password Program

The Password program uses the `if` statement to simulate the login procedure of a highly secure computer system. The program grants the user access if he or she enters the correct password. Figures 3.3 and 3.4 show a few sample runs.

You can find the code for this program on the companion website for this book (www.courseptr.com/downloads), in the Chapter 3 folder; the file name is password.py.

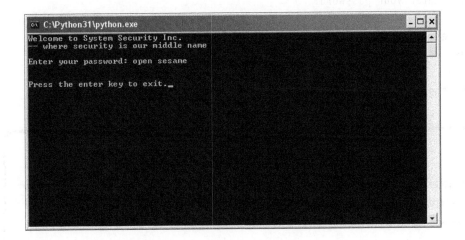

FIGURE 3.3

Ha, you'll never crack the code.

FIGURE 3.4

Guess I should
have picked a
better password
than "secret."

```
# Password
# Demonstrates the if statement

print("Welcome to System Security Inc.")
print("-- where security is our middle name\n")

password = input("Enter your password: ")

if password == "secret":
    print("Access Granted")

input("\n\nPress the enter key to exit.")
```

IN THE REAL WORLD

While the program Password does a good job of demonstrating the if statement, it's not a good example of how to implement computer security. In fact, anyone could simply examine the source code and discover the "secret" password.

To create a password validation system, a programmer would most likely use some form of *cryptography*. Cryptography, an ancient idea that dates back thousands of years, is used to encode information so that only the intended recipients can understand it. Cryptography is an entire field unto itself and some computer scientists devote their careers to it.

Examining the if Statement

The key to program Password is the if statement:

```
if password == "secret":
    print("Access Granted")
```

The if statement is pretty straightforward. You can probably figure out what's happening just by reading the code. If password is equal to "secret", then "Access Granted" is printed and the program continues to the next statement. But, if it isn't equal to "secret", the program does not print the message and continues directly to the next statement following the if statement.

Creating Conditions

All if statements have a *condition*. A condition is just an expression that is either true or false. You're already familiar with conditions. They're pretty common in daily life. In fact, almost any statement you make could be viewed as a condition. For example, the statement "It's 100 degrees outside." could be treated as a condition. It's either true or false.

Python has its own, built-in values to represent truth and falsehood. True represents true and False (drumroll) represents false. A condition can always be evaluated to one of these. In the Password program, the condition used in the if statement is password == "secret". It means that password is equal to, or refers to the value, "secret". This condition evaluates to either True or False, depending on the value of password. If the value of password is equal to "secret", then the condition is True. Otherwise, the condition is False.

Understanding Comparison Operators

Conditions are often created by comparing values. You can compare values using *comparison operators*. You've already seen one comparison operator by way of the Password program. It's the equal-to comparison operator, written as ==.

TRAP The equal-to comparison operator is two equal signs in a row. Using just one equal sign in a condition will result in a syntax error, because one equal sign represents the assignment operator. So, password = "secret" is an assignment statement. It assigns a value. And password == "secret" is a condition. It evaluates to either True or False. Even though the assignment operator and the equal-to operator look similar, they are two different things.

In addition to equal-to, there are other comparison operators. Table 3.1 summarizes some useful ones.

TABLE 3.1	COMPARISON OPERATORS		
Operator	**Meaning**	**Sample Condition**	**Evaluates To**
==	equal to	5 == 5	True
!=	not equal to	8 != 5	True
>	greater than	3 > 10	False
<	less than	5 < 8	True
>=	greater than or equal to	5 >= 10	False
<=	less than or equal to	5 <= 5	True

Using comparison operators, you can compare integers to integers, floating-point numbers to floating-point numbers, as well as integers to floating-point numbers. You can even compare strings—the results are based on alphabetical order. For example, "apple" < "orange" is True because "apple" is alphabetically less than "orange" (it comes before it in the dictionary).

 TRAP Python won't let you make certain comparisons. Objects of different types that don't have an established definition for order can't be compared using the <, <=, >, or >= operators. For example, Python won't let you use these operators to compare strings and integers. Go ahead, try to use the condition 10 > "five" in your program—all you'll do is generate a big, fat error message.

Using Indentation to Create Blocks

You may have noticed that the second line of the if statement, print("Access Granted"), is indented. By indenting the line, it becomes a *block*. A block is one or more consecutive lines indented by the same amount. Indenting sets lines off not only visually, but logically too. Together, they form a single unit.

Blocks can be used, among other ways, as part of an if statement. They're the statement or group of statements that gets executed if the condition is True. In the Password program, the block is the single statement print("Access Granted").

Since blocks can be as many statements as you like, you could add a special welcome for users who enter the proper password by changing the block in the if statement like so:

```
if password == "secret":
    print("Access Granted")
    print("Welcome! You must be someone very important.")
```

Now, users who correctly enter the secret password will see Access Granted followed by Welcome! You must be someone very important. And if a user enters something besides secret, the user won't see either of the messages.

 There's passionate debate within the Python community about whether to use tabs or spaces (and if spaces, the number to use) for indentation. This is really a question of personal style. But there are two guidelines worth following. First, be consistent. If you indent blocks with two spaces, then always use two spaces. Second, don't mix spaces and tabs. Even though you can line up blocks using a combination of both, this can lead to big headaches later. Common indentation styles include one tab, or two spaces, or (the style the creator of Python uses) four spaces. The choice is yours.

Building Your Own if Statement

You've seen a full example of an if statement, but I want to leave the topic by summarizing how to build your own. You can construct an if statement by using if, followed by a condition, followed by a colon, followed by a block of one or more statements. If the condition evaluates to True, then the statements that make up the block are executed. If the condition evaluates to False, then the program moves on to the next statement after the if statement.

USING THE ELSE CLAUSE

Sometimes you'll want your program to "make a choice" based on a condition: do one thing if the condition is true, do something else if it's false. The else clause, when used in an if statement, gives you that power.

Introducing the Granted or Denied Program

The program Password did a good job welcoming a user who entered the correct password, but it didn't do anything if the wrong password was entered. Program Granted or Denied solves this problem by using an else clause. Figures 3.5 and 3.6 show off the new and improved version.

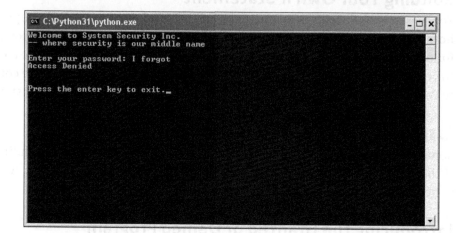

You can find the code for this program on the companion website, in the Chapter 3 folder; the file name is granted_or_denied.py.

```
# Granted or Denied
# Demonstrates an else clause

print("Welcome to System Security Inc.")
print("-- where security is our middle name\n")

password = input("Enter your password: ")

if password == "secret":
```

```
    print("Access Granted")
else:
    print("Access Denied")

input("\n\nPress the enter key to exit.")
```

Examining the else Clause

I only made one change from the Password program. I added an `else` clause to the `if` statement:

```
if password == "secret":
    print("Access Granted")
else:
    print("Access Denied")
```

If the value of password is equal to "secret", the program prints Access Granted, just like before. But thanks to the `else` clause, the program prints Access Denied otherwise.

In an `if` statement with an `else` clause, exactly one of the code blocks will execute. If the condition is true, then the block immediately following the condition is executed. If the condition is false, then the block immediately after the `else` is executed.

You can create an `else` clause immediately following the `if` block with `else`, followed by a colon, followed by a block of statements. The `else` clause must be in the same block as its corresponding `if`. That is, the `else` and `if` must be indented the same amount.

USING THE ELIF CLAUSE

Your program can choose from among several possibilities in an `if` statement with the use of the `elif` clause. This clause comes in quite handy when you have one variable that you want to compare to a bunch of different values.

Introducing the Mood Computer Program

In the mid-1970s (yes, last century), there was a wildly successful fad product called the Mood Ring. The ring revealed the wearer's mood through a color-changing gem. Well, the Mood Computer program takes the technology to the next level by looking into the psyche of the user and displaying his or her mood. Figure 3.7 reveals my mood while writing this very chapter.

FIGURE 3.7

Looks like I was in a
great mood while
writing the Mood
Computer
program.

Okay, the program doesn't really plumb the emotional depths of the user through electro-dermal impulses transmitted via the keyboard. Instead, Mood Computer generates a random number to choose one of three faces to print using an if statement with elif clauses. (By the way, the Mood Ring didn't really reveal the wearer's emotions either. It was just an LCD that changed colors based on body temperature.)

You can find the code for this program on the downloads site (www.courseptr.com/downloads), in the Chapter 3 folder; the file name is mood_computer.py.

```
# Mood Computer
# Demonstrates the elif clause

import random

print("I sense your energy.  Your true emotions are coming across my screen.")
print("You are...")

mood = random.randint(1, 3)

if mood == 1:
    # happy
    print( \
    """
```

```
          ----------
          |          |
          | 0     0  |
          |    <     |
          |          |
          | .      . |
          | `...`    |
          ----------
                    """)
elif mood == 2:
    # neutral
    print( \
    """
          ----------
          |          |
          | 0     0  |
          |    <     |
          |  ------  |
          |          |
          ----------
                    """)
elif mood == 3:
    # sad
    print( \
    """
          ----------
          |          |
          | 0     0  |
          |    <     |
          |   .'.    |
          |  '   '   |
          ----------
                    """)
else:
    print("Illegal mood value!  (You must be in a really bad mood).")
```

```
print("...today.")

input("\n\nPress the enter key to exit.")
```

Examining the elif Clause

An `if` statement with `elif` clauses can contain a sequence of conditions for a program to evaluate. In Mood Computer, the lines containing the different conditions are

- `if mood == 0:`
- `elif mood == 1:`
- `elif mood == 2:`

Notice that you write the first condition using an `if`, but then test the remaining conditions using `elif` (short for "else if") clauses. You can have as many `elif` clauses as you like.

By isolating the conditions, you can see the purpose of the structure: to test `mood` against three different values. The program first checks to see if `mood` is equal to 0. If it is, then the happy face is printed. If not, the program moves to the next condition and checks if `mood` is equal to 1. If it is, the neutral face is printed. If not, the program checks if `mood` is equal to 2. If so, the sad face is printed.

An important feature of an `if` statement with `elif` clauses is that once a condition evaluates to `True`, the computer executes its corresponding block and exits the statement. This means that at most, only one block executes, even if several conditions would evaluate to `True`. In Mood Computer, that's no big deal. `mood` can only be equal to a single number, so only one of the conditions can be true. But it's important to be aware of this behavior because it's possible to create statements where more than one condition can be true at the same time. In that case, only the block associated with the first true condition executes.

If none of the preceding conditions for `mood` turn out to be `True`, then the final `else` clause's block runs and `Illegal mood value! (You must be in a really bad mood).` appears on the screen. This should never happen, since `mood` will always be 0, 1, or 2. But I put the clause in there just in case. I didn't have to, though, since the final `else` clause is optional.

Though it's not necessary to use the final `else` clause, it's a good idea. It works as a catchall for when none of the conditions within the statement are `True`. Even if you think one of your conditions will always be `True`, you can still use the final `else` clause to catch the "impossible" case, like I did.

You've seen three similar, but progressively more powerful branching structures. For a concise review, check out Table 3.2.

TABLE 3.2   BRANCHING STATEMENTS SUMMARY

Statement	Description
if <condition>: <block>	if statement. If <condition> is true, <block> is executed; otherwise it's skipped.

if <condition>:
    <block1>
else:
    <block 2>
	if statement with else clause. If <condition> is true, <block1> is executed; otherwise <block2> is executed.

if <condition 1>:
    <block 1>
elif <condition 2>:
    <block 2>
.
.
.
elif <condition N>:
    <block N>
else:
    <block N+1>
	if statement with elif clauses and optional final else clause. The block of the first true condition is executed. If no condition is true, the optional else clause's block is executed.

CREATING WHILE LOOPS

Loops are all around us. Even your shampoo bottle has looping instructions on it: "While your hair is dirty: Rinse. Lather. Repeat." This may seem like a simple idea—while some condition is true, repeat something—but it's a powerful tool in programming. It would come in quite handy, for example, in making a quiz show game. You might want to tell your program: while there are questions left, keep playing the game. Or, in a banking application, you might want to tell your program: while the user hasn't entered a valid account number, keep asking the user for an account number. The while loop lets you do exactly this.

Introducing the Three-Year-Old Simulator Program

In today's fast-paced world, many people don't get to spend the time they'd like with the children in their lives. A busy lawyer might be stuck at the office and not see her small son. A salesman might be on the road and not see his little niece. Well, the Three-Year-Old Simulator solves that problem by reproducing a conversation with a three-year-old child.

The key to mimicking a three-year-old, it turns out, is the `while` loop. Figure 3.8 shows a sample run.

```
C:\Python31\python.exe                                        _ □ ×
            Welcome to the 'Three-Year-Old Simulator'
This program simulates a conversation with a three-year-old child.
Try to stop the madness.

Why?
Why what?
Why?
I don't know why.
Why?
Really, I don't know.
Why?
Please, I don't know.
Why?
Please, stop.
Why?
Please! I'm begging you to stop.
Why?
Because.
Oh. Okay.

Press the enter key to exit._
```

FIGURE 3.8

If you've ever been in charge of a three-year-old, this should bring back warm memories.

As you can see, the program keeps asking Why? until the answer, Because., is entered. You can find the code for this program on the companion website, in the Chapter 3 folder; the file name is three_year-old.py.

```python
# Three Year-Old Simulator
# Demonstrates the while loop

print("\tWelcome to the 'Three-Year-Old Simulator'\n")
print("This program simulates a conversation with a three-year-old child.")
print("Try to stop the madness.\n")

response = ""
while response != "Because.":
    response = input("Why?\n")

print("Oh.  Okay.")

input("\n\nPress the enter key to exit.")
```

Examining the while Loop
The loop from the Three-Year-Old Simulator program is just two lines:

```
while response != "Because.":
    response = input("Why?\n")
```

If the format of the `while` loop looks familiar, there's a good reason. It bears a striking resemblance to its cousin, the `if` statement. The only difference is that `if` is replaced by `while`. And the similarities aren't just skin-deep. In both statement types, if the condition is true, the block (sometimes call the *loop body* in a loop) is executed. But in the `while` statement, the computer tests the condition and executes the block over and over, until the condition is false. That's why it's called a loop.

In this case, the loop body is just `response = input("Why?\n")`, which will continue to execute until the user enters `Because.`. At that point, `response != "Because."` is false and the loop mercifully ends. Then, the program executes the next statement, `print("Oh. Okay. ")`.

Initializing the Sentry Variable

Often, `while` loops are controlled by a *sentry variable,* a variable used in the condition and compared to some other value or values. Like a human sentry, you can think of your sentry variable as a guard, helping form a barrier around the `while` loop's block. In the Three-Year-Old Simulator program, the sentry variable is `response`. It's used in the condition and is compared to the string `"Because."` before the block is executed each time.

It's important to initialize your sentry variable. Most of the time, sentry variables are initialized right before the loop itself. That's what I did with:

```
response = ""
```

 TRAP If the sentry variable doesn't have a value when the condition is evaluated, your program will generate an error.

It's usually a good idea to initialize your sentry variables to some type of empty value. I assign `""`, the empty string, to `response`. While I could assign the string `"aardvark"`, and the program would work just the same, it would make the code needlessly confusing.

Checking the Sentry Variable

Make sure that it's possible for the `while` condition to evaluate to `True` at some point; otherwise, the block will *never* run. Take, for example, one minor change to the loop you've been working with:

```
response = "Because."
while response != "Because.":
    response = input("Why?\n")
```

Since `response` is equal to `"Because."` right before the loop, the block will never run.

Updating the Sentry Variable

Once you've established your condition, initialized your sentry variable, and are sure that under some conditions the loop block will execute, you have yourself a working loop. Next, make sure the loop will end at some point.

If you write a loop that never stops, you've created an *infinite* loop. Welcome to the club. At one time or another, all programmers have accidentally created an infinite loop and watched their program get stuck doing something over and over. Or they see their programs just plain freeze up.

Here's a simple example of an infinite loop:

```
counter = 0
while counter <= 10
  print(counter)
```

The programmer probably intended the loop to print the numbers from 0 to 10. Unfortunately, what this program does is print 0, forever. The programmer forgot to change `counter`, the sentry variable, inside the loop body. So remember, the values in the condition must be able to change as a result of the code inside the loop body. If they can't ever change, the loop won't end, and you end up with an infinite loop.

AVOIDING INFINITE LOOPS

One type of infinite loop is where the sentry variable is never updated, like you just saw. But there are more insidious forms of the never-ending loop. Check out the next program. It does change the value of the sentry variable in the loop body. But something is wrong, because the loop never ends. See if you can spot the trouble before I explain what's going on.

Introducing the Losing Battle Program

The Losing Battle program describes the last, valiant fight of a hero overwhelmed by an army of trolls, a scenario you might find in a role-playing game. The program narrates the battle action. It describes the struggle, blow-by-blow, as the hero defeats a troll, but then takes more damage. In the end, the program always ends with the death of the hero. Or does it? You can find the code for this program on the companion website, in the Chapter 3 folder; the file name is losing_battle-bad.py.

```
# Losing Battle
# Demonstrates the dreaded infinite loop

print("Your lone hero is surrounded by a massive army of trolls.")
print("Their decaying green bodies stretch out, melting into the horizon.")
print("Your hero unsheathes his sword for the last fight of his life.\n")

health = 10
trolls = 0
damage = 3

while health != 0:
    trolls += 1
    health -= damage

    print("Your hero swings and defeats an evil troll, " \
          "but takes", damage, "damage points.\n")

print("Your hero fought valiantly and defeated", trolls, "trolls.")
print("But alas, your hero is no more.")

input("\n\nPress the enter key to exit.")
```

Figure 3.9 shows a run of the program. This resulted in an infinite loop and I had to stop the process by pressing Ctrl+C, or it would have continued.

FIGURE 3.9

It seems you have an immortal hero. The only way to end the program was to stop the process.

So, what's going on?

Tracing the Program

Well, it looks like the program has a logical error. A good way to track down this kind of error is to trace your program's execution. *Tracing* means you simulate the running of your program and do exactly what it would do, following every statement and keeping track of the values assigned to variables. This way, you can step through the program, understand exactly what is happening at each point, and discover the circumstances that conspire to produce the bug in your code.

The most basic way to trace a program is with old-fashioned pencil and paper. I created columns, one for each variable and condition. So to start, my page looks like this:

health	trolls	damage	health != 0

Right after the condition of the `while` loop is evaluated, my page looks like this:

health	trolls	damage	health != 0
10	0	3	True

Since the condition is `True`, the loop executes for the first time. After one full time through and back up to evaluate the condition again, my trace looks like this:

Health	trolls	damage	health != 0
10	0	3	True
7	1	3	True

After a few more times through the loop, my trace looks like:

health	trolls	damage	health != 0
10	0	3	True
7	1	3	True
4	2	3	True
1	3	3	True
-2	4	3	True
-5	5	3	True
-7	6	3	True

I stopped the trace because it seemed like I was in an infinite loop. Since the value of `health` is negative (and not equal to 0) in the last three lines of the trace, the condition is still `True`. The problem is, `health` will never become 0. It will just grow in the negative direction each time the loop executes. As a result, the condition will never become `False`, and the loop will never end.

Creating Conditions That Can Become False

In addition to making sure values in a while loop's condition change, you should be sure that the condition can eventually evaluate to False; otherwise, you still have an infinite loop on your hands. In the case of the Losing Battle program, the fix is easy. The line with the condition just needs to become

```
while health > 0:
```

You can find the code for this program on the companion website, in the Chapter 3 folder; the file name is losing_battle-good.py.

Now, if health becomes 0 or negative, the condition evaluates to False and the loop ends. To be sure, you can trace the program using this new condition:

health	trolls	damage	health > 0
10	0	3	True
7	1	3	True
4	2	3	True
1	3	3	True
-2	4	3	False

And the program ends as it should. Figure 3.10 shows how the debugged program runs.

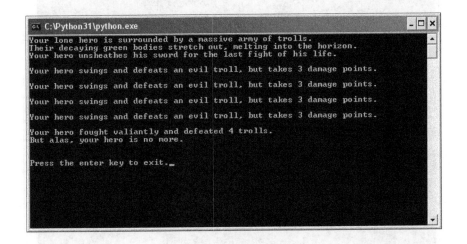

FIGURE 3.10

Now the program runs correctly, avoiding an infinite loop. Your hero's fate, however, is not as bright.

TREATING VALUES AS CONDITIONS

If I asked you to evaluate 35 + 2 you'd come back quickly with 37. But if I asked you to evaluate 37 as either true or false, you'd probably come back with, "Huh?" But the idea of looking at any value as either true or false is valid in Python. Any value, of any type, can be treated this way. So, 2749, 8.6, "banana", 0, and "" can each be interpreted as True or False. This may seem bizarre, but it's easy. The rules that establish True and False are simple. More importantly, interpreting values this way can make for more elegant conditions.

Introducing the Maitre D' Program

If you haven't been snubbed at a fancy, French restaurant lately, then I have just the program for you. Maitre D' welcomes you to the fine eatery and then asks you how much money you slip your host. If you give zero dollars, then you are rightly ignored. If you give some other amount, then your table is waiting. Figures 3.11 and 3.12 show off the program.

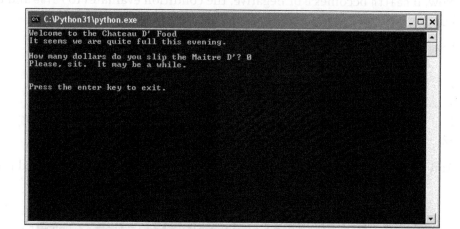

FIGURE 3.11

When you don't tip the maitre d', there are no tables to be found.

FIGURE 3.12

This time, my money has helped cure the maitre d' of his amnesia.

From watching the program run, you might not be impressed. This seems like something you could have already done. The difference is, there is no comparison operator used in this program. Instead, a value (the amount of money) is treated as a condition. You can find the code for this program on the companion website (www.courseptr.com/downloads), in the Chapter 3 folder; the file name is maitre_d.py.

```
# Maitre D'
# Demonstrates treating a value as a condition

print("Welcome to the Chateau D' Food")
print("It seems we are quite full this evening.\n")

money = int(input("How many dollars do you slip the Maitre D'? "))

if money:
    print("Ah, I am reminded of a table.  Right this way.")
else:
    print("Please, sit.  It may be a while.")

input("\n\nPress the enter key to exit.")
```

Interpreting Any Value as True or False

The new concept is demonstrated in the line:

```
if money:
```

Notice that money is not compared to any other value. money is the condition. When it comes to evaluating a number as a condition, 0 is False and everything else is True. So, the above line is equivalent to

```
if money != 0:
```

The first version is simpler, more elegant, and more intuitive. It reads more naturally and could be translated to "if there is money."

The rules for what makes a value True or False are simple. The basic principal is this: any empty or zero value is False, everything else is True. So, 0 evaluates to False, but any other number evaluates to True. The empty string, "", is False, while any other string is True. As you can see, most every value is True. It's only the empty or zero value that's False. You'll find that testing for an empty value is a common thing to do, so this way of treating values can come up a lot in programs.

One last thing to note here is that if you enter a negative dollar amount, the maitre d' will still seat you. Remember, for numbers, only 0 is False. So, all negative numbers are True, just like positive ones.

CREATING INTENTIONAL INFINITE LOOPS

Coming soon after a section called "Avoiding Infinite Loops," you might be more than a bit surprised to see a section about *creating* infinite loops. Aren't infinite loops always a mistake? Well, if a loop were truly infinite—that is, it could never end, then yes, it would be a logical error. But what I call *intentional infinite loops* are infinite loops with an exit condition built into the loop body. The best way to understand an intentional infinite loop is to see an example.

Introducing the Finicky Counter Program

The Finicky Counter program counts from 1 to 10 using an intentional infinite loop. It's finicky because it doesn't like the number 5 and skips it. Figure 3.13 shows a run of the program.

You can find the code for this program on the companion website, in the Chapter 3 folder; the file name is finicky_counter.py.

```
# Finicky Counter
# Demonstrates the break and continue statements

count = 0
while True:
    count += 1
```

```
    # end loop if count greater than 10
    if count > 10:
        break
    # skip 5
    if count == 5:
        continue
    print(count)

input("\n\nPress the enter key to exit.")
```

Using the break Statement to Exit a Loop

I set up the loop with:

```
while True:
```

This technically means that the loop will continue forever, unless there is an exit condition in the loop body. Luckily, I put one in:

```
    # end loop if count greater than 10
    if count > 10:
        break
```

Since count is increased by 1 each time the loop body begins, it will eventually reach 11. When it does, the break statement, which here means "break out of the loop," is executed and the loop ends.

Using the continue Statement to Jump Back to the Top of a Loop

Just before count is printed, I included the lines:

```
    # skip 5
    if count == 5:
        continue
```

The continue statement means "jump back to the top of the loop." At the top of the loop, the while condition is tested and the loop is entered again if it evaluates to True. So when count is equal to 5, the program does not get to the print(count) statement. Instead, it goes right back to the top of the loop so that 5 is never printed.

Understanding When to Use break and continue

You can use break and continue in any loop you create. They aren't just restricted for use in intentional infinite loops. But they should be used sparingly. Both break and continue make it harder for someone (including you!) to see the flow of a loop and understand under what conditions it ends. Plus, you don't actually need `break` and `continue`. Any loop you can write using them can be written without them.

In Python, there are times when an intentional infinite loop can be clearer than a traditional loop. In those cases, where it's really clunky to write the loop with a regular condition, some programmers use intentional infinite loops.

USING COMPOUND CONDITIONS

So far, you've only seen comparisons where exactly two values are involved. These are called *simple conditions*. But you may find yourself wishing for more power. Luckily, you can combine simple conditions together with *logical operators*. Combined, these simple conditions become *compound conditions*. Using compound conditions, your programs can make decisions based on how multiple groups of values compare.

Introducing the Exclusive Network Program

Exclusive clubs are no fun, unless you're a member. So, I created the Exclusive Network program. It simulates an elite computer network where only a select few are members. The membership consists of me and several top game designers in the world today (not bad company).

Like real-world computer systems, each person has to enter a username and a password. A member has to enter both his or her username and password, or the member won't be able to log in. With a successful login, the member is personally greeted. Also like real-world systems, everyone has a security level.

Because I'm not a total elitist, guests are allowed to log in. Guests have the lowest security level, though. Figures 3.14 through 3.16 show off the program.

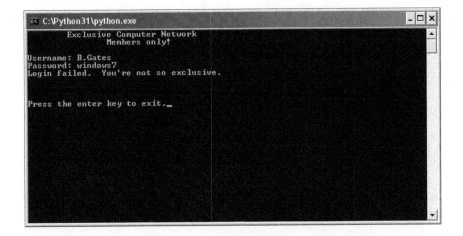

FIGURE 3.14

If you're not a member or a guest, you can't get in.

FIGURE 3.15

A guest can log in, but his security level is set quite low.

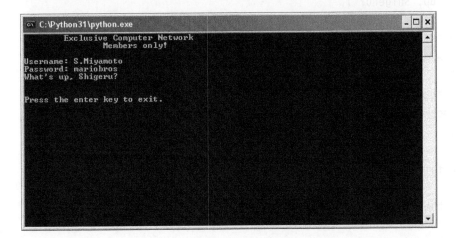

FIGURE 3.16

Looks like one of the guys logged in today.

You can find the code for this program on the companion website, in the Chapter 3 folder; the file name is exclusive_network.py.

```python
# Exclusive Network
# Demonstrates logical operators and compound conditions

print("\tExclusive Computer Network")
print("\t\tMembers only!\n")

security = 0

username = ""
while not username:
    username = input("Username: ")

password = ""
while not password:
    password = input("Password: ")

if username == "M.Dawson" and password == "secret":
    print("Hi, Mike.")
    security = 5
elif username == "S.Meier" and password == "civilization":
    print("Hey, Sid.")
    security = 3
elif username == "S.Miyamoto" and password == "mariobros":
    print("What's up, Shigeru?")
    security = 3
elif username == "W.Wright" and password == "thesims":
    print("How goes it, Will?")
    security = 3
elif username == "guest" or password == "guest":
    print("Welcome, guest.")
    security = 1
else:
    print("Login failed.  You're not so exclusive.\n")

input("\n\nPress the enter key to exit.")
```

IN THE REAL WORLD

If you really want to implement a private network, you wouldn't write usernames and passwords directly into your code. You'd probably use some type of *database management system* (DBMS). Database management systems allow you to organize, access, and update related information. These systems are powerful and could handle thousands or even millions of pairs of usernames and passwords quickly and securely.

Understanding the not Logical Operator

I wanted to make sure that the user enters something for the username and password. Just pressing the Enter key, which results in the empty string, won't do. I wanted a loop that continues to ask for a username until the user enters something:

```
username = ""
while not username:
    username = input("Username: ")
```

In the `while` condition, I used the logical `not` operator. It works a lot like the word "not." In English, putting the word "not" in front of something creates a new phrase that means the opposite of the original. In Python, putting `not` in front of a condition creates a new condition that evaluates to the opposite of the original.

This means `not username` is `True` when `username` is `False`. And `not username` is `False` when `username` is `True`. Here's another way to understand how `not` works:

```
username      not username
True          False
False         True
```

Since `username` is initialized to the empty string in the program, it starts out as `False`. That makes `not username` `True` and the loop runs the first time. Then, the program gets a value for `username` from the user. If the user just presses Enter, `username` is the empty string, just as before. And just as before, `not username` is `True` and the loop keeps running. So, as long as the user just hits Enter, the loop keeps running, and the user keeps getting prompted for a username.

But when the user finally enters something, username becomes something other than the empty string. That makes username evaluate to True and not username evaluate to False. As a result, the loop ends, just like I wanted.

The program does the same thing for the variable password.

Understanding the and Logical Operator

If a member wants to log in to this exclusive network, the member has to enter a username and password that are recognized together. If, for example, Sid Meier wants to log in, he has to enter S.Meier for his username and civilization for his password. If Sid doesn't enter both, just that way, he can't log in. S.Meier and mariobros won't work. Neither will M.Dawson and civilization. The combination civilization and S.Meier fails too. The program checks that Sid enters S.Meier for his username and civilization for his password with the following code:

```
elif username == "S.Meier" and password == "civilization":
```

The line contains a single compound condition made up of two simple conditions. The simple conditions are username == "S.Meier" along with password == "civilization". These are just like conditions you've already seen, but they've been joined together by the and logical operator to form a larger, compound condition, username == "S.Meier" and password == "civilization". This compound condition, though longer than you're used to, is still just a condition, which means that it can be either True or False.

So, when is username == "S.Meier" and password == "civilization" True, and when is it False? Well, just like in English, "and" means both. So, the condition is True only if both username == "S.Meier" and password == "civilization" are True; otherwise, it's False. Here's another way to see how this works:

username == "S.Meier"	password == "civilization"	username == "S.Meier" and password == "civilization"
True	True	True
True	False	False
False	True	False
False	False	False

 HINT   Put and between two conditions when you want to create a new condition that is true only if both simpler conditions are true.

So, when Sid enters S.Meier for his username and civilization for his password, the compound condition is true. Sid is then greeted and assigned a security level.

The program, of course, works for others besides Sid Meier. Through an if-elif-else structure, the program checks four different username and password pairs. If a user enters a recognized pair, the member is personally greeted and assigned a security value.

If a member or guest doesn't properly log in, the computer prints a "failed login" message and tells the person that he or she is not so exclusive.

Understanding the or Logical Operator

Guests are allowed in the network, too, but with a limited security level. To make it easy for a guest to try the network, all he or she has to do is enter guest for either the username or password. The following lines of code log in a guest:

```
elif username == "guest" or password == "guest":
    print("Welcome, guest.")
    security = 1
```

The elif condition, username == "guest" or password == "guest", looks a lot like the other conditions, the ones used for the members. But there's a major difference. The guest condition is created by using the logical or operator.

A compound condition created with an or is True as long as at least one of the simpler conditions is True. Again, the operator works just like in English. "Or" means either, so if either condition is True, the compound condition is True. In this particular case, if username == "guest" is True or if password == "guest" is True, or even if both are True, then username == "guest" or password == "guest" is True; otherwise, it's False. Here's another way to look at how or works:

username == "guest"	password == "guest"	username == "guest" or password == "guest"
True	True	True
True	False	True
False	True	True
False	False	False

PLANNING YOUR PROGRAMS

So far, all the programs you've seen have been pretty simple. The idea of planning any of them formally on paper probably seems like overkill. It's not. Planning your programs, even the small ones, will almost always result in time (and often frustration) saved.

Programming is a lot like construction. So, imagine a contractor building a house for you without a blueprint. Yikes! You're liable to end up with a house that has 12 bathrooms, no windows, and a front door on the second floor. Plus, it will cost you 10 times the estimated price.

Programming is the same way. Without a plan, you'll likely struggle through the process, wasting time. You might even end up with a program that doesn't quite work.

Program planning is so important that there's an entire field of software engineering dedicated to it. But even a beginning programmer can benefit from a few simple planning tools and techniques.

Creating Algorithms with Pseudocode

An *algorithm* is a set of clear, easy-to-follow instructions for accomplishing some task. An algorithm is like an outline for your program. It's something you planned out, before programming, to guide you along as you code.

An algorithm isn't just a goal—it's a concrete list of steps to be followed in order. So, for example, "Be a millionaire" is not really an algorithm. It's more like a goal. But a worthy one. So I wrote the Make a Million Dollars algorithm. Here it is:

```
if you can think of a new and useful  product
    then that's your product
otherwise
    repackage an existing product as  your product
make an infomercial about your product
show the infomercial on TV
charge $100 per unit of your product
sell 10,000 units of your product
```

There you go. It's a clear series of finite steps that can be followed to achieve the goal.

Algorithms are generally written in something called *pseudocode,* and mine is no exception. Pseudocode falls somewhere between English and a programming language. Anyone who understands English can understand my algorithm. But at the same time, my algorithm should feel vaguely like a program. The first four lines resemble an if-else structure, and that's intentional.

Applying Stepwise Refinement to Your Algorithms

Like any outline or plan, your algorithm might not be finished after one draft. Often, algorithms need multiple passes before they can be implemented in code. *Stepwise refinement* is one process used to rewrite algorithms so that they're ready for implementation. Basically, it means "make it more detailed." By taking each step in an algorithm and breaking it down into a series of simpler steps, the algorithm becomes closer to programming code. In stepwise refinement, you keep breaking down each step until you feel that the entire algorithm could be fairly easily translated into a program. As an example, take a step from the Make a Million Dollars algorithm:

```
create an infomercial about your product
```

This might seem like too vague a task. How do you create an infomercial? Using stepwise refinement, the single step can be broken down into several others. So, it becomes the following:

```
write a script for an infomercial about your product
rent a TV studio for a day
hire a production crew
hire an enthusiastic audience
film the infomercial
```

If you feel that these five steps are clear and achievable, then that part of the algorithm has been thoroughly refined. If you're still unclear about a step, refine it some more. Continue with this process and you will have a complete algorithm and a million dollars.

RETURNING TO THE GUESS MY NUMBER GAME

The Guess My Number game combines many of the concepts you learned in this chapter. But, more importantly, it represents the first full game that you can use to show off to your friends, family, and members of the opposite sex.

Planning the Program

To plan the game, I wrote some pseudocode first:

```
pick a random number
while the player hasn't guessed the number
    let the player guess
congratulate the player
```

This isn't a bad first pass, but it's missing some important elements. First, the program needs to tell the player if the guess is too high or too low. Second, the program should keep track of how many guesses the player has made and then tell the player this number at the end of the game.

     It's okay if your first program plan isn't complete. Start planning with the major ideas first, then fill in the gaps until it feels done.

Okay, here's a refinement of my algorithm:

```
welcome the player to the game and explain it
 pick a random number between 1 and 100
 ask the player for a guess
 set the number of guesses to 1
     while the player's guess does not equal the number
         if the guess is greater than the number
             tell the player to guess lower
         otherwise
             tell the player to guess higher
         get a new guess from the player
         increase the number of guesses by 1
congratulate the player on guessing the number
let the player know how many guesses it took
```

Now I feel ready to write the program. Take a look over the next few sections and see how directly pseudocode can be translated into Python. You can find the code for this program on the companion website, in the Chapter 3 folder; the file name is guess_my_ number.py.

Creating the Initial Comment Block

Like all good programs, this one begins with a block of comments:

```
# Guess My Number
#
# The computer picks a random number between 1 and 100
# The player tries to guess it and the computer lets
# the player know if the guess is too high, too low
# or right on the money
```

Importing the random Module

To be fun, the program needs to generate a random number. So, I imported the `random` module:

```
import random
```

Explaining the Game

The game is simple, but a little explanation wouldn't hurt:

```
print("\tWelcome to 'Guess My Number'!")
print("\nI'm thinking of a number between 1 and 100.")
print("Try to guess it in as few attempts as possible.\n")
```

Setting the Initial Values

Next, I set all the variables to their initial values:

```
# set the initial values
the_number = random.randint(1, 100)
guess = int(input("Take a guess: "))
tries = 1
```

`the_number` represents the number the player has to guess. I assign it a random integer from 1 to 100 with a call to `random.randint()`. Next, `input()` gets the player's first guess. `int()` converts the guess to an integer. I assign this number to `guess`. I assign `tries`, which represents the number of guesses so far, the value 1.

Creating a Guessing Loop

This is the core of the program. The loop executes as long as the player hasn't correctly guessed the computer's number. In the loop body, the player's guess is compared to the computer's number. If the guess is higher than the number, `Lower` is printed; otherwise, `Higher` is printed. The player enters the next guess, and the number of guesses counter is incremented.

```
# guessing loop
while guess != the_number:
    if guess > the_number:
        print("Lower...")
    else:
        print("Higher...")

    guess = int(input("Take a guess: "))
    tries += 1
```

Congratulating the Player

When the player guesses the number, guess is equal to the_number, which means that the loop condition, guess != the_number, is False and the loop ends. At that point, the player needs to be congratulated:

```
print("You guessed it!  The number was", the_number)
print("And it only took you", tries, "tries!\n")
```

The computer tells the player what the secret number was and how many tries it took the player to guess it.

Waiting for the Player to Quit

As always, the last line waits patiently for the player to press the Enter key:

```
input("\n\nPress the enter key to exit.")
```

SUMMARY

In this chapter, you saw how to change the flow of your program. You learned that the key to changing the flow is the computer's ability to evaluate conditions. You saw how to create simple and compound conditions. You learned about the if, if-else, and if-elif-else statements, which allow programs to make a decision. You met the while loop, useful for repeating code sections. You learned about the importance of program planning. You saw how to plan a program by creating an algorithm in pseudocode. You also learned how to generate random numbers to add some excitement to your programs.

CHALLENGES

1. Write a program that simulates a fortune cookie. The program should display one of five unique fortunes, at random, each time it's run.
2. Write a program that flips a coin 100 times and then tells you the number of heads and tails.
3. Modify the Guess My Number game so that the player has a limited number of guesses. If the player fails to guess in time, the program should display an appropriately chastising message.
4. Here's a bigger challenge. Write the pseudocode for a program where the player and the computer trade places in the number guessing game. That is, the player picks a random number between 1 and 100 that the computer has to guess. Before you start, think about how you guess. If all goes well, try coding the game.

FOR LOOPS, STRINGS, AND TUPLES: THE WORD JUMBLE GAME

You've seen how variables are a great way to access information, but as your programs grow in size and complexity, so can the number of your variables. Keeping track of all of them can become a lot of work. Therefore, in this chapter, you'll learn about the idea of sequences and meet a new type, called the *tuple*, which let's you organize and manipulate information in ordered groups. You'll also see how a type you've already encountered, the string, is really a sequence too. You'll learn about a new kind of loop that's built just for working with sequences. Specifically, you'll learn how to do the following:

- Construct for loops to move through a sequence
- Use the range() function to create a sequence of numbers
- Treat strings as sequences
- Use tuples to harness the power of sequences
- Use sequence functions and operators
- Index and slice sequences

INTRODUCING THE WORD JUMBLE GAME

The Word Jumble game, featured in Figure 4.1, utilizes many of the new ideas you'll learn in this chapter.

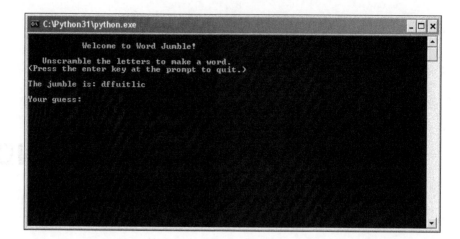

```
            Welcome to Word Jumble!

   Unscramble the letters to make a word.
(Press the enter key at the prompt to quit.)

The jumble is: dffuitlic

Your guess:
```

FIGURE 4.1

The Word Jumble
game. This jumble
looks "difficult."

This game re-creates the typical word jumble you might find in the Sunday paper (you know, that thing people used to read before the Internet). The computer picks a random word from a group and then creates a jumbled version of it, where the letters are in random order. The player has to guess the original word to win the game.

USING FOR LOOPS

In the last chapter, you saw one kind of loop, the `while` loop, which repeats part of your code based on a condition. As long as the condition is true, some code repeats. The `for` loop also repeats code, but not based on a condition. Instead, the `for` loop repeats part of a program based on a *sequence,* an ordered list of things. If you've ever written a list of, say, your top 10 favorite movies, then you've created a sequence.

A `for` loop repeats its loop body for each *element* of the sequence, in order. When it reaches the end of the sequence, the loop ends. As an example, consider your movie list sequence again. A `for` loop could go through this sequence of movie titles, one at a time, and print each one. But the best way to understand a `for` loop is to see one in action.

Introducing the Loopy String Program

This program takes a word from the user and prints its letters, in order, on separate lines. Look at a sample run in Figure 4.2.

FIGURE 4.2

A for loop goes through a word the user enters, one character at a time.

This simple program provides a good example of a for loop. You can find the code for the program on the companion website (www.courseptr.com/downloads) in the Chapter 4 folder; the file name is loopy_string.py.

```
# Loopy String
# Demonstrates the for loop with a string

word = input("Enter a word: ")

print("\nHere's each letter in your word:")
for letter in word:
    print(letter)


input("\n\nPress the enter key to exit.")
```

Understanding for Loops

The new idea in this program is the for loop, which is just the following two short lines:

```
for letter in word:
    print(letter)
```

Even before you know anything about for loops, the code is pretty clear, but I'll explain exactly how it works. All sequences are made up of elements. A string is a sequence in which each element is one character. In the case of the string "Loop", the first element is the character "L", the second is "o", and so on.

A for loop marches through (or *iterates over*) a sequence one element at a time. In my program, the loop iterates over the string "Loop", one character at a time. A for loop uses a variable that gets each successive element of the sequence. In my loop, letter is the variable that gets each successive character of "Loop". Inside the loop body, the loop can then do something with each successive element. In my loop body, I simply print letter. Now, the variable you use to get each element of the sequence is like any other variable—and if it doesn't exist before the loop, it's created.

So, when my loop begins, letter is created and gets the first character in word, which is "L". Then, in the loop body, the print statement displays L. Next, with the loop body finished, control jumps back to the top of the loop and letter gets the next character in word, which is "o". The computer displays o, and the loop continues until each character in the string "Loop" is displayed.

In the Real World

Most modern languages offer a form of the for loop. However, these loops tend to be more restrictive. The loops generally only allow a counter variable, which must be assigned a number. Then, the counter changes by the same amount, each time the loop executes. The ability to loop directly through a sequence makes the Python for loop more flexible than this other, more traditional type of loop.

Creating a for Loop

To create a for loop, you can follow the example in the program. Start with for, followed by a variable for each element, followed by in, followed by the sequence you want to loop through, followed by a colon, and finally, the loop body. That's all there is to it.

Counting with a for Loop

When you write a program, you may find that you need to count. In combination with the for loop, you can use Python's range() function to count in all kinds of ways.

Introducing the Counter Program

The Counter program is nothing fancy, but it shows you how to use the range() function with a for loop to count forwards or backwards, or even to skip numbers if you like. Take a look at Figure 4.3 to see the results of the program.

FIGURE 4.3

The range()
function and for
loop allow you to
count forwards, by
fives, and
backwards.

You can find the code for the program on the companion website (www.courseptr.com/downloads) in the Chapter 4 folder; the file name is counter.py.

```python
# Counter
# Demonstrates the range() function

print("Counting:")
for i in range(10):
    print(i, end=" ")

print("\n\nCounting by fives:")
for i in range(0, 50, 5):
    print(i, end=" ")

print("\n\nCounting backwards:")
for i in range(10, 0, -1):
    print(i, end=" ")

input("\n\nPress the enter key to exit.\n")
```

IN THE REAL WORLD

It's traditional to name generic counter and loop variables i, j, or k. Normally, you want to create descriptive, clear variable names. Believe it or not, i, j, and k are clear to experienced programmers, who know when reading your code that you just need a quick, counter variable.

Counting Forwards

The first loop in the program counts forwards:

```
for i in range(10):
    print(i, end=" ")
```

This for loop works like the for loop you saw in the Loopy String program. But this time, the sequence the loop iterates over is generated by the return value of the range() function. You can imagine that the range() function returns a sequence of numbers. If you give range() a positive integer, you can imagine that it returns a sequence starting with 0, up to, but not including, the number you gave it. So, you can imagine that the code range(10) returns the sequence [0, 1, 2, 3, 4, 5, 6, 7, 8, 9]. This should help you visualize what happens in the loop: in the first iteration of the loop, i gets 0 and its value is printed, then, in the next iteration, i gets 1 and its value is printed and so on until the final iteration, where i gets 9, its value is printed, and the loop ends.

While it can be helpful to imagine that the result of the range() function is a sequence of integers, that's not what it produces. The function actually returns something that produces the next number in the sequence, as needed. For our purposes, imagining the entire sequence of numbers all at once is fine. If you want to learn more about the inner workings of the range() function, check out the documentation at http://www.python.org.

You can create your own sequence of values, called a list, by enclosing the values in brackets, separated by commas. But don't go off creating a bunch of lists just yet. You'll learn all about lists in Chapter 5, "Lists and Dictionaries: The Hangman Game," I promise.

Counting by Fives

The next loop counts by fives:

```
for i in range(0, 50, 5):
    print(i, end=" ")
```

If you give `range()` three values, it will treat them as a start point, an end point, and the number by which to count. The start point is always the first value in our imagined sequence while the end point is never included. So here, our imagined sequence is [0, 5, 10, 15, 20, 25, 30, 35, 40, 45]. Notice though that the sequence ends at 45. Remember, 50 is the end point, so it's not included. If you want to include 50, your end point needs to be greater than 50. So, for example, `range(0, 51, 5)` would do the trick.

Counting Backwards

The last loop in the program counts backwards:

```
for i in range(10, 0, -1):
    print(i, end=" ")
```

It does this because the last argument in the `range()` call is -1. This tells the function to go from the start point to the end point by adding −1 each time. This is the same as saying "subtract 1." You can imagine the call to `range()` produces the sequence [10, 9, 8, 7, 6, 5, 4, 3, 2, 1]. So, the loop counts from 10 down to 1 and does not include 0.

TRICK   There's no law that says you have to use the loop variable inside a for loop. You might find that you want to repeat some action a specific number of times. To do this, create a for loop and just ignore the loop variable in the loop body. For example, let's say I just wanted to print "Hi!" 10 times. The following two lines are all I would need:

```
for i in range(10):
    print("Hi!")
```

USING SEQUENCE OPERATORS AND FUNCTIONS WITH STRINGS

As you just learned, strings are one type of sequence, made up of individual characters. Python offers some useful functions and operators that work with any kind of sequence, including strings. These operators and functions can tell you basic but important things about a sequence, such as how long it is or whether a certain element is in it.

Introducing the Message Analyzer Program

This next program analyzes any message that you enter. It tells you how long the message is and whether or not it contains the most common letter in the English language (the letter "e"). The program accomplishes this with a new sequence function and sequence operator. Figure 4.4 shows off the program.

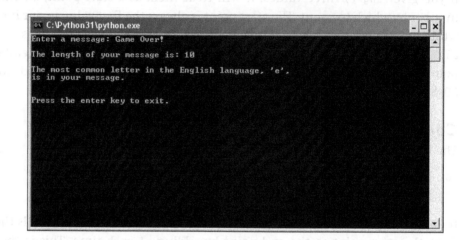

FIGURE 4.4

This program uses the len() function and the in operator to produce some information about your message.

You can find the code for the program on the companion website (www.courseptr.com/downloads) in the Chapter 4 folder; the file name is message_analyzer.py.

```python
# Message Analyzer
# Demonstrates the len() function and the in operator

message = input("Enter a message: ")

print("\nThe length of your message is:", len(message))

print("\nThe most common letter in the English language, 'e',")
if "e" in message:
    print("is in your message.")
else:
    print("is not in your message.")

input("\n\nPress the enter key to exit.")
```

Using the len() Function

After the program imports the random module and gets the user's message, it prints the message length with

```
print("\nThe length of your message is:", len(message))
```

You can pass any sequence you want to the len() function and it will return the length of the sequence. A sequence's length is the number of elements it has. Since message has 10 characters in it (you count every character, including a space or an exclamation point), it has a length of 10.

Using the in Operator

The letter "e" is the most common letter in English. The program uses the following lines to test whether "e" is in the message the user entered:

```
if "e" in message:
    print("is in your message.")
else:
    print("is not in your message.")
```

The condition in the if statement is "e" in message. If message contains the character "e", it's true. If message doesn't contain "e", it's false. In the sample run, the value of message is "Game Over!", which does contain the character "e". So, the condition "e" in message evaluated to True and the computer printed "is in your message." If the condition had been false (for example, if message had been equal to "Python Programming"), then the computer would have displayed is not in your message. If an element is in a sequence, it's said to be a *member* of the sequence.

You can use in anywhere in your own programs to check if an element is a member of a sequence. Just put the element you want to check for, followed by in, followed by the sequence. This creates a condition. If the element is a member, the condition is true; otherwise, it's false.

INDEXING STRINGS

By using a for loop, you're able to go through a string, one character at a time, in order. This is known as *sequential access,* which means you have to go through a sequence one element at a time. Sequential access is like going through a stack of heavy boxes that you can only lift one at a time. To get to the bottom box in a stack of five, you'd have to lift the top box, then the next box, followed by the next box, then one more to finally get to the last box. Wouldn't it be nice to just grab the last box without messing with any of the others? This kind of direct access is called *random access.* Random access allows you to get to any element in a sequence directly. Fortunately, there's a way to randomly access elements of a sequence. It's called *indexing*. Through indexing, you specify a position (or index) number in a sequence and get the element at that position. In the box example, you could get the bottom box directly by asking for box number five.

Introducing the Random Access Program

The Random Access program uses sequence indexing to directly access random characters in a string. The program picks a random position from the string "index", and prints the letter and the position number. The program does this 10 times to give a good sampling of random positions. Figure 4.5 shows the program in action.

```
C:\Python31\python.exe
The word is:   index

word[ -3 ]        d
word[ 3 ]         e
word[ -4 ]        n
word[ 2 ]         d
word[ 3 ]         e
word[ -3 ]        d
word[ 0 ]         i
word[ -5 ]        i
word[ -5 ]        i
word[ -1 ]        x

Press the enter key to exit.
```

FIGURE 4.5

You can directly access any character in a string through indexing.

You can find the code for the program on the companion website (www.courseptr.com/downloads) in the Chapter 4 folder; the file name is random_access.py.

```python
# Random Access
# Demonstrates string indexing

import random

word = "index"
print("The word is: ", word, "\n")

high = len(word)
low = -len(word)
```

```
for i in range(10):
    position = random.randrange(low, high)
    print("word[", position, "]\t", word[position])

input("\n\nPress the enter key to exit.")
```

Working with Positive Position Numbers

In this program, one of the first things I do is assign a string value to a variable:

```
word = "index"
```

Nothing new here. But by doing this, I create a sequence (like every time I create a string) where each character has a numbered position. The first letter, "i," is at position 0. (Remember, computers usually start counting from 0.) The second letter, "n," is at position 1. The third letter, "d," is at position 2, and so on.

Accessing an individual character of a string is easy. To access the letter in position 0 from the variable word, you'd just type word[0]. For any other position, you'd just substitute that number. To help cement the idea, take a look at part of an interactive session I had:

```
>>> word = "index "
>>> print(word[0])
i
>>> print(word[1])
n
>>> print(word[2])
d
>>> print(word[3])
e
>>> print(word[4])
x
```

 TRAP   Since there are five letters in the string "index", you might think that the last letter, "x," would be at position 5. But you'd be wrong. There is no position 5 in this string, because the computer begins counting at 0. Valid positive positions are 0, 1, 2, 3, and 4. Any attempt to access a position 5 will cause an error. Take a look at an interactive session for proof:

```
>>> word = "index "
>>> print(word[5])
Traceback (most recent call last):
        File "<pyshell#1>", line 1, in ?
```

```
print word[5]
IndexError: string index out of range
```

Somewhat rudely, the computer is saying there is no position 5. So remember, the last element in a sequence is at the position number of its length minus one.

Working with Negative Position Numbers

Except for the idea that the first letter of a string is at position 0 and not 1, working with positive position numbers seems pretty natural. But there's also a way to access elements of a sequence through negative position numbers. With positive position numbers, your point of reference is the beginning of the sequence. For strings, this means that the first letter is where you start counting. But with negative position numbers, you start counting from the end. For strings, that means you start counting from the last letter and work backwards.

The best way to understand how negative position numbers work is to see an example. Take a look at another interactive session I had, again, using the string "index ":

```
>>> word = "index "
>>> print(word[-1])
x
>>> print(word[-2])
e
>>> print(word[-3])
d
>>> print(word[-4])
n
>>> print(word[-5])
i
```

You can see from this session that word[-1] accesses the last letter of "index", the "x." When using negative position numbers, -1 means the last element, the index -2 means the second to the last element, the index -3 means the third to the last element, and so on. Sometimes it makes more sense for your reference point to be the end of a sequence. For those times, you can use negative position numbers.

Figure 4.6 provides a nice way to see the string "index" broken up by position numbers, both positive and negative.

0	1	2	3	4
i	n	d	e	x

-5   -4   -3   -2   -1

FIGURE 4.6

You can access any letter of "index" with a positive or negative position number.

Accessing a Random String Element

It's time to get back to the Random Access program. To access a random letter from the "index", I need to generate random numbers. So, the first thing I did in the program was import the random module:

```
import random
```

Next, I wanted a way to pick any valid position number in word, negative or positive. I wanted my program to be able to generate a random number between –5 and 4, inclusive, because those are all the possible position values of word. Luckily, the random.randrange() function can take two end points and produce a random number from between them. So, I created two end points:

```
high = len(word)
low = -len(word)
```

high gets the value 5, because "index" has five characters in it. The variable low gets the negative value of the length of the word (that's what putting a minus sign in front of a numeric value does). So low gets the value of –5. This represents the range from which I want to grab a random number.

Actually, I want to generate a random number between, and including, –5 up to, but not including, 5. And that's exactly the way the random.randrange() function works. If you pass it two arguments, it will produce a random number from and including the low end point, up to, but not including, the high end point. So in my sample run, the line.

```
position = random.randrange(low, high)
```

produces either –5, –4, –3, –2, –1, 0, 1, 2, 3, or 4. This is exactly what I want, since these are all the possible valid position numbers for the string "index".

Finally, I created a for loop that executes 10 times. In the loop body, the program picks a random position value and prints that position value and corresponding letter:

```
for i in range(10):
    position = random.randrange(low, high)
    print("word[", position, "]\t", word[position])
```

UNDERSTANDING STRING IMMUTABILITY

Sequences fall into one of two categories: mutable or immutable. (Again, more fancy computer jargon.) *Mutable* means changeable. So, a sequence that's a mutable sequence is one that can change. *Immutable* means unchangeable. So, a sequence that's immutable is one that can't change. Strings are immutable sequences, which means that they can't change. So, for example, the string "Game Over! " will always be the string "Game Over! ". You can't change it. In fact, you can't change any string you create. Now, you might think, from your experience with strings, that I'm totally wrong on this. You might even run an interactive session to prove that you *can* change a string, maybe something resembling this:

```
>>> name = "Chris "
>>> print(name)
Chris
>>> name = "Jackson "
>>> print(name)
Jackson
```

You might offer this as proof that you can change a string. After all, you changed the string "Chris" to "Jackson ". But, you didn't change any strings in this session. You just created two different strings. First, you created a string "Chris " and assigned it to the variable name. Then, you created another string, "Jackson ", and assigned it to name. Now, both "Chris" and "Jackson" are great names, but they're different names and always will be, just as they are different strings and always will be. Take a look at Figure 4.7 for a visual representation of what happened in the interactive session.

FIGURE 4.7

First, name gets the string "Chris", then it gets a different string, "Jackson". But no string values ever change.

Another way to think about this is to imagine that strings are written in ink on pieces of paper. You can throw out a piece of paper with a string on it and replace it with another piece of paper with a new string on it, but you can't change the words once they've been written.

You might think this is much ado about nothing. So what if a string is immutable? But string immutability does have consequences. Since you can't change a string, you can't assign a new character to a string through indexing. Here's an interactive session to show you what I mean:

```
>>> word = "game "
>>> word[0] = "l "
Traceback (most recent call last):
  File "<pyshell#1>", line 1, in <module>
    word[0] = "l"
TypeError: 'str' object does not support item assignment
```

In this session, I wanted to change the string "game" to the string "lame" (obviously, I didn't much like the game I was referring to). All I needed to do was change the letter "g" to an "l." So I just assigned "l" to the first position in the string, word[0]. But as you can see, this resulted in a big, fat error. The interpreter even tells me that strings don't support item assignment (you can't assign a new value to a character in a string).

But, just because you can't alter a string doesn't mean you can't create new strings from existing ones.

BUILDING A NEW STRING

You've already seen how you can concatenate two strings with the + operator. Sometimes, you may want to build a new string, one character at a time. Since strings are immutable, what you'll really be doing is creating a new string every time you use the concatenation operator.

Introducing the No Vowels Program

This next program, No Vowels, takes a message from the user and prints it, minus any vowels. Figure 4.8 shows the program in action.

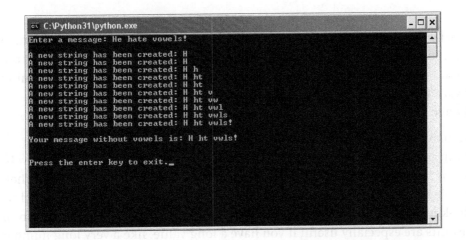

FIGURE 4.8

Using a for loop, new strings are created. The program skips the concatenation operation for any vowels.

The program creates a new string of the original message, without the vowels. Really what it does is create a series of new strings. You can find the code for the program on the companion website (www.courseptr.com/downloads) in the Chapter 4 folder; the file name is no_vowels.py.

```
# No Vowels
# Demonstrates creating new strings with a for loop

message = input("Enter a message: ")
new_message = ""
VOWELS = "aeiou"

print()
for letter in message:
    if letter.lower() not in VOWELS:
        new_message += letter
        print("A new string has been created:", new_message)

print("\nYour message without vowels is:", new_message)

input("\n\nPress the enter key to exit.")
```

Creating Constants

After the program gets the message from the user and creates an empty new message, it creates a string:

```
VOWELS = "aeiou"
```

This variable, VOWELS, gets a string of all the vowels. You probably notice that the variable name is in all caps, contrary to what you have learned: that, traditionally, variable names are in lowercase. Well, I haven't veered from tradition here. In fact, there's a special meaning associated with variable names in all caps. They're called *constants* and refer to a value that is not meant to change (their value is constant).

Constants are valuable to programmers in two ways. First, they make programs clearer. In this program, I can use the variable name VOWELS anywhere I need the sequence of vowels, instead of the string "aeiou". Using the variable name instead of the string is clearer. When you see the variable name, you understand what it means, but you might be confused by seeing the odd-looking string itself. Second, constants save retyping (and possibly errors from mistyping). Constants are especially useful if you have a long value, like a very long number or string. Use a constant in programs where you have the same, unchanging value used in multiple places.

 You have to be careful when you create constants by making an all-caps variable name. Even though you're saying to yourself and other programmers that this variable will always refer to the same value, there's nothing in Python that will stop you from changing it in your program. This naming practice is simply a convention. So, once you create a variable with a name in all caps, make sure to treat it as unchangeable.

IN THE REAL WORLD

In some programming languages, constants are exactly that. They can't be changed once they're defined. That's the safest way to create and use constants. In Python, though, there isn't a simple way to create true constants of your own.

Creating New Strings from Existing Ones

The real work of the program happens in the loop. The program creates a new message, without any vowels, as the loop runs. Each time through, the computer checks the next letter in the original message. If it's not a vowel, it adds this letter to the new message it's creating. If it is a vowel, the program moves on to the next letter. You know that a program can't literally add a character to a string, so, more precisely, when the program comes across a character that's not a vowel, it concatenates the new message it has so far with this character to create a new string. The code that accomplishes this is:

```
for letter in message:
    if letter.lower() not in VOWELS:
        new_message += letter
        print("A new string has been created:", new_message)
```

There are two new ideas in the loop, so let me go over both of them. First, Python is picky when dealing with strings and characters. "A" is not the same as "a". Since VOWELS is assigned a string that contains only lowercase letters, I needed to make sure that I checked only lowercase letters when using the in operator. That's why I used letter.lower().

TRICK
Often, when you compare two strings, you don't care about the case matching, only the letters. If you ask a player if he or she wants to continue a game, the string "Yes" is as good as the string "yes". Well, in these instances, just make sure to convert both strings to the same case (upper- or lowercase, it doesn't matter) before you compare them.

Here's an example. Let's say I want to compare two strings, name and winner, to see if they are equal, and I don't care about matching the case. I could create the condition:

```
name.lower() == winner.lower()
```

This condition is true whenever name and winner each have the same sequence of characters, regardless of case. So, "Larry" and "larry" is a match. "LARRY" and "larry" is too. Even "LaRrY" and "lArRy" works.

Second, you also might notice that I used the augmented assignment operator, +=, in the program for string concatenation. You saw the augmented assignment operators with numbers, but they also work with strings. So, this line:

```
new_message += letter
```

is exactly the same as

```
new_message = new_message + letter
```

SLICING STRINGS

Indexing is a useful technique, but you aren't restricted to copying just one element at a time from a sequence. You can make copies of continuous sections of elements (called *slices*). You can copy (or *slice*) one element (just like indexing) or part of a sequence (like, say, the middle three elements). You can even create a slice that is a copy of the entire sequence. So, for strings, that means you can grab anything ranging from a single character, to a group of consecutive characters, to the entire string.

Introducing the Pizza Slicer Program

The Pizza Slicer program lets you slice the string "pizza" any way you want. It's a great, interactive way to help you understand slicing. All you do is enter the starting and ending positions of the slice, and the program displays the results. Figure 4.9 shows off the program.

FIGURE 4.9

Fresh, hot slices of "pizza", made just the way you asked. The program also offers a "cheat sheet" so you can visualize how a slice will be created.

You can find the code for the program on the companion website (www.courseptr.com/downloads) in the Chapter 4 folder; the file name is pizza_slicer.py.

```
# Pizza Slicer
# Demonstrates string slicing

word = "pizza"

print(
"""
  Slicing 'Cheat Sheet'

  0   1   2   3   4   5
  +---+---+---+---+---+
  | p | i | z | z | a |
  +---+---+---+---+---+
  -5  -4  -3  -2  -1

"""
)
```

```
print("Enter the beginning and ending index for your slice of 'pizza'.")
print("Press the enter key at 'Start' to exit.")
start = None
while start != "":
    start = (input("\nStart: "))

    if start:
        start = int(start)

        finish = int(input("Finish: "))

        print("word[", start, ":", finish, "] is", end=" ")
        print(word[start:finish])

input("\n\nPress the enter key to exit.")
```

Introducing None

Before you get to the code about slicing, take a look at this line, which introduces a new idea:

```
start = None
```

The line assigns a special value, called None, to start. None is Python's way of representing nothing. None makes a good placeholder for a value. It also evaluates to False when treated as a condition. I used it here because I wanted to initialize start for use in the while loop condition.

Understanding Slicing

Creating a slice is similar to indexing. But instead of using a single position number, you supply a starting position and ending position. Every element between the two points becomes part of the slice. Figure 4.10 shows a way to look at slicing end point numbers for the string "pizza". Notice that it's a slightly different numbering system than the index numbering in Figure 4.6.

To specify the end points of a slice, include both in brackets, separated by a colon. Here's a quick interactive session to show you what I mean:

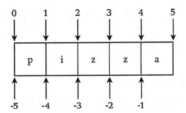

FIGURE 4.10

An example of slicing end point numbers for the string "pizza". You can use any combination of positive and negative end points for your slice.

```
>>> word = "pizza"
>>> print(word[0:5])
pizza
>>> print(word[1:3])
iz
>>> print(word[-4:-2])
iz
>>> print(word[-4:3])
iz
```

word[0:5] returns the entire string because all its characters are between those two end points. word[1:3] returns the string "iz" because those two characters are between the end points. Just like with indexing, you can use negative numbers. word[-4:-2] also produces the string "iz" because those characters are between the two negative positions. You can also mix and match positive and negative end points. This works just like creating any other slice; the elements between the two position numbers will be in the slice. So, word[-4:3] also produces the string "iz", because they are the two characters between those two end points.

TRAP   If you create an "impossible" slice, where the starting point is bigger than the ending point, like word[2:1], you won't cause an error. Instead, Python will quietly return an empty sequence. For strings, that means you'll get the empty string. So be careful, because this is probably not the kind of result you're after.

Creating Slices

Inside the loop of Pizza Slicer, the program prints the syntax for creating a slice based on the beginning and ending positions the user entered, through the following line:

```
print("word[", start, ":", finish, "] is", end=" ")
```

Then, the program prints the actual slice using the variables start and finish:

```
print(word[start:finish])
```

Using Slicing Shorthand

Although you can get every possible slice by specifying two numbers, there are a few slicing shortcuts you can use. You can omit the beginning point for the slice to start the slice at the beginning of the sequence. So, given that word has been assigned "pizza", the slice word[:4] is exactly the same as word[0:4]. You can omit the ending point so that the slice ends with the very last element. So, word[2:] is just shorthand for word[2:5]. You can even omit both numbers to get a slice that is the entire sequence. So, word[:] is shorthand for word[0:5].

Here's an interactive session to back up this proposition:

```
>>> word = "pizza"
>>>print(word[0:4])
pizz
>>>print(word[:4])
pizz
>>>print(word[2:5])
zza
>>>print(word[2:])
zza
>>>print(word[0:5])
pizza
>>> print(word[:])
Pizza
```

 TRICK   If there's one bit of slicing shorthand you should remember, it's that [:] returns a complete copy of a sequence. As you program, you'll find you may need to make a copy of a sequence, and this is a quick and efficient way to do just that.

Creating Tuples

Tuples are a type of sequence, like strings. But unlike strings, which can only contain characters, tuples can contain elements of any type. That means you can have a tuple that stores a bunch of high scores for a game, or one that stores a group of employee names. But tuple elements don't have to all be of the same type. You could create a tuple with both strings and numbers, if you wanted. And you don't have to stop at strings and numbers. You can create a tuple that contains a sequence of graphic images, sound files, or even a group of aliens (once you learn how to create these things, which you will in later chapters). Whatever you can assign to a variable, you can group together and store as a sequence in a tuple.

Introducing the Hero's Inventory Program

Hero's Inventory maintains the inventory of a hero from a typical role-playing game. Like most role-playing games ever created, the hero is from a small, insignificant village. His father was, of course, killed by an evil warlord. (What's a quest without a dead father?) And now that the hero has come of age, it's time for him to seek his revenge.

In this program, the hero's inventory is represented by a tuple. The tuple contains strings, one for each item in the hero's possession. The hero starts out with nothing, but then I give him a few items. Figure 4.11 shows the humble beginnings of our hero's journey.

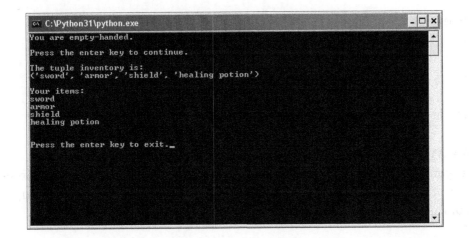

FIGURE 4.11

At first, the hero has no items in his inventory. Then, the program creates a new tuple with string elements and our hero is stocked.

You can find the code for the program on the companion website (www.courseptr.com/downloads) in the Chapter 4 folder; the file name is hero's_inventory.py.

```
# Hero's Inventory
# Demonstrates tuple creation

# create an empty tuple
inventory = ()

# treat the tuple as a condition
if not inventory:
    print("You are empty-handed.")

input("\nPress the enter key to continue.")
```

```
# create a tuple with some items
inventory = ("sword",
             "armor",
             "shield",
             "healing potion")

# print the tuple
print("\nThe tuple inventory is:")
print(inventory)

# print each element in the tuple
print("\nYour items:")
for item in inventory:
    print(item)

input("\n\nPress the enter key to exit.")
```

Creating an Empty Tuple

To create a tuple, you just surround a sequence of values, separated by commas, with parentheses. Even a pair of lone parentheses is a valid (but empty) tuple. I created an empty tuple in the first part of the program to represent that the hero has nothing:

```
inventory = ()
```

It's as simple as that. So in this line, the variable inventory gets an empty tuple.

Treating a Tuple as a Condition

When you learned about conditions, you saw that you could treat any value in Python as a condition. That means you can treat a tuple as a condition, too. And that's what I did in the next lines:

```
if not inventory:
    print("You are empty-handed.")
```

As a condition, an empty tuple is False. A tuple with at least one element is True. Since the tuple assigned to inventory is empty, it's False. That means not inventory is True. So the computer prints the string, "You are empty-handed.", just as it should.

Creating a Tuple with Elements

An unarmed hero is a boring hero. So next, I created a new tuple with string elements that represent useful items for our hero. I assigned this new tuple to inventory with the following:

```
inventory = ("sword",
             "armor",
             "shield",
             "healing potion")
```

Each element in the tuple is separated by a comma. That makes the first element the string "sword", the next "armor", the next "shield", and the last element "healing potion". So each string is a single element in this tuple.

Also, notice that the tuple spans multiple lines. You can write a tuple in one line, or span it across multiple lines like I did, as long as you end each line after a comma. This is one of the few cases where Python lets you break up a statement across multiple lines.

 TRICK Make your programs easier to read by creating tuples across multiple lines. You don't have to write exactly one element per line, though. It might make sense to write several on a line. Just end each line at one of the commas separating elements and you'll be fine.

Printing a Tuple

Though a tuple can contain many elements, you can print the entire tuple just like you would any single value. That's what I did in the next line:

```
print("\nThe tuple inventory is:")
print(inventory)
```

The computer displays all of the elements, surrounded by parentheses.

Looping Through a Tuple's Elements

Finally, I wrote a for loop to march through the elements in inventory and print each one individually:

```
print("\nYour items:")
for item in inventory:
    print(item)
```

This loop prints each element (each string) in inventory on a separate line. This loop looks just like the ones you've seen with strings. In fact, you can use this kind of loop to go through the elements of any sequence.

Even though I created a tuple where all the elements are of the same type (strings in this case), tuples don't have to be filled with values of the same type. A single tuple can just as easily contain strings, integers, and floating-point numbers, for example.

TRAP Other programming languages offer structures similar to tuples. Some go by the name "arrays" or "vectors." However, those other languages usually restrict the elements of these sequences to just one type. So, for example, you couldn't mix strings and numbers together. Just be aware that these other structures don't usually offer all the flexibility that Python sequences do.

USING TUPLES

Since tuples are simply another kind of sequence, everything you learned about sequences from strings works with tuples. You can get the length of a tuple, print each element with a for loop, and use the in operator to test if an element is in a tuple. You can index, slice, and concatenate tuples, too.

Introducing the Hero's Inventory 2.0

Our hero's journey continues. In this program, his inventory is counted, tested, indexed, and sliced. Our hero will also happen upon a chest with items in it (represented by another tuple). Through tuple concatenation, our hero's inventory will be replaced with all of his current items plus the treasure he finds in the chest. Figure 4.12 shows a sample run of the program.

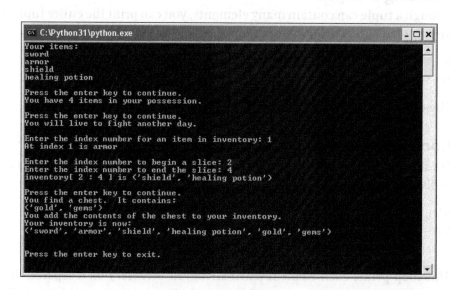

FIGURE 4.12

The hero's inventory is a tuple, which means it can be counted, indexed, sliced, and even concatenated with another tuple.

Since this program is a little long, I'll go through the code one section at a time rather than show you the whole thing at once. You can find the code for the program on the companion website (www.courseptr.com/downloads) in the Chapter 4 folder; the file name is hero's_inventory2.py.

Setting Up the Program

The first part of the program works just like it did in the previous program, Hero's Inventory. These lines create a tuple and print out each element:

```
# Hero's Inventory 2.0
# Demonstrates tuples

# create a tuple with some items and display with a for loop
inventory = ("sword",
             "armor",
             "shield",
             "healing potion")
print("Your items:")
for item in inventory:
    print(item)

input("\nPress the enter key to continue.")
```

Using the len() Function with Tuples

The len() function works with tuples just the way it does with strings. If you want to know the length of a tuple, place it inside the parentheses. The function returns the number of elements in the tuple. Empty tuples, or any empty sequences for that matter, have a length of 0. The following lines use the len() function with the tuple:

```
# get the length of a tuple
print("You have", len(inventory), "items in your possession.")

input("\nPress the enter key to continue.")
```

Since this tuple has four elements (the four strings: "sword", "armor", "shield", and "healing potion"), the message You have 4 items in your possession. is displayed.

TRAP Notice that in the tuple inventory, the string "healing potion" is counted as a single element, even though it's two words.

Using the in Operator with Tuples

Just like with strings, you can use the in operator with tuples to test for element membership. And, just like before, the in operator is usually used to create a condition. That's how I used it here:

```
# test for membership with in
if "healing potion" in inventory:
    print("You will live to fight another day.")
```

The condition "healing potion" in inventory tests if the entire string "healing potion" is an element in inventory. Since it is, the message You will live to fight another day. is displayed.

Indexing Tuples

Indexing tuples works like indexing strings. You specify a position number, in brackets, to access a particular element. In the following lines, I let the user choose the index number and then the computer displays the corresponding element:

```
# display one item through an index
index = int(input("\nEnter the index number for an item in inventory: "))
print("At index", index, "is", inventory[index])
```

Figure 4.13 shows this tuple with index numbers.

FIGURE 4.13

Each string is a single element in the tuple.

	0	1	2	3	
	"sword"	"armor"	"shield"	"healing potion"	
	-4	-3	-2	-1	

Slicing Tuples

Slicing works just like you saw with strings. You give a beginning and ending position. The result is a tuple containing every element between those two positions.

Just as in the Pizza Slicer program from earlier in this chapter, I let the user pick the beginning and ending position numbers. Then, like before, the program displays the slice:

```
# display a slice
start = int(input("\nEnter the index number to begin a slice: "))
finish = int(input("Enter the index number to end the slice: "))
print("inventory[", start, ":", finish, "] is", end=" ")
print(inventory[start:finish])

input("\nPress the enter key to continue.")
```

Using this tuple as an example, Figure 4.14 provides a visual way to understand tuple slicing.

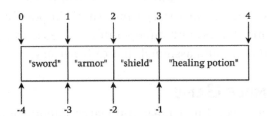

Slicing positions for tuples are defined between elements, just as they are for strings.

Understanding Tuple Immutability

Like strings, tuples are immutable. That means you can't change a tuple. Here's an interactive session to prove my point:

```
>>> inventory = ("sword", "armor", "shield", "healing potion")
>>> print(inventory)
('sword', 'armor', 'shield', 'healing potion')
>>> inventory[0] = "battleax"
Traceback (most recent call last):
  File "<pyshell#3>", line 1, in ?
    inventory[0] = "battleax"
TypeError: object doesn't support item assignment
```

Although you can't change tuples, like strings, you can create new tuples from existing ones.

Concatenating Tuples

You can concatenate tuples the same way you concatenate strings. You simply join them together with +, the concatenation operator:

```
# concatenate two tuples
chest = ("gold", "gems")
print("You find a chest.  It contains:")
print(chest)
```

```
print("You add the contents of the chest to your inventory.")
inventory += chest
print("Your inventory is now:")
print(inventory)

input("\n\nPress the enter key to exit.")
```

The first thing I did was create a new tuple, `chest`, with the two string elements `"gold"` and `"gems"`. Next, I printed `chest` to show its elements. After that, I used an augmented assignment operator to concatenate `inventory` with `chest` and assign the result back to `inventory`. I did not modify the original tuple assigned to `inventory` (since that's impossible, because tuples are immutable). Instead, the augmented assignment operator created a brand-new tuple with the elements from `inventory` and `chest` and assigned that to `inventory`.

BACK TO THE WORD JUMBLE GAME

The Word Jumble game combines several new ideas you learned about in this chapter. You can easily modify the program to contain your own list of words to guess. The code for the program is on the companion website (www.courseptr.com/downloads) in the Chapter 4 folder; the file name is word_jumble.py.

Setting Up the Program

After my initial comments, I import the `random` module:

```
# Word Jumble
#
# The computer picks a random word and then "jumbles" it
# The player has to guess the original word

import random
```

Next, I used a tuple to create a sequence of words. Notice that the variable name `WORD` is in all caps, implying that I'll treat it as a constant.

```
# create a sequence of words to choose from
WORDS = ("python", "jumble", "easy", "difficult", "answer", "xylophone")
```

Next, I use a new function, `random.choice()`, to grab a random word from `WORDS`:

```
# pick one word randomly from the sequence
word = random.choice(WORDS)
```

This function is new to you, but it's pretty simple. The computer looks at whatever sequence you give and picks a random element.

Once the computer has chosen a random word, it assigns it to word. This is the word the player will have to guess. Lastly, I assign word to correct, which I'll use later to see if the player makes a correct guess:

```
# create a variable to use later to see if the guess is correct
correct = word
```

Planning the Jumble Creation Section

The next section of code uses the new concepts in the chapter and is the most interesting part of the program. It's the section that actually creates the jumbled word from the original, randomly chosen word.

But, before I wrote any code, I planned out this part of the program in pseudocode (yes, I actually use all that stuff I write about). Here's my first pass at the algorithm to create a jumbled word from the chosen word:

```
create an empty jumble word
while the chosen word has letters in it
    extract a random letter from the chosen word
    add the random letter to the jumble word
```

Conceptually, this is pretty good, but I have to watch my semantics. Because strings are immutable, I can't actually "extract a random letter" from the string the user entered. But, I can create a new string that doesn't contain the randomly chosen letter. And while I can't "add the random letter" to the jumble word string either, I can create a new string by concatenating the current jumble word with the "extracted" letter.

Creating an Empty Jumble String

The very first part of the algorithm is easy:

```
# create a jumbled version of the word
jumble =""
```

The program creates the empty string and assigns it to jumble, which will refer to the final, jumbled word.

Setting Up the Loop

The jumble creation process is controlled by a `while` loop. The loop condition is pretty simple, as you can see:

```
while word:
```

I set the loop up this way so that it will continue until `word` is equal to the empty string. This is perfect, because each time the loop executes, the computer creates a new version of `word` with one letter "extracted" and assigns it back to `word`. Eventually, `word` will become the empty string and the jumbling will be done.

Generating a Random Position in word

The first line in the loop body generates a random position in `word`, based on its length:

```
position = random.randrange(len(word))
```

So, the letter `word[position]` is the letter that is going to be "extracted" from `word` and "added to" `jumble`.

Creating a New Version of jumble

The next line in the loop creates a new version of the string `jumble`. It becomes equal to its old self, plus the letter `word[position]`.

```
jumble += word[position]
```

Creating a New Version of word

The next line in the loop,

```
word = word[:position] + word[(position + 1):]
```

creates a new version of `word` minus the one letter at position `position`. Using slicing, the computer creates two new strings from `word`. The first slice, `word[:position]`, is every letter up to, but not including, `word[position]`. The next slice, `word[(position + 1):]`, is every letter after `word[position]`. These two strings are joined together and assigned to `word`, which is now equal to its old self, minus the one letter `word[position]`.

Welcoming the Player

After the jumbled word has been created, the next section of the program welcomes the player to the game and displays the jumbled word to be rearranged:

```
# start the game
print(
"""
          Welcome to Word Jumble!

   Unscramble the letters to make a word.
(Press the enter key at the prompt to quit.)
"""
)
print("The jumble is:", jumble)
```

Getting the Player's Guess

Next, the computer gets the player's guess. The computer keeps asking the player for a guess as long as the player doesn't enter the correct word or press the Enter key at the prompt:

```
guess = input("\nYour guess: ")
while guess != correct and guess != "":
    print("Sorry, that's not it.")
    guess = input("Your guess: ")
```

Congratulating the Player

At this point in the program, the player has either correctly guessed the word or quit the game. If the player has guessed the word, then the computer offers its hearty congratulations:

```
if guess == correct:
    print("That's it!  You guessed it!\n")
```

Ending the Game

Finally, the program thanks the player for playing the game and ends:

```
print("Thanks for playing.")

input("\n\nPress the enter key to exit.")
```

SUMMARY

In this chapter, you learned about the concept of sequences. You saw how to create a sequence of numbers with the range() function. You saw how strings are really just sequences of characters. You learned about tuples, which let you organize a sequence of any type. You saw how to go through the elements of a sequence with a for loop. You learned how to get the length of a sequence and how to check if an element is a member of a sequence. You saw how to copy pieces of a sequence through indexing and slicing. You learned about immutability and some of the limitations it places on you. But you also saw how to create new sequences from existing ones through concatenation, in spite of this immutability. Finally, you put everything together to create a challenging word jumble game.

CHALLENGES

1. Write a program that counts for the user. Let the user enter the starting number, the ending number, and the amount by which to count.

2. Create a program that gets a message from the user and then prints it out backwards.

3. Improve "Word Jumble" so that each word is paired with a hint. The player should be able to see the hint if he or she is stuck. Add a scoring system that rewards players who solve a jumble without asking for the hint.

4. Create a game where the computer picks a random word and the player has to guess that word. The computer tells the player how many letters are in the word. Then the player gets five chances to ask if a letter is in the word. The computer can only respond with "yes" or "no". Then, the player must guess the word.

LISTS AND DICTIONARIES: THE HANGMAN GAME

Tuples are a great way to work with sequences of any type, but their immutability can be limiting. Fortunately, another kind of sequence, the *list*, does everything that the tuple can plus more. That's because lists are mutable. Elements can be added or removed from a list. You can even sort a list. You'll also be introduced to another type, *dictionaries*. Whereas lists work with sequences of information, dictionaries work with pairs of data. Dictionaries, like their real-life counterparts, let you look up one value with another. Specifically in this chapter, you'll learn to do the following:

- Create, index, and slice a list
- Add and delete elements from a list
- Use list methods to append and sort a list
- Use nested sequences to represent even more complex information
- Use dictionaries to work with pairs of data
- Add and delete dictionary items

INTRODUCING THE HANGMAN GAME

The project for this chapter is the game of hangman. The computer picks a secret word and the player has to try to guess it, one letter at a time. Each time the player makes an incorrect guess, the computer shows a new image of a figure being hanged. If the player doesn't guess the word in time, the stick figure is a goner. Figures 5.1 through 5.3 show off the game in all its glory.

Not only is this game fun, but by the end of the chapter, you'll know how to create your own version. You can have a personalized group of secret words, and even update my marginally adequate artwork.

```
C:\Python31\python.exe

Enter your guess: N

Yes! N is in the word!

       |    |
       |    O
       |   -+-
       |
       |
       |
       |
-----------

You've used the following letters:
['R', 'S', 'T', 'P', 'Y', 'H', 'N']

So far, the word is:
 PYTH-N

Enter your guess:
```

FIGURE 5.1

The "Hangman" game in action. Hmm . . . I wonder what the word could be.

```
C:\Python31\python.exe

-----------
       |    |
       |    O
       |   -+-
       |
       |
       |
       |
-----------

You've used the following letters:
['R', 'S', 'T', 'P', 'Y', 'H', 'N']

So far, the word is:
 PYTH-N

Enter your guess: O

Yes! O is in the word!

You guessed it!

The word was PYTHON

Press the enter key to exit._
```

FIGURE 5.2

I won this game!

FIGURE 5.3

This game ended badly, especially for the little guy made of text.

USING LISTS

Lists are sequences, just like tuples—but lists are mutable. They can be modified. So, lists can do everything tuples can, plus more. Lists work just like tuples, so everything you learned about tuples is applicable to lists, which makes learning to use them a snap.

Introducing the Hero's Inventory 3.0 Program

This program is based on the Hero's Inventory 2.0 program, introduced in Chapter 4, in the "Creating Tuples" section. But instead of using tuples to store the hero's inventory, this program uses lists. The first part of Hero's Inventory 3.0 creates the same results as version 2.0. In fact, the code is almost exactly the same. The only difference is that it uses lists instead of tuples. Figure 5.4 shows off the results of the first part of the program. The second part of the program takes advantage of the mutability of lists and does some brand-new things with sequences. Figure 5.5 shows that part in action.

```
C:\Python31\python.exe

Your items:
sword
armor
shield
healing potion

Press the enter key to continue.
You have 4 items in your possession.

Press the enter key to continue.
You will live to fight another day.

Enter the index number for an item in inventory: 1
At index 1 is armor

Enter the index number to begin a slice: 2
Enter the index number to end the slice: 4
inventory[ 2 : 4 ] is ['shield', 'healing potion']

Press the enter key to continue.
You find a chest which contains:
['gold', 'gems']
You add the contents of the chest to your inventory.
Your inventory is now:
['sword', 'armor', 'shield', 'healing potion', 'gold', 'gems']

Press the enter key to continue._
```

FIGURE 5.4

The hero's inventory is now represented by a list. The results look almost exactly the same as when the inventory was represented by a tuple in Hero's Inventory 2.0.

```
C:\Python31\python.exe

Press the enter key to continue.
You trade your sword for a crossbow.
Your inventory is now:
['crossbow', 'armor', 'shield', 'healing potion', 'gold', 'gems']

Press the enter key to continue.
You use your gold and gems to buy an orb of future telling.
Your inventory is now:
['crossbow', 'armor', 'shield', 'healing potion', 'orb of future telling']

Press the enter key to continue.
In a great battle, your shield is destroyed.
Your inventory is now:
['crossbow', 'armor', 'healing potion', 'orb of future telling']

Press the enter key to continue.
Your crossbow and armor are stolen by thieves.
Your inventory is now:
['healing potion', 'orb of future telling']

Press the enter key to exit._
```

FIGURE 5.5

Since the hero's inventory is represented by a list, items can be added, modified, and deleted.

Creating a List

The first lines of the program create a new list, assign it to inventory, and print each element. This works almost exactly like it did in Hero's Inventory 2.0. The only difference is that I surrounded the elements with square brackets instead of parentheses, to create a list instead of a tuple. You can find the code for the program on the companion website (www.courseptr.com/downloads) in the Chapter 5 folder; the file name is hero's_inventory3.py.

```
# Hero's Inventory 3.0
# Demonstrates lists
```

```
# create a list with some items and display with a for loop
inventory = ["sword", "armor", "shield", "healing potion"]
print("Your items:")
for item in inventory:
    print(item)

input("\nPress the enter key to continue.")
```

Using the len() Function with Lists

The following code is exactly the same as the corresponding code in Hero's Inventory 2.0. The len() function works the same with lists as it does with tuples.

```
# get the length of a list
print("You have", len(inventory), "items in your possession.")

input("\nPress the enter key to continue.")
```

Using the in Operator with Lists

Again, the code for this section is exactly the same as in the previous version. The in operator works the same with lists as it does with tuples.

```
# test for membership with in
if "healing potion" in inventory:
    print("You will live to fight another day.")
```

Indexing Lists

Once again, the code is exactly the same as it was with tuples. Indexing a list is the same as indexing a tuple—just supply the position number of the element you're after in brackets.

```
# display one item through an index
index = int(input("\nEnter the index number for an item in inventory: "))
print("At index", index, "is", inventory[index])
```

Slicing Lists

Would you believe that slicing a list is exactly the same as slicing a tuple? Again, you just supply the two end points, separated by a colon, in brackets:

```
# display a slice
start = int(input("\nEnter the index number to begin a slice: "))
finish = int(input("Enter the index number to end the slice: "))
```

```
print("inventory[", start, ":", finish, "] is", end=" ")
print(inventory[start:finish])

input("\nPress the enter key to continue.")
```

Concatenating Lists

Concatenating lists works the same way concatenating tuples does. The only real difference here is that I created a list (rather than a tuple) and assigned it to chest. This is a small but important difference, because you can only concatenate sequences of the same type.

```
# concatenate two lists
chest = ["gold", "gems"]
print("You find a chest which contains:")
print(chest)
print("You add the contents of the chest to your inventory.")
inventory += chest
print("Your inventory is now:")
print(inventory)

input("\nPress the enter key to continue.")
```

Understanding List Mutability

At this point, you may be getting a bit tired of reading the phrase "works exactly the same as it did with tuples." So far, with the exception of using brackets instead of parentheses, lists seem no different than tuples. But there is one huge difference between them. Lists are mutable. They can change. As a result, there are many things you can do with lists that you can't do with tuples.

Assigning a New List Element by Index

Because lists are mutable, you can assign an existing element a new value:

```
# assign by index
print("You trade your sword for a crossbow.")
inventory[0] = "crossbow"
print("Your inventory is now:")
print(inventory)

input("\nPress the enter key to continue.")
```

The following line from the preceding code assigns the string `"crossbow"` to the element in `inventory` at position 0:

```
inventory[0] = "crossbow"
```

The new string replaces the previous value (which was `"sword"`). You can see the results when the `print` function displays the new version of `inventory`.

 TRAP You can assign an existing list element a new value with indexing, but you can't create a new element in this way. An attempt to assign a value to a nonexistent element will result in an error.

Assigning a New List Slice

In addition to assigning a new value to a single element, you can assign a new value to a slice. I assigned the list `["orb of future telling"]` to the slice `inventory[4:6]`:

```
# assign by slice
print("You use your gold and gems to buy an orb of future telling.")
inventory[4:6] = ["orb of future telling"]
print("Your inventory is now:")
print(inventory)

input("\nPress the enter key to continue.")
```

This assignment statement replaces the two items `inventory[4]` and `inventory[5]` with the string `"orb of future telling"`. Because I assigned a list with one element to a slice with two elements, the length of the list shrunk by one.

Deleting a List Element

You can delete an element from a list with `del`—simply designate the element after `del`:

```
# delete an element
print("In a great battle, your shield is destroyed.")
del inventory[2]
print("Your inventory is now:")
print(inventory)

input("\nPress the enter key to continue.")
```

After this code executes, the element that was at position number 2, the string "shield", is removed from inventory. Deleting an element doesn't create a gap in a sequence. The length of the list shrinks by one, and all of the elements after the deleted one "slide down" one position. So, in this case, there is still an element in position 2; it's just the element that was at position 3.

Deleting a List Slice

You can also delete a slice from a list:

```
# delete a slice
print("Your crossbow and armor are stolen by thieves.")
del inventory[:2]
print("Your inventory is now:")
print(inventory)

input("\n\nPress the enter key to exit.")
```

The following line removes the slice inventory[:2], which is ["crossbow", "armor"], from inventory:

```
del inventory[:2]
```

Just as with deleting an element, the length of the list shrinks and the remaining elements form a new, continuous list, starting from position 0.

USING LIST METHODS

Lists have methods that allow you to manipulate them. Through list methods, you can add an element, remove an element based on its value, sort a list, and even reverse the order of a list.

Introducing the High Scores Program

The High Scores program uses list methods to create and maintain a list of the user's best scores for a computer game. The program uses a simple, menu-driven interface. The user has a few choices. He or she can add a new score, delete a score, sort the scores, or quit the program. Figure 5.6 shows the program in action.

FIGURE 5.6

The user chooses from a menu to maintain the high scores list. Behind the scenes, list methods do the bulk of the work.

Setting Up the Program

The setup code for the program is pretty simple. After the initial comments, I create two variables. scores is a list that will contain the scores. I set it to an empty list to start out. choice represents the user's choice from the menu. I initialized it to None. You can find the code for the program on the companion website (www.courseptr.com/downloads) in the Chapter 5 folder; the file name is high_scores.py.

```
# High Scores
# Demonstrates list methods

scores = []

choice = None
```

Displaying the Menu

The while loop is the core of the program. It continues until the user enters 0. The rest of this code prints the menu and gets the user's choice:

```
while choice != "0":

    print(
    """
```

```
High Scores

0 - Exit
1 - Show Scores
2 - Add a Score
3 - Delete a Score
4 - Sort Scores
"""
)

choice = input("Choice: ")
print()
```

Exiting the Program

I first check if the user wants to quit. If the user enters 0, the computer says "Good-bye.":

```
# exit
if choice == "0":
    print("Good-bye.")
```

If the user enters 0, then the `while` loop's condition will be false the next time it's tested. The loop will end and so will the program.

Displaying the Scores

If the user enters 1, then this `elif` block executes and the computer displays the scores:

```
# list high-score table
elif choice == "1":
    print("High Scores")
    for score in scores:
        print(score)
```

Adding a Score

If the user enters 2, the computer asks the user for a new score and assigns it to `score`. The last line uses the `append()` list method to add `score` to the end of `scores`. The list becomes one element longer.

```
# add a score
elif choice == "2":
    score = int(input("What score did you get?: "))
    scores.append(score)
```

Removing a Score

When the user enters 3, the computer gets a score from the user to remove. If the score is in the list, the computer removes the first occurrence of it. If the score isn't in the list, the user is informed.

```
# remove a score
elif choice == "3":
    score = int(input("Remove which score?: "))
    if score in scores:
        scores.remove(score)
    else:
        print(score, "isn't in the high scores list.")
```

The code first checks to see if the score is in the list. If it is, the list method remove() is invoked. The method goes through the list, starting at position 0, and searches for the value passed to it—in this case, score. When the method finds the first occurrence of the value, that element is deleted from the list. If the value is in the list more than once, only the first occurrence is removed. So, only the first occurrence of score is removed. If the method successfully removes an element from the list, the list becomes one element shorter.

Also, notice how remove() is different from del. The remove() method doesn't delete an element based on a position, but rather on a value.

TRAP Watch out when you use the remove() method. If you try to remove a value that isn't in a list, you'll generate an error. Here's a safe way to do just that:

```
if score in scores:
    scores.remove(score)
```

Sorting the Scores

The scores in the list are in the exact order the user entered them. To sort the scores, all the user has to do is enter 4:

```
# sort scores
elif choice == "4":
    scores.sort(reverse=True)
```

The sort() method sorts the elements in the list. This is great, except that by default sort() orders the elements in ascending—smallest values first. But what I want is the highest scores first. Luckily, you can tell the sort() method to sort values in descending order—largest values first. You can do this by passing True to the method's reverse parameter. That's just what I did here and, as a result, the scores are sorted with the highest values first.

If you want to sort a list in ascending order (smallest values first), you can simply call the method without passing values to any parameters. So, if I wanted to sort a list called `numbers` in ascending order, I could just use the following line:

```
numbers.sort()
```

Dealing with an Invalid Choice

If the user enters a number that isn't a valid choice, the `else` clause catches it. The program lets the user know that the choice isn't understood.

```
# some unknown choice
else:
    print("Sorry, but", choice, "isn't a valid choice.")
```

Waiting for the User

After the user enters 0 to exit, the loop ends. As always, the program waits for the user:

```
input("\n\nPress the enter key to exit.")
```

You've seen a bunch of useful list methods in action. To get a summary of these methods (plus a few more), take a look at Table 5.1.

	TABLE 5.1 SELECTED LIST METHODS

Method	Description
append(*value*)	Adds *value* to end of a list.
sort()	Sorts the elements, smallest value first. Optionally, you can pass a Boolean value to the parameter `reverse`. If you pass `True`, the list will be sorted with the largest value first.
reverse()	Reverses the order of a list.
count(*value*)	Returns the number of occurrences of *value*.
index(*value*)	Returns the first position number of where *value* occurs.
insert(*i*, *value*)	Inserts *value* at position *i*.
pop([*i*])	Returns value at position *i* and removes value from the list. Providing the position number *i* is optional. Without it, the last element in the list is removed and returned.
remove(*value*)	Removes the first occurrence of *value* from the list.

Understanding When to Use Tuples Instead of Lists

At this point, you may be thinking, "Why use tuples at all?" It's true that lists can do everything tuples can, plus more. But don't be so quick to dismiss tuples. There is a place for them in your Python programming world. There are a few occasions where tuples make more sense than lists.

- Tuples are faster than lists. Because the computer knows they won't change, tuples can be stored in a way that makes using them faster than using lists. For simple programs, this speed difference won't matter, but in more complex applications, with very large sequences of information, it could.

- Tuples' immutability makes them perfect for creating constants since they can't change. Using tuples can add a level of safety and clarity to your code.

- Sometimes tuples are required. In some cases, Python requires immutable values. Okay, you haven't actually seen any of those cases yet, but there is a common situation you'll see when you learn about dictionaries, later in this chapter in the "Using Dictionaries" section. Dictionaries require immutable types, so tuples will be essential when creating some kinds of dictionaries.

But, because lists are so flexible, you're probably best off using them rather than tuples the majority of the time.

Using Nested Sequences

Before, I said that lists or tuples can be sequences of anything. If that's true, then lists can contain other lists or tuples, and tuples can contain other tuples or lists. Well, they can, and when they do, they're called *nested sequences*. Nested sequences are sequences inside other sequences. Nested sequences are a great way to organize more complex collections of information.

Although the term sounds like another cryptic piece of computer jargon, I bet you create and use nested sequences all the time. Let me give you an example. Say you're making a holiday shopping list. You start by making a list of names. Under each name, you list a few possible gifts. Well, you've just created a nested sequence: you have a list of names and each name represents a list of gifts. That's all there is to it.

Introducing the High Scores 2.0 Program

The last program, High Scores, uses only scores. But most high score lists store a name along with a score. That's what this new version does. It also has a few other improvements. It automatically sorts the scores and even limits the list to just the top five. Figure 5.7 shows a sample run.

```
C:\Python31\python.exe                                    _ □ ×
     High Scores 2.0

     0 - Quit
     1 - List Scores
     2 - Add a Score

Choice: 2

What is the player's name?: Curly
What score did the player get?: 3000

     High Scores 2.0

     0 - Quit
     1 - List Scores
     2 - Add a Score

Choice: 1

High Scores

NAME     SCORE
Curly    3000
Larry    2000
Moe      1000

     High Scores 2.0

     0 - Quit
     1 - List Scores
     2 - Add a Score

Choice:
```

FIGURE 5.7

The new and
improved version
of High Scores
stores a name with
a score through
nested sequences.

Creating Nested Sequences

You can create a nested list or tuple like always: type each element, followed by a comma. The difference with nested sequences is that you include entire lists or tuples as elements. Here's an example:

```
>>> nested = ["first", ("second", "third"), ["fourth", "fifth", "sixth"]]
>>> print(nested)
['first', ('second', 'third'), ['fourth', 'fifth', 'sixth']]
```

So, although you see six strings here, nested has only three elements. The first element is the string "first", the second element is the tuple ("second", "third"), and the third element is the list ["fourth", "fifth", "sixth"].

While you can create a list or tuple with any number of lists and tuples, useful nested sequences often have a consistent pattern. Take a look at the next example:

```
>>> scores = [("Moe", 1000), ("Larry", 1500), ("Curly", 3000)]
>>> print(scores)
[('Moe', 1000), ('Larry', 1500), ('Curly', 3000)]
```

scores is a list with three elements. Each element is a tuple. Each tuple has exactly two elements, a string and a number.

This sequence, by the way, represents a high score table with names and scores (like a real high score table should!). In this particular instance, Moe got a score of 1,000; Larry got 1,500; and Curly got a high score of 3,000.

TRAP   Although you can create nested sequences inside nested sequences many times over, as in the following example, this usually isn't a good idea.

```
nested = ("deep", ("deeper", ("deepest", "still deepest")))
```

Things can get confusing fast. Even experienced programmers rarely use sequences more than a level or two deep. For most programs you'll write, one level of nesting (like the scores list you just saw) is really all you'll need.

Accessing Nested Elements

You access elements of a nested sequence just like any other sequence, through indexing:

```
>>> scores = [("Moe", 1000), ("Larry", 1500), ("Curly", 3000)]
>>> print(scores[0])
('Moe', 1000)
>>> print(scores[1])
('Larry', 1500)
>>> print(scores[2])
('Curly', 3000)
```

Each element is a tuple, so that's exactly what you get when you access one. But what if you want to access one of the elements of one of the tuples? One way is to assign the tuple to a variable and index it, as in:

```
>>> a_score = scores[2]
>>> print(a_score)
('Curly ', 3000)
>>> print(a_score[0])
Curly
```

But there's a direct way to access "Curly" right from scores:

```
>>> print(scores[2][0])
Curly
```

By supplying two indices with scores[2][0], you're telling the computer to go get the element from scores at position 2 (which is ("Curly", 3000)) and then, from that, to get the element at position 0 (which is "Curly"). You can use this kind of multiple indexing with nested sequences to get directly to a nested element.

Unpacking a Sequence

If you know how many elements are in a sequence, you can assign each to its own variable in a single line of code:

```
>>> name, score = ("Shemp", 175)
>>> print(name)
Shemp
>>> print(score)
175
```

This is called *unpacking* and works with any sequence type. Just remember to use the same number of variables as elements in the sequence, because otherwise you'll generate an error.

Setting Up the Program

Just as in the original High Scores program, I set up the variables and `while` loop. As before, if the user enters 0, the computer prints `"Good-bye."`. You can find the code for the program on the companion website (www.courseptr.com/downloads) in the Chapter 5 folder; the file name is high_scores2.py.

```
# High Scores 2.0
# Demonstrates nested sequences

scores = []

choice = None
while choice != "0":

    print(
    """
    High Scores 2.0

    0 - Quit
    1 - List Scores
    2 - Add a Score
    """
    )

    choice = input("Choice: ")
    print()
```

```
# exit
if choice == "0":
    print("Good-bye.")
```

Displaying the Scores by Accessing Nested Tuples

If the user enters 1, the computer goes through each element in scores and unpacks the score and name into the variables score and name. Then the computer prints them out.

```
# display high-score table
elif choice == "1":
    print("High Scores\n")
    print("NAME\tSCORE")
    for entry in scores:
        score, name = entry
        print(name, "\t", score)
```

Adding a Score by Appending a Nested Tuple

If the user enters 2, the computer lets the user enter a new score and name. With these two values, the computer creates a tuple, entry. I chose to store the score first in this tuple because I wanted the entries to be sorted by score, then name. Next, the computer appends this new high score entry to the list. The computer sorts the list and reverses it so that the highest scores are first. The final statement slices and assigns the list so that only the top five scores are kept.

```
# add a score
elif choice == "2":
    name = input("What is the player's name?: ")
    score = int(input("What score did the player get?: "))
    entry = (score, name)
    scores.append(entry)
    scores.sort(reverse=True)
    scores = scores[:5]      # keep only top 5 scores
```

Dealing with an Invalid Choice

If the user enters something other than 0, 1, or 2, the else clause catches it. The program lets the user know that the choice wasn't understood.

```
# some unknown choice
else:
    print("Sorry, but", choice, "isn't a valid choice.")
```

Waiting for the User

After the user enters 0 to exit, the loop ends and the program waits for the user:

```
input("\n\nPress the enter key to exit.")
```

UNDERSTANDING SHARED REFERENCES

In Chapter 2, you learned that a variable refers to a value. This means that, technically, a variable doesn't store a copy of a value, but just refers to the place in your computer's memory where the value is stored. For example, `language = "Python"` stores the string `"Python"` in your computer's memory somewhere and then creates the variable `language`, which refers to that place in memory. Take a look at Figure 5.8 for a visual representation.

FIGURE 5.8

The variable language refers to a place in memory where the string value "Python" is stored.

To say the variable `language` stores the string `"Python"`, like a piece of Tupperware stores a chicken leg, is not accurate. In some programming languages, this might be a good analogy, but not in Python. A better way to think about it is like this: A variable refers to a value the same way a person's name refers to a person. It would be wrong (and silly) to say that a person's name "stores" the person. Using a person's name, you can get to a person. Using a variable name, you can get to a value.

So what does all this mean? Well, for immutable values that you've been using, like numbers, strings, and tuples, it doesn't mean much. But it does mean something for mutable values, like lists. When several variables refer to the same mutable value, they share the same reference. They all refer to the one, single copy of that value. And a change to the value through one of the variables results in a change for all the variables, since there is only one, shared copy to begin with.

Here's an example to show how this works. Suppose that I'm throwing a hip, happening party with my friends and dignitaries from around the world. (Hey, this is my book. I can make up any example I want.) Different people at the party call me by different names, even though I'm only one person. Let's say that a friend calls me "Mike," a dignitary calls me "Mr. Dawson," and my Pulitzer Prize winning, supermodel girlfriend, just back from her literacy, fundraising world-tour (again, my book, my fictional girlfriend) calls me "Honey." So, all three people refer to me with different names. This is the same way that three variables could all refer to the same list. Here's the beginning of an interactive session to show you what I mean:

```
>>> mike = ["khakis", "dress shirt", "jacket"]
>>> mr_dawson = mike
>>> honey = mike
>>> print(mike)
['khakis', 'dress shirt', 'jacket']
>>> print(mr_dawson)
['khakis', 'dress shirt', 'jacket']
>>> print(honey)
['khakis', 'dress shirt', 'jacket']
```

So, all three variables, mike, mr_dawson, and honey, refer to the same, single list, representing me (or at least what I'm wearing at this party). Figure 5.9 helps drive this idea home.

FIGURE 5.9

The variables mike, mr_dawson, and honey all refer to the same list.

This means that a change to the list using any of these three variables will change the list they all refer to. Back at the party, let's say that my girlfriend gets my attention by calling "Honey." She asks me to change my jacket for a red sweater she knitted (yes, she knits too). I, of course, do what she asks. In my interactive session, this could be expressed as follows:

```
>>> honey[2] = "red sweater"
>>> print(honey)
['khakis', 'dress shirt', 'red sweater']
```

The results are what you would expect. The element in position number 2 of the list referred to by honey is no longer "jacket", but is now "red sweater".

Now, at the party, if a friend were to get my attention by calling "Mike" or a dignitary were to call me over with "Mr. Dawson," both would see me in my red sweater, even though neither had anything to do with me changing my clothes. The same is true in Python. Even though I changed the value of the element in position number 2 by using the variable honey, that change is reflected by any variable that refers to this list. So, to continue my interactive session:

```
>>> print(mike)
['khakis', 'dress shirt', 'red sweater']
>>> print(mr_dawson)
['khakis', 'dress shirt', 'red sweater']
```

The element in position number 2 of the list referred to by mike and mr_dawson is "red sweater". It has to be since there's only one list.

So, the moral of this story is: be aware of shared references when using mutable values. If you change the value through one variable, it will be changed for all.

However, you can avoid this effect if you make a copy of a list through slicing. For example:

```
>>> mike = ["khakis", "dress shirt", "jacket"]
>>> honey = mike[:]
>>> honey[2] = "red sweater"
>>> print(honey)
['khakis', 'dress shirt', 'red sweater']
>>> print(mike)
['khakis', 'dress shirt', 'jacket']
```

Here, honey is assigned a copy of mike. honey does not refer to the same list. Instead, it refers to a copy. So, a change to honey has no effect on mike. It's like I've been cloned. Now, my girlfriend is dressing my clone in a red sweater, while the original me is still in a jacket. Okay, this party is getting pretty weird with my clone walking around in a red sweater that my fictional girlfriend knitted for me, so I think it's time to end this bizarre yet useful analogy.

One last thing to remember is that sometimes you'll want this shared-reference effect, while other times you won't. Now that you understand how it works, you can control it.

Using Dictionaries

By now you probably realize that programmers love to organize information. You saw that lists and tuples let you organize things into sequences. Well, dictionaries let you organize information too, but in a different way. With a dictionary, you don't store information in a sequence; instead, you store it in pairs. It's a lot like an actual dictionary where each entry is a pair: a word and its definition. When you look up a word, you get its definition. Python dictionaries work the same way: you look up a *key* and get its *value*.

Introducing the Geek Translator Program

The high-tech world has created many things that impact our lives, including a culture of its own. As the result of technology, new words and concepts have been born. The Geek Translator is here to help you understand the technophile in your life. The program creates a dictionary with geek terms and definitions. The program not only lets the user look up a term, but also add a term, replace a definition, and delete a term. Figure 5.10 illustrates the program in action.

FIGURE 5.10

So "uninstalled" means fired. I was totally 404 on that.

Creating Dictionaries

The first thing I did in the program was create a dictionary of terms and definitions. The geek terms are on the left, and their definitions are on the right. You can find the code for the program on the companion website (www.courseptr.com/downloads) in the Chapter 5 folder; the file name is geek_translator.py.

```
# Geek Translator
# Demonstrates using dictionaries

geek = {"404": "clueless.  From the web error message 404, meaning page not found.",
        "Googling": "searching the Internet for background information on a person.",
        "Keyboard Plaque" : "the collection of debris found in computer keyboards.",
        "Link Rot" : "the process by which web page links become obsolete.",
        "Percussive Maintenance" : "the act of striking an electronic device to make
it work.",
        "Uninstalled" : "being fired.  Especially popular during the dot-bomb era."}
```

This code creates a dictionary named geek. It consists of six pairs, called *items*. As an example, one of the items is "Keyboard Plaque" : "the collection of debris found in computer keyboards. " Each item is made up of a key and a value. The keys are on the left side of the colons.

The values are on the right. So, `"Keyboard Plaque"` is a key, and its value is `"the collection of debris found in computer keyboards."` The key is literally the "key" to getting the value. That means you could use the key `"Keyboard Plaque"` to get its value `"the collection of debris found in computer keyboards."`

To create your own dictionary, follow the pattern I used. Type a key, followed by a colon, followed by the key's value. Use commas to separate all of the key-value pairs, and surround the whole thing with curly brackets. Like tuples and lists, you can either type the whole thing on one line or use separate lines after any of the commas.

Accessing Dictionary Values

One of the most common things you'll do with a dictionary is use a key to get its value. There are a few different ways you can do this. I'll show you an example of each in this section, using the interactive interpreter.

Using a Key to Retrieve a Value

The simplest way to retrieve a value from a dictionary is by directly accessing it with a key. To get a key's value, just put the key in brackets, following the name of the dictionary. Here's an interactive session to show you what I mean (assume that I've already defined the dictionary geek):

```
>>> geek["404"]
'clueless. From the web error message 404, meaning page not found. '
>>> geek["Link Rot"]
'the process by which web page links become obsolete. '
```

This looks similar to indexing a sequence, but there's an important difference. When you index a sequence, you use a position number. When you look up a value in a dictionary, you use a key. This is the only direct way to retrieve a value from a dictionary. In fact, dictionaries don't have position numbers at all.

One thing that sometimes trips up beginning programmers is that a value can't be used to get a key in a dictionary. That would be like trying to use a definition to find a word in a real-life dictionary. Real-life dictionaries just aren't set up for that kind of thing, and neither are Python dictionaries. So remember, it's give a key and get a value, only.

TRAP   If you try to get a value from a dictionary by directly accessing it with a key that doesn't exist, you'll generate an error:

```
>>> geek["Dancing Baloney"]
Traceback (most recent call last):
```

```
File "<pyshell#1>", line 1, in <module>
  geek["Dancing Baloney"]
KeyError: 'Dancing Baloney'
```

Since "Dancing Baloney" isn't a key in the dictionary, this results in an error. ("Dancing Baloney," by the way, means animated graphics and other visual effects that have no substantive value, often used by web designers to impress clients.)

Testing for a Key with the in Operator Before Retrieving a Value

Since using a nonexistent key can lead to an error, it's usually best not to directly access a dictionary without taking some precautions. One thing you can do is check to see if a key exists before attempting to retrieve its value. You can check for the existence of a key with the in operator:

```
>>> if "Dancing Baloney" in geek:
      print("I know what Dancing Baloney is. ")
    else:
      print("I have no idea what Dancing Baloney is. ")


I have no idea what Dancing Baloney is.
```

Because the dictionary doesn't contain "Dancing Baloney" as a key, the condition "Dancing Baloney" in geek is false. So, the computer says it doesn't know what it is.

You use the in operator with dictionaries much the same way you've used it with lists and tuples. You type the value you're checking for, followed by in, followed by the dictionary. This creates a condition. The condition is true if the key is in the dictionary; otherwise, it's false. This is a handy thing to do before trying to get a value. But remember, in only checks for keys; it can't check for values used this way.

Using the get() Method to Retrieve a Value

There's another way to retrieve a value from a dictionary. You can use the dictionary method get(). The method has a built-in safety net for handling situations where you ask for a value of a key that doesn't exist. If the key doesn't exist, the method returns a default value, which you can define. Take a look at another attempt:

```
>>> print(geek.get("Dancing Baloney", "I have no idea."))
I have no idea.
```

By using the get() method here, I was guaranteed to get a value back. If this term was in the dictionary as a key, then I'd get its definition. Since it wasn't, I got back the default value that I defined, the string "I have no idea."

To use the get() method, all you have to do is supply the key you're looking for followed by an optional default value. If the key is in the dictionary, you get its value. If the key isn't in the dictionary, you get the default value. But here's the twist: If you don't supply a default value (it's your option), then you get back None. Here's an example I created without providing a default value:

```
>>> print(geek.get("Dancing Baloney"))
None
```

Setting Up the Program

Time to get back to the code for the Geek Translator program. After I created the geek dictionary, I implemented the menu system you've seen before, this time with five choices. Like before, if the user chooses 0, the computer says good-bye.

```
choice = None
while choice != "0":

    print(
    """
    Geek Translator

    0 - Quit
    1 - Look Up a Geek Term
    2 - Add a Geek Term
    3 - Redefine a Geek Term
    4 - Delete a Geek Term
    """
    )

    choice = input("Choice: ")
    print()

    # exit
    if choice == "0":
        print("Good-bye.")
```

Getting a Value

If the user enters 1, the next section asks for a term to look up. The computer checks to see if the term is in the dictionary. If it is, the program accesses the dictionary, using the term as the key, gets its definition, and prints it out. If the term is not in the dictionary, the computer informs the user.

```
# get a definition
elif choice == "1":
    term = input("What term do you want me to translate?: ")
    if term in geek:
        definition = geek[term]
        print("\n", term, "means", definition)
    else:
        print("\nSorry, I don't know", term)
```

Adding a Key-Value Pair

Dictionaries are mutable, so you can modify them. If the user enters 2, the next section adds a new term to the dictionary:

```
# add a term-definition pair
elif choice == "2":
    term = input("What term do you want me to add?: ")
    if term not in geek:
        definition = input("\nWhat's the definition?: ")
        geek[term] = definition
        print("\n", term, "has been added.")
    else:
        print("\nThat term already exists!  Try redefining it.")
```

The computer asks the user for the new term to add. If the term is not already in the dictionary, the computer gets the definition and adds the pair through the line:

```
geek[term] = definition
```

This creates a new item in geek. The term is the key and the definition is its value. This is exactly how you assign a new item to a dictionary. You use the dictionary, followed by the key in square brackets, followed by the assignment operator, followed by the key's value.

I wrote the program so that the computer refuses to add a term if it's already in the dictionary. This is a safety measure I created to ensure that the user doesn't accidentally overwrite an existing term. If the user really wants to redefine an existing term, he or she should choose menu option 3.

TRICK   A dash of pessimism is a good thing, at least when you're programming. As you saw here, I assumed that the user might try to add a new term without realizing it's already in the dictionary. If I hadn't checked for this, a user could overwrite a term without realizing it. When you're writing your own programs, try to think of things that could go wrong, then try to make sure your program can deal with them. So be a pessimist, just a little bit.

Replacing a Key-Value Pair

If the user enters 3, then the next section replaces an existing key-value pair:

```
# redefine an existing term
elif choice == "3":
    term = input("What term do you want me to redefine?: ")
    if term in geek:
        definition = input("What's the new definition?: ")
        geek[term] = definition
        print("\n", term, "has been redefined.")
    else:
        print("\nThat term doesn't exist!  Try adding it.")
```

To replace a key-value pair, I used the exact same line of code that I used for adding a new pair:

```
        geek[term] = definition
```

Python replaces the current value (the definition) with the new one.

 TRIP   If you assign a value to a dictionary using a key that already exists, Python replaces the current value without complaint. So you have to watch out, because you might overwrite the value of an existing key without realizing it.

Deleting a Key-Value Pair

If the user enters 4, then this `elif` block runs:

```
# delete a term-definition pair
elif choice == "4":
    term = input("What term do you want me to delete?: ")
    if term in geek:
        del geek[term]
        print("\nOkay, I deleted", term)
    else:
        print("\nI can't do that!", term, "doesn't exist in the dictionary.")
```

The program asks the user for the geek term to delete. Next, the program checks to see if the term is actually in the dictionary with the `in` operator. If it is, the item is deleted with

```
del geek[term]
```

This deletes the item with the key `term` from the dictionary `geek`. You can delete any item in a dictionary this way. Just put `del` in front of the dictionary followed by the key of the item you wish to delete in square brackets.

If the geek term doesn't exist in the first place, the `else` clause executes and the computer lets the user know.

 Trying to delete a dictionary item through a key that doesn't exist will give you an error. It's a smart move to be sure the key you're using exists.

Wrapping Up the Program

The final `else` clause lets the user know that he or she entered an invalid choice:

```
# some unknown choice
else:
    print("\nSorry, but", choice, "isn't a valid choice.")

input("\n\nPress the enter key to exit.")
```

Understanding Dictionary Requirements

There are a few things you should keep in mind when creating dictionaries:

- A dictionary can't contain multiple items with the same key. Think again about a real dictionary. It becomes pretty meaningless if you can keep adding the same word with totally new definitions whenever you want.

- A key has to be immutable. It can be a string, a number, or a tuple, which gives you lots of possibilities. A key has to be immutable because, if it weren't, you could sneak into a dictionary later and change its keys, possibly ending up with two identical keys. And you just learned you can't have that!

- Values don't have to be unique. Also, values can be mutable or immutable. They can be anything you want.

There's even more you can do with dictionaries. Table 5.2 summarizes some useful methods that can help you get more out of this type.

TABLE 5.2	SELECTED DICTIONARY METHODS
Method	**Description**
get(*key*, [*default*])	Returns the value of *key*. If *key* doesn't exist, then the optional *default* is returned. If *key* doesn't exist and *default* isn't specified, then None is returned.
keys()	Returns a view of all the keys in a dictionary.
values()	Returns a view of all the values in a dictionary.
items()	Returns a view of all the items in a dictionary. Each item is a two-element tuple, where the first element is a key and the second element is the key's value.

Dictionary views—returned by keys(), values(), and items()—are, in some ways, like lists. They can be iterated over with a for loop. However, they are not lists. They can't, for example, be indexed. In addition, views are dynamic, which means that their contents are not independent of their associated dictionaries. So, a change to a dictionary is reflected by views of that dictionary. To learn more about views, see the documentation section of the official Python website (www.python.org).

BACK TO THE HANGMAN GAME

By putting together all you've learned so far, you can create the Hangman game presented at the beginning of the chapter. This program is much longer than anything you've seen, but don't be intimidated by its size. The code isn't much more complex than that of the other projects you've worked through. The biggest part of the program is just my modest ASCII art, the eight versions of the stick figured being hanged. The real meat of the program is not much more than a screenful of code.

Setting Up the Program

First things first. As always, I started with opening comments, explaining the program. Next, I imported the random module. I need the module to pick a random word from a sequence. You can find the code for the program on the companion website (www.courseptr.com/downloads) in the Chapter 5 folder; the file name is hangman.py.

```
# Hangman Game
#
# The classic game of Hangman.  The computer picks a random word
# and the player wrong to guess it, one letter at a time.  If the player
# can't guess the word in time, the little stick figure gets hanged.


# imports
import random
```

Creating Constants

Though there are several screenfuls of code in this next section, I only create three constants in all that programming. First, I created the biggest tuple you've seen. It's really just a sequence of eight elements, but each element is a triple-quoted string that spans 12 lines.

Each string is a representation of the gallows where the stick figure is being hanged. Each subsequent string shows a more complete figure. Each time the player guesses incorrectly, the next string is displayed. By the eighth entry, the image is complete and the figure is a goner. If this final string is displayed, the player has lost and the game is over. I assigned this tuple to HANGMAN, a variable name in all caps, because I'll be using it as a constant.

```
# constants
HANGMAN = (
"""
 ------
 |    |
 |
 |
 |
 |
 |
 |
 |
 ----------
""",
"""
 ------
 |    |
 |    0
 |
```

```
     |
     |
     |
     |
     |
  ---------
""",
"""

  ------
  |    |
  |    0
  |  -+-
  |
  |
  ---------
""",
"""

  ------
  |    |
  |    0
  |  /-+-
  |
  |
  |
  |
  |
  ---------
""",
"""

  ------
  |    |
  |    0
  |  /-+-/
  |
  |
  |
```

```
      |
      |
    ---------
""",
"""
    ------
    |   |
    |   0
    | /-+-/
    |   |
    |
    |
    |
    ---------
""",
"""
    ------
    |   |
    |   0
    | /-+-/
    |   |
    |   |
    |   |
    |
    ---------
""",
"""
    ------
    |   |
    |   0
    | /-+-/
    |   |
    |   |
    |   | |
    |
    ---------
""")
```

Next, I created a constant to represent the maximum number of wrong guesses a player can make before the game is over:

```
MAX_WRONG = len(HANGMAN) - 1
```

The maximum number of incorrect guesses is one less than the length of HANGMAN. This is because the first image of the empty gallows is displayed even before the player makes a first guess. So although there are eight images in HANGMAN, the player only gets seven wrong guesses before the game is over.

Finally, I created a tuple containing all of the possible words that the computer can pick from for the player to guess. Feel free to modify the program and make up your own list.

```
WORDS = ("OVERUSED", "CLAM", "GUAM", "TAFFETA", "PYTHON")
```

Initializing the Variables

Next, I initialized the variables. I used the random.choice() function to pick a random word from the list of possible words. I assigned this secret word to the variable word.

```
# initialize variables
word = random.choice(WORDS)    # the word to be guessed
```

I created another string, so_far, to represent what the player has guessed so far in the game. The string starts out as just a series of dashes, one for each letter in the word. When the player correctly guesses a letter, the dashes in the positions of that letter are replaced with the letter itself.

```
so_far = "-" * len(word)       # one dash for each letter in word to be
guessed
```

I created wrong and assigned it the number 0. wrong keeps track of the number of wrong guesses the player makes.

```
wrong = 0                      # number of wrong guesses player has made
```

I created an empty list, used, to contain all the letters the player has guessed:

```
used = []                      # letters already guessed
```

Creating the Main Loop

I created a loop that continues until either the player has guessed too many wrong letters or the player has guessed all the letters in the word:

```
print("Welcome to Hangman.   Good luck!")

while wrong < MAX_WRONG and so_far != word:
    print(HANGMAN[wrong])
    print("\nYou've used the following letters:\n", used)
    print("\nSo far, the word is:\n", so_far)
```

Next, I print the current stick figure, based on the number of wrong guesses the player has made. The more wrong guesses the player has made, the closer the stick figure is to being done in. After that, I display the list of letters that the player has used in this game. And then I show what the partially guessed word looks like so far.

Getting the Player's Guess

I get the player's guess and convert it to uppercase so that it can be found in the secret word (which is in all caps). After that, I make sure that the player hasn't already used this letter. If the player has already guessed this letter, then I make the player enter a new character until the player enters one he or she hasn't used yet. Once the player enters a valid guess, I convert the guess to uppercase and add it to the list of used letters.

```
guess = input("\n\nEnter your guess: ")
guess = guess.upper()

while guess in used:
    print("You've already guessed the letter", guess)
    guess = input("Enter your guess: ")
    guess = guess.upper()

used.append(guess)
```

Checking the Guess

Next, I check to see if the guess is in the secret word. If it is, I let the player know. Then I go about creating a new version of so_far to include this new letter in all the places where the letter is in the secret word.

```
if guess in word:
    print("\nYes!", guess, "is in the word!")

    # create a new so_far to include guess
    new = ""
```

```
    for i in range(len(word)):
        if guess == word[i]:
            new += guess
        else:
            new += so_far[i]
    so_far = new
```

If the player's guess isn't in the word, then I let the player know and increase the number of wrong guesses by one.

```
    else:
        print("\nSorry,", guess, "isn't in the word.")
        wrong += 1
```

Ending the Game

At this point, the game is over. If the number of wrong guesses has reached the maximum, the player has lost. In that case, I print the final image of the stick figure. Otherwise, I congratulate the player. In either case, I let the player know what the secret word was.

```
if wrong == MAX_WRONG:
    print(HANGMAN[wrong])
    print("\nYou've been hanged!")
else:
    print("\nYou guessed it!")

print("\nThe word was", word)

input("\n\nPress the enter key to exit.")
```

SUMMARY

In this chapter, you learned all about lists and dictionaries, two new types. You learned that lists are mutable sequences. You saw how to add, delete, sort, and even reverse list elements. But even with all that lists offer, you learned that there are some cases where the less flexible tuple is actually the better (or required) choice. You also learned about shared references that can occur with mutable types and saw how to avoid them when necessary. You saw how to create and use nested sequences to work with even more interesting information, like a high score list. You learned how to create and modify dictionaries that let you work with pairs of data, too.

CHALLENGES

1. Create a program that prints a list of words in random order. The program should print all the words and not repeat any.

2. Write a Character Creator program for a role-playing game. The player should be given a pool of 30 points to spend on four attributes: Strength, Health, Wisdom, and Dexterity. The player should be able to spend points from the pool on any attribute and should also be able to take points from an attribute and put them back into the pool.

3. Write a Who's Your Daddy? program that lets the user enter the name of a male and produces the name of his father. (You can use celebrities, fictional characters, or even historical figures for fun.) Allow the user to add, replace, and delete son-father pairs.

4. Improve the Who's Your Daddy program by adding a choice that lets the user enter a name and get back a grandfather. Your program should still only use one dictionary of son-father pairs. Make sure to include several generations in your dictionary so that a match can be found.

Functions: The Tic-Tac-Toe Game

Every program you've written so far has been one large, continuous series of instructions. Once your programs reach a certain size or level of complexity, it becomes hard to work with them this way. Fortunately, there are ways to break up big programs into smaller, manageable chunks of code. In this chapter, you learn one way of doing this by creating your own functions. Specifically in this chapter, you'll learn to do the following:

- Write your own functions
- Accept values into your functions through parameters
- Return information from your functions through return values
- Work with global variables and constants
- Create a computer opponent that plays a strategy game

Introducing the Tic-Tac-Toe Game

In this chapter project, you'll learn how to create a computer opponent using a dash of artificial intelligence (AI). In the game, the player and computer square off in a high-stakes, human-machine showdown of Tic-Tac-Toe. The computer plays a formidable, though not perfect, game, and comes with enough attitude to make any match fun. Figures 6.1 through 6.3 illustrate the gameplay.

FIGURE 6.1

The computer is full of . . . confidence.

FIGURE 6.2

I did not see that coming. Even with simple programming techniques, the computer makes some pretty good moves.

FIGURE 6.3

I found the computer's weakness and won this time.

CREATING FUNCTIONS

You've already seen several built-in functions in action, including `len()` and `range()`. Well, if these aren't enough for you, Python lets you create functions of your very own. Your functions work just like the ones that come standard with the language. They go off and perform a task and then return control to your program. Creating your own functions offers you many advantages. One of the biggest is that it allows you to break up your code into manageable, bite-sized chunks. Programs that are one, long series of instructions with no logical breaks are hard to write, understand, and maintain. Programs that are made up of functions can be easier to create and work with. Just like the functions you've already met, your new functions should do one job well.

Introducing the Instructions Program

From the screen shots of the Tic-Tac-Toe game, you can probably tell that the computer opponent has a little attitude. It comes across quite clearly in the instructions the computer gives before the game. You'll get a look at the code that produces those instructions in this next program, Instructions. The code is a little different than you might expect. That's because I created a function to display the instructions. I used that same function here in Instructions. Take a look at Figure 6.4 to see a sample run of the program.

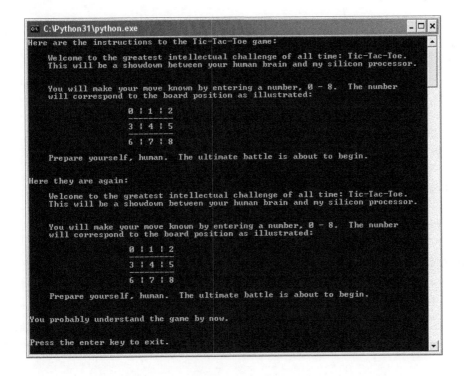

FIGURE 6.4

The instructions are displayed each time with just a single line of code: a call to a function I created.

You can find the code for the program on the companion website (www.courseptr.com/downloads) in the Chapter 6 folder; the file name is instructions.py.

```
# Instructions
# Demonstrates programmer-created functions

def instructions():
    """Display game instructions."""
    print(
    """
    Welcome to the greatest intellectual challenge of all time: Tic-Tac-Toe.
    This will be a showdown between your human brain and my silicon processor.

    You will make your move known by entering a number, 0 - 8.  The number
    will correspond to the board position as illustrated:

                    0 | 1 | 2
                    ---------
                    3 | 4 | 5
                    ---------
                    6 | 7 | 8

    Prepare yourself, human.  The ultimate battle is about to begin. \n
    """
    )

# main
print("Here are the instructions to the Tic-Tac-Toe game:")
instructions()
print("Here they are again:")
instructions()
print("You probably understand the game by now.")

input("\n\nPress the enter key to exit.")
```

Defining a Function

I began the definition of my new function with a single line:

```
def instructions():
```

This line tells the computer that the block of code that follows is to be used together as the function `instructions()`. I'm basically naming this block of statements. This means that whenever I call the function `instructions()` in this program, the block of code runs.

This line and its block are a *function definition*. They define what the function does, but don't run the function. When the computer sees the function definition, it makes a note that this function exists so it can use it later. It won't actually run the function until it sees a function call for it, later in the program.

To define a function of your own, follow my example. Start with `def`, followed by your function name, followed by a pair of parentheses, followed by a colon, and then your indented block of statements. To name a function, follow the basic rules for naming variables. Also, try to use a name that conveys what the function produces or does.

Documenting a Function

Functions have a special mechanism that allows you to document them with what's called a *docstring* (or *documentation string*). I created the following docstring for `instructions()`:

```
"""Display game instructions."""
```

A docstring is typically a triple-quoted string and, if you use one, must be the first line in your function. For simple functions, you can do what I did here: write a single sentence that describes what the function does. Functions work just fine without docstrings, but using them is a good idea. It gets you in the habit of commenting your code and makes you describe the function's one, well-defined job. Also, a function's docstring can pop up as interactive documentation while you type your call to it in IDLE.

Calling a Programmer-Created Function

Calling a programmer-created function works just like calling a built-in function. Use the name of the function followed by a set of parentheses. I called my new function several times, each time with the line:

```
instructions()
```

This tells the computer to go off and execute the function I defined earlier. So each time I call it, the computer prints the instructions to the game.

Understanding Abstraction

By writing and calling functions, you practice what's known as *abstraction*. Abstraction lets you think about the big picture without worrying about the details. So, in this program, I can just use the function instructions() without worrying about the details of displaying the text. All I have to do is call the function with one line of code, and it gets the job done.

You might be surprised where you find abstraction, but people use it all the time. For example, consider two employees at a fast food place. If one tells the other that he just filled a #3, and "sized it," the other employee knows that the first employee took a customer's order, went to the heat lamps, grabbed a burger, went over to the deep fryer, filled their biggest cardboard container with French fries, went to the soda fountain, grabbed their biggest cup, filled it with soda, gave it all to the customer, took the customer's money, and gave the customer change. Not only would this version be a boring conversation, but it's unnecessary. Both employees understand what it means to fill a #3 and "size it." They don't have to concern themselves with all the details because they're using abstraction.

USING PARAMETERS AND RETURN VALUES

As you've seen with built-in functions, you can provide a function values and get values back from them. With the len() function, for example, you provide a sequence, and the function returns its length. Your own functions can also receive and return values. This allows your functions to communicate with the rest of your program.

Introducing the Receive and Return Program

I created three functions in the program Receive and Return to show the various combinations of receiving and returning values. One function receives a value. The next function returns a value. And the last function both receives and returns a value. Take a look at Figure 6.5 to see exactly what happens as a result of the program.

FIGURE 6.5	
| Each function uses a parameter, a return value, or both to communicate with the main part of the program. | ```
C:\Python31\python.exe
Here's a message for you.
Here's what I got from give_me_five(): 5
Please enter 'y' or 'n': y
Thanks for entering: y
Press the enter key to exit.
``` |

You can find the code for the program on the companion website (www.courseptr.com/downloads) in the Chapter 6 folder; the file name is receive_and_return.py.
```

```
# Receive and Return
# Demonstrates parameters and return values

def display(message):
    print(message)

def give_me_five():
    five = 5
    return five

def ask_yes_no(question):
    """Ask a yes or no question."""
    response = None
    while response not in ("y", "n"):
        response = input(question).lower()
    return response

# main
display("Here's a message for you.\n")

number = give_me_five()
print("Here's what I got from give_me_five():", number)

answer = ask_yes_no("\nPlease enter 'y' or 'n': ")
print("Thanks for entering:", answer)

input("\n\nPress the enter key to exit.")
```

Receiving Information through Parameters

The first function I defined, display(), receives a value and prints it. It receives a value through its *parameter*. Parameters are essentially variable names inside the parentheses of a function header:

```
def display(message):
```

Parameters catch the values sent to the function from a function call through its arguments. So here, when display() is called, message is assigned the value provided through the argument "Here's a message for you.\n"

In the main part of the program, I call `display()` with

```
display("Here's a message for you.\n")
```

As a result, `message` gets the string `"Here's a message for you.\n"`. Then, the function runs. `message`, like any parameter, exists inside the function as a variable. So, the line

```
print(message)
```

prints the string `"Here's a message for you.\n"`.

If I hadn't passed `message` a value, I would have generated an error. The function `display()` requires exactly one argument value.

Although `display()` has only one parameter, functions can have many. To define a function with multiple parameters, list them out, separated by commas.

Returning Information through Return Values

The next function I wrote, `give_me_five()`, returns a value. It returns a value through (believe it or not) the `return` statement:

```
return five
```

When this line runs, the function passes the value of `five` back to the part of the program that called it, and then ends. A function always ends after it hits a `return` statement.

It's up to the part of the program that called a function to catch the values it returns and do something with them. Here's the main part of the program, where I called the function:

```
number = give_me_five()
print("Here's what I got from give_me_five():", number)
```

I set up a way to catch the return value of the function by assigning the result of the function call to `number`. So, when the function finishes, `number` gets the return value of `give_me_five()`, which is equal to 5. The next line prints `number` to show that it got the return value okay.

You can pass more than one value back from a function. Just list all the values you want to return, separated by commas.

TRAP Make sure to have enough variables to catch all the return values of a function. If you don't have the right number when you try to assign them, you'll generate an error.

Understanding Encapsulation

You might not see the need for return values when using your own functions. Why not just use the variable five back in the main part of the program? Because you can't. five doesn't exist outside of its function give_me_five(). In fact, no variable you create in a function, including its parameters, can be directly accessed outside its function. This is a good thing and is called *encapsulation*. Encapsulation helps keep independent code truly separate by hiding or encapsulating the details. That's why you use parameters and return values: to communicate just the information that needs to be exchanged. Plus, you don't have to keep track of variables you create within a function in the rest of your program. As your programs get large, this is a great benefit.

Encapsulation might sound a lot like abstraction. That's because they're closely related. Encapsulation is a principal of abstraction. Abstraction saves you from worrying about the details. Encapsulation hides details from you. As an example, consider a remote control for a TV with volume up and down buttons. When you use a TV remote to change the volume, you're employing abstraction, because you don't need to know what happens inside the TV for it to work. Now suppose the TV remote has 10 volume levels. You can get to them all through the remote, but you can't directly access them. That is, you can't get a specific volume number directly. You can only press the up volume and down volume buttons to eventually get to the level you want. The actual volume number is encapsulated and not directly available to you.

HINT Don't worry if you don't totally get the subtle difference between abstraction and encapsulation right now. They're intertwined concepts, so it can be a little tricky. Plus, you'll get to see them in action again when you learn about software objects and object oriented programming in Chapters 8 and 9.

Receiving and Returning Values in the Same Function

The final function I wrote, ask_yes_no(), receives one value and returns another. It receives a question and returns a response from the user, either "y" or "n". The function receives the question through its parameter:

```
def ask_yes_no(question):
```

question gets the value of the argument passed to the function. In this case, it's the string, "\nPlease enter 'y' or 'n': ". The next part of the function uses this string to prompt the user for a response:

```
response = None
while response not in ("y", "n"):
    response = input(question).lower()
```

The `while` loop keeps asking the question until the user enters either y, Y, n, or N. The function always converts the user's entry to lowercase.

Finally, when the user has entered a valid response, the function sends a string back to the part of the program that called it with

```
return response
```

and the function ends.

In the main part of the program, the return value is assigned to answer and printed:

```
answer = ask_yes_no("\nPlease enter 'y' or 'n': ")
print("Thanks for entering:", answer)
```

Understanding Software Reuse

Another great thing about functions is that they can easily be reused in other programs. For example, since asking the user a yes or no question is such a common thing to do, you could grab the `ask_yes_no()` function and use it in another program without doing any extra coding. This type of thing is called *software reuse.* So writing good functions not only saves you time and energy in your current project, but can also save you effort in future ones!

IN THE REAL WORLD

It's always a waste of time to "reinvent the wheel," so software reuse, using existing software and other project elements in new projects, is a technique that business has taken to heart. Software reuse can do the following:

- Increase company productivity. By reusing code and other elements that already exist, companies can get their projects done with less effort.

- Improve software quality. If a company already has a tested piece of code, then it can use the code with the knowledge that it's bug-free.

- Provide consistency across software products. By using the same user interface, for example, companies can create new software that users feel comfortable with right out of the box.

- Improve software performance. Once a company has a good way of doing something through software, using it again not only saves the company the trouble of reinventing the wheel, but also saves it from the possibility of reinventing a less efficient wheel.

One way to reuse functions you've written is to copy them into your new program. But there is a better way. You can create your own modules and `import` your functions into a new program, just like you `import` standard Python modules and use their functions. You'll learn how to create your own modules and import reusable code you've written in Chapter 9, in the "Creating Modules" section.

USING KEYWORD ARGUMENTS AND DEFAULT PARAMETER VALUES

Passing values through arguments to parameters allows you to give information to a function. But so far, you've only seen the most basic way to do that. Python allows greater control and flexibility with the way you pass information, through default parameter values and keyword arguments.

Introducing the Birthday Wishes Program

The program Birthday Wishes, a sample run of which is pictured in Figure 6.6, sends birthday greetings through two very similar functions. The first function uses the type of parameters you saw in the last section, called *positional parameters*. The second version of the function uses *default parameter values*. The best way to appreciate the difference is to see examples of them in action.

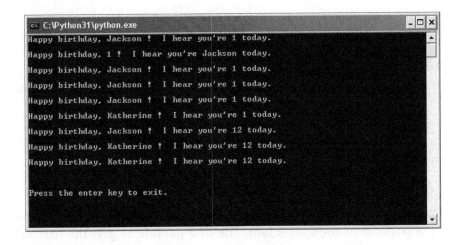

FIGURE 6.6

Functions can be called in different ways with the flexibility of keyword arguments and default parameter values.

You can find the code for the program on the companion website (www.courseptr.com/downloads) in the Chapter 6 folder; the file name is birthday_wishes.py.

```
# Birthday Wishes
# Demonstrates keyword arguments and default parameter values
```

```
# positional parameters
def birthday1(name, age):
    print("Happy birthday,", name, "!", " I hear you're", age, "today.\n")

# parameters with default values
def birthday2(name = "Jackson", age = 1):
    print("Happy birthday,", name, "!", " I hear you're", age, "today.\n")


birthday1("Jackson", 1)
birthday1(1, "Jackson")
birthday1(name = "Jackson", age = 1)
birthday1(age = 1, name = "Jackson")


birthday2()
birthday2(name = "Katherine")
birthday2(age = 12)
birthday2(name = "Katherine", age = 12)
birthday2("Katherine", 12)


input("\n\nPress the enter key to exit.")
```

Using Positional Parameters and Positional Arguments

If you just list out a series of variable names in a function's header, you create positional parameters:

```
def birthday1(name, age):
```

If you call a function with just a series of values, you create positional arguments:

```
birthday1("Jackson", 1)
```

Using positional parameters and positional arguments means that parameters get their values based solely on the position of the values sent. The first parameter gets the first value sent, the second parameter gets the second value sent, and so on.

With this particular function call, it means that name gets "Jackson" and age gets 1. This results in the message: Happy Birthday, Jackson ! I hear you're 1 today. If you switch the positions of two arguments, the parameters get different values. So with the call

```
birthday1(1, "Jackson")
```

name gets the first value, 1, and age gets the second value, "Jackson". As a result, you end up with a message you probably didn't intend: Happy Birthday, 1 ! I hear you're Jackson today.

You've seen this way of creating and calling functions already. But there are other ways to create parameter and argument lists in your programs.

Using Positional Parameters and Keyword Arguments

Positional parameters get values sent to them in order, unless you tell the function otherwise. You can tell the function to assign certain values to specific parameters, regardless of order, if you use keyword arguments. With keyword arguments, you use the actual parameter names from the function header to link a value to a parameter. So, by calling the same function birthday1() with

```
birthday1(name = "Jackson", age = 1)
```

name gets "Jackson" and age gets 1 and the function displays the message Happy Birthday, Jackson ! I hear you're 1 today. This isn't terribly impressive. You could achieve the same results without keyword arguments by just sending these values in this order. But the beauty of keyword arguments is that their order doesn't matter; it's the keywords that link values to parameters. So the call

```
birthday1(age = 1, name = "Jackson")
```

also produces the message Happy Birthday, Jackson ! I hear you're 1 today. even though the values are listed in opposite order.

Keyword arguments let you pass values in any order. But their biggest benefit is clarity. When you see a function call using keyword arguments, you get a much better understanding of what the values represent.

 TRAP You can combine keyword arguments and positional arguments in a single function call, but this can get tricky. Once you use a keyword argument, all the remaining arguments in the call must be keyword arguments, too. To keep things simple, try to use all keyword or all positional arguments in your function calls.

Using Default Parameter Values

Finally, you have the option to assign default values to your parameters, values that get assigned to the parameters if no value is passed to them. That's just what I did with the birthday2() function. I made changes in the header only:

```
def birthday2(name = "Jackson", age = 1):
```

This means that if no value is supplied to `name`, it gets `"Jackson"`. And if no value is supplied for `age`, it gets `1`. So the call

`birthday2()`

doesn't generate an error; instead, the default values are assigned to the parameters, and the function displays the message `Happy Birthday, Jackson ! I hear you're 1 today.`

Once you assign a default value to a parameter in the list, you have to assign default values to all the parameters listed after it. So, this function header is perfectly fine:

```
def monkey_around(bananas = 100, barrel_of = "yes", ↲
    uncle = "monkey's"):
```

But this isn't:

```
def monkey_around(bananas = 100, barrel_of, uncle):
```

The above header will generate an error.

So far, so good. But you can add a wrinkle here by overriding the default values of any or all the parameters. With the call

`birthday2(name = "Katherine")`

the default value of `name` is overridden. `name` gets `"Katherine"`, `age` still gets its default value of `1`, and the message `Happy Birthday, Katherine ! I hear you're 1 today.` is displayed.

With this function call:

`birthday2(age = 12)`

the default value of `age` is overridden. `age` gets the value of `12`. `name` gets its default value of `"Jackson"`. And the message `Happy Birthday, Jackson ! I hear you're 12 today.` is displayed.

With the call

`birthday2(name = "Katherine", age = 12)`

both default values are overridden. `name` gets `"Katherine"` and `age` gets `12`. The message `Happy Birthday, Katherine ! I hear you're 12 today.` is displayed.

And with the call

`birthday2("Katherine", 12)`

you get the exact same results as you did with the previous call. Both default values are overridden. `name` gets `"Katherine"` and `age` gets `12`. And the message `Happy Birthday, Katherine ! I hear you're 12 today.` is displayed.

 Default parameter values are great if you have a function where almost every time it's called, some parameter gets sent the same value. To save programmers using your function the trouble of typing this value every time, you could use a default parameter value instead.

Using Global Variables and Constants

Through the magic of encapsulation, the functions you've seen are all totally sealed off and independent from each other and the main part of your program. The only way to get information into them is through their parameters, and the only way to get information out of them is from their return values. Well, that's not completely true. There is another way that you can share information among parts of your program: through global variables.

Understanding Scopes

Scopes represent different areas of your program that are separate from each other. For example, each function you define has its own scope. That's why the functions you've seen can't directly access each other's variables. A visual representation really helps to gel this idea, so take a look at Figure 6.7.

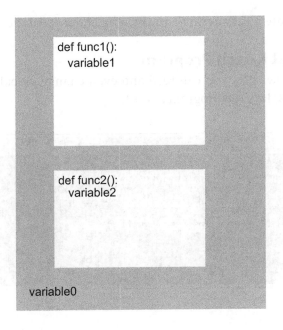

Figure 6.7

This simple program has three different scopes: one for each function, plus one for the global scope.

Figure 6.7 shows a program with three different scopes. The first is defined by function func1(), the second is defined by function func2(), and the third is the global scope (which all programs automatically have). In this program, you're in the global scope when you're not inside any function. The shaded area in the figure represents the global scope. Any variable that you create in the global scope is called a *global variable*, while any variable you create inside a function is called a *local variable* (it's local to that function).

Since variable1 is defined inside func1(), it's a local variable that lives only in the scope of func1(). variable1 can't be accessed from any other scope. So, no command in func2() can get at it, and no command in the global space can access or modify it either.

A good way to remember how this works is to think of scopes as houses and encapsulation as tinted windows, giving each house privacy. As a result, you can see anything inside a house if you're in it. But if you're outside a house, you can't see what's inside. This is the way it works with functions. When you're in a function, you have access to all of its variables. But when you're outside a function, like in the global scope, you can't see any of the variables inside a function.

If two variables have the same name inside two separate functions, they're totally different variables with no connection to each other. For example, if I created a variable called variable2 inside function func1(), it would be different and completely separate from the variable named variable2 in function func2(). Because of encapsulation, it would be like they exist in different worlds and have no effect on each other.

Global variables, however, create a little wrinkle in the idea of encapsulation, as you'll see.

Introducing the Global Reach Program

The Global Reach program shows how you can read and even change global variables from inside functions. Figure 6.8 displays the program's results.

```
C:\Python31\python.exe                                          - □ ×
In the global scope, value has been set to: 10

From inside the local scope of read_global(), value is: 10
Back in the global scope, value is still: 10

From inside the local scope of shadow_global(), value is: -10
Back in the global scope, value is still: 10

From inside the local scope of change_global(), value is: -10
Back in the global scope, value has now changed to: -10

Press the enter key to exit._
```

FIGURE 6.8

You can read, shadow, or even change the value of a global variable from inside a function.

You can find the code for the program on the companion website (www.courseptr.com/downloads) in the Chapter 6 folder; the file name is global_reach.py.

```
# Global Reach
# Demonstrates global variables

def read_global():
    print("From inside the local scope of read_global(), value is:", value)

def shadow_global():
    value = -10
    print("From inside the local scope of shadow_global(), value is:", value)

def change_global():
    global value
    value = -10
    print("From inside the local scope of change_global(), value is:", value)

# main
# value is a global variable because we're in the global scope here
value = 10
print("In the global scope, value has been set to:", value, "\n")

read_global()
print("Back in the global scope, value is still:", value, "\n")

shadow_global()
print("Back in the global scope, value is still:", value, "\n")

change_global()
print("Back in the global scope, value has now changed to:", value)

input("\n\nPress the enter key to exit.")
```

Reading a Global Variable from Inside a Function

Although by now you're probably quite comfortable with the idea of encapsulation, I'm going to throw you a little curve ball: you can read the value of a global variable from within any scope in your program. But fear not, this can still work with the concept of houses and tinted windows. Remember, tinted windows keep the houses (or functions) private. But tinted windows also let you see out. So, you can always see outside of a function to the global scope and see the value of a global variable. That's what I did when I created the function read_global(). It prints the global variable value without a problem.

While you can always read the value of a global variable in any function, you can't change it directly (at least not without asking specifically for that kind of access). So, in read_global(), doing something like the following would generate a nasty error:

```
value += 1
```

Back to the houses and tinted glass idea, this means that you can see a global variable from within a function through the tinted window, but you can't touch it because it's outside. So, although you can read the value of a global variable from inside a function, you can't change its value without asking for special access to it.

Shadowing a Global Variable from Inside a Function

If you give a variable inside a function the same name as a global variable, you *shadow* the global variable. That is, you hide it with your new variable. It might look like you can change the value of a global variable by doing this, but you only change the local variable you've created. That's what I did in the function shadow_global(). When I assigned –10 to value with

```
value = -10
```

I didn't change the global version of value. Instead, I created a new, local version of value inside the function and that got –10. You can see that this is what happened, because when the function finishes, the main program prints out the global version of value with

```
print("Back in the global scope, value is still:", value, "\n")
```

and it's still 10.

TRAP   It's not a good idea to shadow a global variable inside a function. It can lead to confusion. You might think you're using a global variable when you're really not. Be aware of any global variables in your program and make sure not to use the name anywhere else in your code.

Changing a Global Variable from Inside a Function

To gain complete access to a global variable, use the keyword `global` like I did in the function `change_global()`:

```
global value
```

At this point, the function has complete access to `value`. So when I changed it with

```
value = -10
```

the global variable `value` got `-10`. When the program prints `value` again back in the main part of the code with

```
print("Back in the global scope, value has now changed to:", value)
```

`-10` is printed. The global variable was changed from inside the function.

Understanding When to Use Global Variables and Constants

Just because you can, doesn't mean you should. This is a good programming motto. Sometimes things are technically possible, but not good ideas. Using global variables is an example of this. In general, global variables make programs confusing because it can be hard to keep track of their changing values. You should limit your use of them as much as you can.

Global constants (global variables that you treat as constants), on the other hand, can make programs less confusing. For example, say you're writing a business application that calculates someone's taxes. Like a good programmer, you have written a variety of functions in your code, all of which use the somewhat cryptic value .28 as the tax rate. Instead, you could create a global constant called TAX_RATE and set it to .28. Then, in each function, you could replace the number .28 with TAX_RATE. This produces two benefits. It makes your code clearer and it makes changes (like a new tax rate) no sweat.

BACK TO THE TIC-TAC-TOE GAME

The Tic-Tac-Toe game presented at the beginning of the chapter is your most ambitious chapter project yet. You certainly have all the skills you need to create the game, but instead of jumping straight into the code, I'm going to go through a planning section to help you get the bigger picture and understand how to create a larger program.

Planning the Tic-Tac-Toe Game

If you haven't figured this out by now, I'll bore you with it again: the most important part of programming is planning to program. Without a roadmap, you'll never get to where you want to go (or it'll take you a lot longer as you travel the scenic route).

Writing the Pseudocode

It's back to your favorite language that's not really a language: pseudocode. Since I'll be using functions for most of the tasks in the program, I can afford to think about the program at a pretty general level. Each line of pseudocode should feel like one function call. Then, later, I'll just have to write the functions that the plan implies. Here's the pseudocode:

```
display the game instructions
determine who goes first
create an empty tic-tac-toe board
display the board
while nobody's won and it's not a tie
    if it's the human's turn
        get the human's move
        update the board with the move
    otherwise
        calculate the computer's move
        update the board with the move
    display the board
    switch turns
congratulate the winner or declare a tie
```

Representing the Data

Alright, I have a good plan, but it is pretty abstract and talks about throwing around different elements that aren't really defined in my mind yet. I see the idea of making a move as placing a piece on a game board. But how exactly am I going to represent the game board? Or a piece? Or a move?

Since I'm going to print the game board on the screen, why not just represent a piece as one character, an "X" or an "0"? An empty piece could just be a space. The board itself should be a list since it's going to change as each player makes a move. There are nine squares on a tic-tac-toe board, so the list should be nine elements long. Each square on the board will correspond to a position in the list that represents the board. Figure 6.9 illustrates what I mean.

FIGURE 6.9

Each square number corresponds to a position in a list that represents the board.

0	1	2
3	4	5
6	7	8

So, each square or position on the board is represented by a number, 0–8. That means the list will be nine elements long and have position numbers 0–8. Since each move indicates a square in which to put a piece, a move is also just a number, 0–8.

The sides the player and computer play could also be represented by "X" and "O", just like a game piece. And a variable to represent the side of the current turn would be either an "X" or an "O".

Creating a List of Functions

The pseudocode inspires the different functions I'll need. I created a list of them, thinking about what they would do, what parameters they would have, and what values they would return. Table 6.1 shows the results of my efforts.

TABLE 6.1 TIC-TAC-TOE FUNCTIONS	
Function	**Description**
display_instruct()	Displays the game instructions.
ask_yes_no(*question*)	Asks a yes or no question. Receives a question. Returns either a "y" or a "n".
ask_number(*question, low, high*)	Asks for a number within a range. Receives a question, a low number, and a high number. Returns a number in the range from *low* to *high*.
pieces()	Determines who goes first. Returns the computer's piece and human's piece.
new_board()	Creates a new, empty game board. Returns a board.
display_board(*board*)	Displays the board on the screen. Receives a board.
legal_moves(*board*)	Creates a list of legal moves. Receives a board. Returns a list of legal moves.
winner(*board*)	Determines the game winner. Receives a board. Returns a piece, "TIE" or None.
human_move(*board, human*)	Gets the human's move from the player. Receives a board and the human's piece. Returns the human's move.
computer_move(*board, computer, human*)	Calculates the computer's move. Receives a board, the computer piece, and the human piece. Returns the computer's move.
next_turn(*turn*)	Switches turns based on the current turn. Receives a piece. Returns a piece.
congrat_winner(*the_winner, computer, human*)	Congratulates the winner or declares a tie. Receives the winning piece, the computer's piece, and the human's piece.

Setting Up the Program

The first thing I did in writing the program was set up some global constants. These are values that more than one function will use. Creating them will make the functions clearer and any changes involving these values easier. You can find the code for the program on the companion website (www.courseptr.com/downloads) in the Chapter 6 folder; the file name is tic-tac-toe.py.

```
# Tic-Tac-Toe
# Plays the game of tic-tac-toe against a human opponent

# global constants
X = "X"
O = "O"
EMPTY = " "
TIE = "TIE"
NUM_SQUARES = 9
```

X is just shorthand for "X", one of the two pieces in the game. O represents "O", the other piece in the game. EMPTY represents an empty square on the board. It's a space because when it's printed, it will look like an empty square. TIE represents a tie game. And NUM_SQUARES is the number of squares on the tic-tac-toe board.

The display_instruct() Function

This function displays the game instructions. You've seen it before:

```
def display_instruct():
    """Display game instructions."""
    print(
    """
Welcome to the greatest intellectual challenge of all time: Tic-Tac-Toe.
This will be a showdown between your human brain and my silicon processor.

You will make your move known by entering a number, 0 - 8.  The number
will correspond to the board position as illustrated:

                    0 | 1 | 2
                    ---------
                    3 | 4 | 5
                    ---------
                    6 | 7 | 8
```

```
    Prepare yourself, human.   The ultimate battle is about to begin. \n
    """
    )
```

The only thing I did was change the function name for the sake of consistency in the program.

The ask_yes_no() Function

This function asks a yes or no question. It receives a question and returns either a "y" or a "n". You've seen this function before too.

```
def ask_yes_no(question):
    """Ask a yes or no question."""
    response = None
    while response not in ("y", "n"):
        response = input(question).lower()
    return response
```

The ask_number() Function

This function asks for a number within a range. It receives a question, a low number, and a high number. It returns a number within the range specified.

```
def ask_number(question, low, high):
    """Ask for a number within a range."""
    response = None
    while response not in range(low, high):
        response = int(input(question))
    return response
```

The pieces() Function

This function asks the player if he or she wants to go first and returns the computer's piece and human's piece, based on that choice. As the great tradition of tic-tac-toe dictates, the X's go first.

```
def pieces():
    """Determine if player or computer goes first."""
    go_first = ask_yes_no("Do you require the first move? (y/n): ")
    if go_first == "y":
        print("\nThen take the first move.  You will need it.")
        human = X
        computer = 0
```

```
    else:
        print("\nYour bravery will be your undoing... I will go first.")
        computer = X
        human = O
    return computer, human
```

Notice that this function calls another one of my functions, ask_yes_no(). This is perfectly fine. One function can call another.

The new_board() Function

This function creates a new board (a list) with all nine elements set to EMPTY and returns it:

```
def new_board():
    """Create new game board."""
    board = []
    for square in range(NUM_SQUARES):
        board.append(EMPTY)
    return board
```

The display_board() Function

This function displays the board passed to it. Since each element in the board is either a space, the character "X", or the character "O", the function can print each one. A few other characters on my keyboard are used to draw a decent-looking tic- tac-toe board.

```
def display_board(board):
    """Display game board on screen."""
    print("\n\t", board[0], "|", board[1], "|", board[2])
    print("\t", "---------")
    print("\t", board[3], "|", board[4], "|", board[5])
    print("\t", "---------")
    print("\t", board[6], "|", board[7], "|", board[8], "\n")
```

The legal_moves() Function

This function receives a board and returns a list of legal moves. This function is used by other functions. It's used by the human_move() function to make sure that the player chooses a valid move. It's also used by the computer_move() function so that the computer can consider only valid moves in its decision making.

A legal move is represented by the number of an empty square. For example, if the center square were open, then 4 would be a legal move. If only the corner squares were open, the list of legal moves would be [0, 2, 6, 8]. (Take a look at Figure 6.9 if you're unclear about this.)

So, this function just loops over the list representing the board. Each time it finds an empty square, it adds that square number to the list of legal moves. Then it returns the list of legal moves.

```
def legal_moves(board):
    """Create list of legal moves."""
    moves = []
    for square in range(NUM_SQUARES):
        if board[square] == EMPTY:
            moves.append(square)
    return moves
```

The winner() Function

This function receives a board and returns the winner. There are four possible values for a winner. The function will return either X or 0 if one of the players has won. If every square is filled and no one has won, it returns TIE. Finally, if no one has won and there is at least one empty square, the function returns None.

The very first thing I do in this function is define a constant called WAYS_TO_WIN, which represents all eight ways to get three in a row. Each way to win is represented by a tuple. Each tuple is a sequence of the three board positions that form a winning three in a row. Take the first tuple in the sequence, (0, 1, 2). This represents the top row: board positions 0, 1, and 2. The next tuple (3, 4, 5) represents the middle row. And so on.

```
def winner(board):
    """Determine the game winner."""
    WAYS_TO_WIN = ((0, 1, 2),
                   (3, 4, 5),
                   (6, 7, 8),
                   (0, 3, 6),
                   (1, 4, 7),
                   (2, 5, 8),
                   (0, 4, 8),
                   (2, 4, 6))
```

Next, I use a for loop to go through each possible way a player can win, to see if either player has three in a row. The if statement checks to see if the three squares in question all contain the same value and are not empty. If so, that means that the row has either three X's or O's in it and somebody has won. The computer assigns one of the pieces in this winning row to winner, returns winner, and ends.

```
for row in WAYS_TO_WIN:
    if board[row[0]] == board[row[1]] == board[row[2]] != EMPTY:
        winner = board[row[0]]
        return winner
```

If neither player has won, then the function continues. Next, it checks to see if there are any empty squares left on the board. If there aren't any, the game is a tie (because the function has already determined that there is no winner, back in the for loop) and TIE is returned.

```
if EMPTY not in board:
    return TIE
```

If the game isn't a tie, the function continues. Finally, if neither player has won and the game isn't a tie, there is no winner yet. So, the function returns None.

```
return None
```

The human_move() Function

This next function receives a board and the human's piece. It returns the square number where the player wants to move.

First, the function gets a list of all the legal moves for this board. Then, it continues to ask the user for the square number to which he or she wants to move until that response is in this list of legal moves. Once that happens, the function returns the move.

```
def human_move(board, human):
    """Get human move."""
    legal = legal_moves(board)
    move = None
    while move not in legal:
        move = ask_number("Where will you move? (0 - 8):", 0, NUM_SQUARES)
        if move not in legal:
            print("\nThat square is already occupied, foolish human. Choose another.\n")
    print("Fine...")
    return move
```

The computer_move() Function

The computer_move() function receives the board, the computer's piece, and the human's piece. It returns the computer's move.

TRICK

This is definitely the meatiest function in the program. Knowing it would be, I initially created a short, temporary function that chooses a random but legal move. I wanted time to think about this function, but didn't want to slow the progress of the entire project. So, I dropped in the temporary function and got the game up and running. Later, I came back and plugged in a better function that actually picks moves for a reason.

I had this flexibility because of the modular design afforded by writing with functions. I knew that computer_move() was a totally independent component and could be substituted later without a problem. In fact, I could even drop a new function in right now, one that chooses even better moves. (Sounds an awful lot like a challenge, now doesn't it?)

I have to be careful here because the board (a list) is mutable and I change it in this function as I search for the best computer move. The problem with this is that any change I make to the board will be reflected in the part of the program that called this function. This is the result of shared references, which you learned about in Chapter 5, in the "Understanding Shared References" section. Basically, there's only one copy of the list, and any change I make here changes that single copy. So, the very first thing I do is make my own local copy to work with:

```
def computer_move(board, computer, human):
    """Make computer move."""
    # make a copy to work with since function will be changing list
    board = board[:]
```

HINT

Any time you get a mutable value passed to a function, you have to be careful. If you know you're going to change the value as you work with it, make a copy and use that instead.

TRAP

You might think that changing the board would be a good thing. You could change it so that it contains the new computer move. This way, you don't need to send the board back as a return value.

Changing a mutable parameter directly like this is considered creating a *side effect*. Not all side effects are bad, but this type is generally frowned upon (I'm frowning right now, just thinking about it). It's best to communicate with the rest of your program through return values; that way, it's clear exactly what information you're giving back.

Okay, here's the basic strategy I came up with for the computer:

1. If there's a move that allows the computer to win this turn, the computer should choose that move.
2. If there's a move that allows the human to win next turn, the computer should choose that move.
3. Otherwise, the computer should choose the best empty square as its move. The best square is the center. The next best squares are the corners. And the next best squares are the rest.

So next in the code, I define a tuple to represent the best squares, in order:

```
# the best positions to have, in order
BEST_MOVES = (4, 0, 2, 6, 8, 1, 3, 5, 7)

print("I shall take square number", end=" ")
```

Next, I create a list of all the legal moves. In a loop, I try the computer's piece in each empty square number I got from the legal moves list and check for a win. If the computer can win, then that's the move to make. If that's the case, the function returns that move and ends. Otherwise, I undo the move I just tried and try the next one in the list.

```
# if computer can win, take that move
for move in legal_moves(board):
    board[move] = computer
    if winner(board) == computer:
        print(move)
        return move
    # done checking this move, undo it
    board[move] = EMPTY
```

If I get to this point in the function, it means the computer can't win on its next move. So, I check to see if the player can win on his or her next move. The code loops through the list of the legal moves, putting the human's piece in each empty square, checking for a win. If the human can win, then that's the move to take for a block. If this is the case, the function returns the move and ends. Otherwise, I undo the move and try the next legal move in the list.

```
# if human can win, block that move
for move in legal_moves(board):
    board[move] = human
    if winner(board) == human:
        print(move)
```

```
        return move
    # done checking this move, undo it
    board[move] = EMPTY
```

If I get to this point in the function, then neither side can win on its next move. So, I look through the list of best moves and take the first legal one. The computer loops through BEST_MOVES, and as soon as it finds one that's legal, it returns that move.

```
    # since no one can win on next move, pick best open square
    for move in BEST_MOVES:
        if move in legal_moves(board):
            print(move)
            return move
```

IN THE REAL WORLD

The Tic-Tac-Toe program considers only the next possible move in the game. Programs that play serious games of strategy, like chess, look far deeper into the consequences of individual moves, considering many levels of moves and countermoves. And today's computers can examine a huge number of game positions. Specialized machines, like IBM's chess-playing Deep Blue computer, which beat world champion Garry Kasparov, can examine far more. Deep Blue is able to explore over 200,000,000 board positions per second. That sounds quite impressive, until you realize that the total number of board positions in a complete search for chess is estimated to be over 100,000,000,000,000,000, 000,000,000,000,000,000,000,000,000, which means it would take Deep Blue more than 1,585,489,599,188,229 years to look at all those possible positions. (The universe, by the way, is estimated to be only 15,000,000,000 years old.)

The next_turn() Function

This function receives the current turn and returns the next turn. A turn represents whose turn it is and is either X or 0.

```
def next_turn(turn):
    """Switch turns."""
    if turn == X:
        return 0
```

```
    else:
        return X
```

The function is used to switch turns after one player has made a move.

The congrat_winner() Function

This function receives the winner of the game, the computer's piece, and the human's piece. This function is called only when the game is over, so the_winner will be passed either X or O if one of the players has won the game, or TIE if the game ended in a tie.

```
def congrat_winner(the_winner, computer, human):
    """Congratulate the winner."""
    if the_winner != TIE:
        print(the_winner, "won!\n")
    else:
        print("It's a tie!\n")

    if the_winner == computer:
        print("As I predicted, human, I am triumphant once more.  \n" \
                "Proof that computers are superior to humans in all regards.")

    elif the_winner == human:
        print("No, no!  It cannot be!  Somehow you tricked me, human. \n" \
                "But never again!  I, the computer, so swear it!")

    elif the_winner == TIE:
        print("You were most lucky, human, and somehow managed to tie me. \n" \
                "Celebrate today... for this is the best you will ever achieve.")
```

The main() Function

I put the main part of the program into its own function, instead of leaving it at the global level. This encapsulates the main code too. Unless you're writing a short, simple program, it's usually a good idea to encapsulate even the main part of it. If you do put your main code into a function like this, you don't have to call it main(). There's no magic to the name. But it's a pretty common practice, so it's a good idea to use it.

Okay, here's the code for the main part of the program. As you can see, it's almost exactly, line for line, the pseudocode I wrote earlier:

```
def main():
    display_instruct()
    computer, human = pieces()
    turn = X
    board = new_board()
    display_board(board)

    while not winner(board):
        if turn == human:
            move = human_move(board, human)
            board[move] = human
        else:
            move = computer_move(board, computer, human)
            board[move] = computer
        display_board(board)
        turn = next_turn(turn)

    the_winner = winner(board)
    congrat_winner(the_winner, computer, human)
```

Starting the Program

The next line calls the main function (which in turn calls the other functions) from the global level:

```
# start the program
main()
input("\n\nPress the enter key to quit.")
```

SUMMARY

In this chapter, you learned to write your own functions. You then saw how to accept and return values in your functions. You learned about scopes and saw how global variables can be accessed and changed from within functions. You also learned to limit your use of global variables, but saw how to use global constants when necessary. You even dabbled ever so slightly in some artificial intelligence concepts to create a computer opponent in a game of strategy.

CHALLENGES

1. Improve the function `ask_number()` so that the function can be called with a step value. Make the default value of step 1.

2. Modify the Guess My Number chapter project from Chapter 3 by reusing the function `ask_number()`.

3. Modify the new version of Guess My Number you created in the last challenge so that the program's code is in a function called `main()`. Don't forget to call `main()` so that you can play the game.

4. Write a new `computer_move()` function for the Tic-Tac-Toe game to plug the hole in the computer's strategy. See if you can create an opponent that is unbeatable!

FILES AND EXCEPTIONS: THE TRIVIA CHALLENGE GAME

Variables provide a great way to store and access information while a program runs, but often, you'll want to save data so that you can retrieve it later. In this chapter, you'll learn to use files for this kind of permanent storage. You'll also learn how to handle errors that your code may generate. Specifically, you'll learn to do the following:

- Read from text files
- Write to text files
- Read and write more complex data with files
- Intercept and handle errors during a program's execution

INTRODUCING THE TRIVIA CHALLENGE GAME

The Trivia Challenge game tests a player's knowledge with a series of multiple-choice questions. The game delivers the questions as a single "episode." The episode I created to show off the program is about the mafia and is called "An Episode You Can't Refuse." All of the questions relate in some way to the mafia (although a bit indirectly at times).

The cool thing about the game is that the questions for an episode are stored in a separate file, independent of the game code. This way, it's easy to play different ones. Even better, this means that anyone with a text editor (like Notepad on Windows machines) can create their own trivia episode about whatever topic they choose—anything from anime to zoology. Figure 7.1 shows the game (and my episode) in action.

READING FROM TEXT FILES

With Python, it's easy to read strings from *plain text files*—files that are made up of only ASCII characters. (Although there are different types of text files, when I use the term "text file," I mean a plain text file.) Text files are a good choice for permanently storing simple information, for a number of reasons. First, text files are cross-platform. A text file on a Windows machine is the same text file on a Mac and is the same text file under Unix. Second, text files are easy to use. Most operating systems come with basic tools to view and edit them.

Introducing the Read It Program

The Read It program demonstrates several ways you can read strings from a text file. The program demonstrates how to read anything from a single character to the entire file. It also shows several different ways to read one line at a time. Figure 7.2 illustrates the program.

The program reads a simple text file I created on my system using a text editor. You can find the file on the companion website (www.courseptr.com/downloads) in the Chapter 7 folder; the file name is read_it.txt. Here are the contents of the file:

```
Line 1
This is line 2
That makes this line 3
```

```
Opening and closing the file.

Reading characters from the file.
L
ine 1

Reading the entire file at once.
Line 1
This is line 2
That makes this line 3

Reading characters from a line.
L
ine 1

Reading one line at a time.
Line 1

This is line 2

That makes this line 3


Reading the entire file into a list.
['Line 1\n', 'This is line 2\n', 'That makes this line 3\n']
3
Line 1

This is line 2

That makes this line 3

Looping through the file, line by line.
Line 1

This is line 2

That makes this line 3


Press the enter key to exit.
```

FIGURE 7.2

The file is read using a few different techniques.

You can find the code for the program on the companion website (www.courseptr.com/downloads) in the Chapter 7 folder; the file name is read_it.py:

```python
# Read It
# Demonstrates reading from a text file

print("Opening and closing the file.")
text_file = open("read_it.txt", "r")
text_file.close()

print("\nReading characters from the file.")
text_file = open("read_it.txt", "r")
print(text_file.read(1))
print(text_file.read(5))
text_file.close()

print("\nReading the entire file at once.")
```

```python
text_file = open("read_it.txt", "r")
whole_thing = text_file.read()
print(whole_thing)
text_file.close()

print("\nReading characters from a line.")
text_file = open("read_it.txt", "r")
print(text_file.readline(1))
print(text_file.readline(5))
text_file.close()

print("\nReading one line at a time.")
text_file = open("read_it.txt", "r")
print(text_file.readline())
print(text_file.readline())
print(text_file.readline())
text_file.close()

print("\nReading the entire file into a list.")
text_file = open("read_it.txt", "r")
lines = text_file.readlines()
print(lines)
print(len(lines))
for line in lines:
    print(line)
text_file.close()

print("\nLooping through the file, line by line.")
text_file = open("read_it.txt", "r")
for line in text_file:
    print(line)
text_file.close()

input("\n\nPress the enter key to exit.")
```

I'll show you exactly how the code works through an interactive session.

Opening and Closing a File

Before you can read from (or write to) a file, you need to open it. That's the first thing I do in the Read It program:

```
>>> text_file = open("read_it.txt", "r")
```

I use the open() function to open a file and assign the results to text_file. In the function call, I provide two string arguments: a file name and an access mode.

The file argument, "read_it.txt", is pretty straightforward. Since I don't include any path information, Python looks in the current directory for the file. I can access a file in any directory by providing the proper path information.

Next, I provide "r" for the access mode, which tells Python that I want to open the file for reading. You can open a file for reading, writing, or both. Table 7.1 describes selected valid text file access modes.

TABLE 7.1 SELECTED TEXT FILE ACCESS MODES

Mode	Description
"r"	Read from a text file. If the file doesn't exist, Python will complain with an error.
"w"	Write to a text file. If the file exists, its contents are overwritten. If the file doesn't exist, it's created.
"a"	Append a text file. If the file exists, new data is appended to it. If the file doesn't exist, it's created.
"r+"	Read from and write to a text file. If the file doesn't exist, Python will complain with an error.
"w+"	Write to and read from a text file. If the file exists, its contents are overwritten. If the file doesn't exist, it's created.
"a+"	Append and read from a text file. If the file exists, new data is appended to it. If the file doesn't exist, it's created.

After opening the file, I access it through the variable text_file, which represents a file object. There are many useful file object methods that I can invoke, but the simplest is close(), which closes the file, sealing it off from further reading or writing until the file is opened again. That's what I do next in the program:

```
>>> text_file.close()
```

Whenever you're done with a file, it's good programming practice to close it.

Reading Characters from a File

For a file to be of any use, you need to do something with its contents between opening and closing it. So next, I open the file and read its contents with the read() file object method. read() allows you to read a specified number of characters from a file, which the method returns as a string. After opening the file again, I read and print exactly one character from it:

```
>>> text_file = open("read_it.txt", "r")
>>> print(text_file.read(1))
L
```

All I have to do is specify the number of characters between the parentheses. Next, I read and print the next five characters:

```
>>> print(text_file.read(5))
ine 1
```

Notice that I read the five characters following the "L". Python remembers where I last left off. It's like the computer puts a bookmark in the file and each subsequent read() begins where the last ended. When you read to the end of a file, subsequent reads return the empty string.

To start back at the beginning of a file, you can close and open it. That's just what I did next:

```
>>> text_file.close()
>>> text_file = open("read_it.txt", "r")
```

If you don't specify the number of characters to be read, Python returns the entire file as a string. Next, I read the entire file, assign the returned string to a variable, and print the variable:

```
>>> whole_thing = text_file.read()
>>> print(whole_thing)
Line 1
This is line 2
That makes this line 3
```

If a file is small enough, reading the entire thing at once may make sense. Since I've read the entire file, any subsequent reads will just return the empty string. So, I close the file again:

```
>>> text_file.close()
```

Reading Characters from a Line

Often, you'll want to work with one line of a text file at a time. The `readline()` method lets you read characters from the current line. You just pass the number of characters you want read from the current line and the method returns them as a string. If you don't pass a number, the method reads from the current position to the end of the line. Once you read all of the characters of a line, the next line becomes the current line. After opening the file again, I read the first character of the current line:

```
>>> text_file = open("read_it.txt", "r")
>>> print(text_file.readline(1))
L
```

Then I read the next five characters of the current line:

```
>>> print(text_file.readline(5))
ine 1
>>> text_file.close()
```

At this point, `readline()` may seem no different than `read()`, but `readline()` reads characters from the current line only, while `read()` reads characters from the entire file. Because of this, `readline()` is usually invoked to read one line of text at a time. In the next few lines of code, I read the file, one line at a time:

```
>>> text_file = open("read_it.txt", "r")
>>> print(text_file.readline())
Line 1

>>> print(text_file.readline())
This is line 2

>>> print(text_file.readline())
That makes this line 3

>>> text_file.close()
```

Notice that a blank line appears after each line. That's because each line in the text file ends with a newline character (`"\n"`).

Reading All Lines into a List

Another way to work with individual lines of a text file is the `readlines()` method, which reads a text file into a list, where each line of the file becomes a string element in the list. Next, I invoke the `readlines()` method:

```
>>> text_file = open("read_it.txt", "r")
>>> lines = text_file.readlines()
```

`lines` now refers to a list with an element for each line in the text file:

```
>>> print(lines)
['Line 1\n', 'This is line 2\n', 'That makes this line 3\n']
```

`lines` is like any list. You can find the length of it and even loop through it:

```
>>> print(len(lines))
3
>>> for line in lines:
        print(line)


Line 1

This is line 2

That makes this line 3

>>> text_file.close()
```

Looping through a File

You can also loop directly through the lines of a file using a `for` loop:

```
>>> text_file = open("read_it.txt", "r")
>>> for line in text_file:
        print(line)

Line 1

This is line 2

That makes this line 3

>>> text_file.close()
```

As you can see, the loop variable (line in this code) gets each line of the file, in succession. The first iteration of the loop it gets the first line; the second iteration it gets the second line; and so on. This technique is the most elegant solution if you want to move through a file one line at a time.

WRITING TO A TEXT FILE

For text files to be a viable form of storage, you need to be able to get information into them. With Python, it's also a simple matter to write strings to text files. I'll demonstrate two basic ways to do just that.

Introducing the Write It Program

The Write It program creates a text file with the same contents of the read_it.txt file that I used in the Read It program. Actually, the program creates and prints this new file twice, using a different file writing method each time. Figure 7.3 shows the results of the program. You can find the code for the program on the companion website (www.courseptr.com/down-loads) in the Chapter 7 folder; the file name is write_it.py.

FIGURE 7.3

The same file is created twice, each time with a different file object method.

Writing Strings to a File

Just as before, in order to use a file, I have to open it in the correct mode. So, the first thing I do in the program is open a file in write mode:

```
# Write It
# Demonstrates writing to a text file

print("Creating a text file with the write() method.")
text_file = open("write_it.txt", "w")
```

The file `write_it.txt` springs into existence as an empty text file just waiting for the program to write to it. If the file `write_it.txt` had already existed, it would have been replaced with a brand-new, empty file and all of its original contents would have been erased.

Next, I use the `write()` file object method, which writes a string to the file:

```
text_file.write("Line 1\n")
text_file.write("This is line 2\n")
text_file.write("That makes this line 3\n")
```

The `write()` method does not automatically insert a newline character at the end of a string it writes. You have to put newlines in where you want them. If I had left the three newline characters out of the previous lines of code, the program would write one, long line to the file.

Also, you don't have to end every string you write to a file with a newline character. To achieve the same end result, I could just as easily have stuck all three of the previous strings together to form one long string, `"Line 1\n This is line 2\n That makes this line 3\n"`, and written that string to the file with a single `write()` method.

Finally, I close the file:

```
text_file.close()
```

Next, just to prove that the writing worked, I read and print the entire contents of the file:

```
print("\nReading the newly created file.")
text_file = open("write_it.txt", "r")
print(text_file.read())
text_file.close()
```

Writing a List of Strings to a File

Next, I create the same file, using the `writelines()` file object method. Like its counterpart, `readlines()`, `writelines()` works with a list of strings. But instead of reading a text file into a list, the method writes a list of strings to a file.

The first thing I do is open the file for writing:

```
print("\nCreating a text file with the writelines() method.")
text_file = open("write_it.txt", "w")
```

I open the same file, `write_it.txt`, which means I wipe out the existing file and start with a new, empty one. Next, I create a list of strings to be written, in order, to the file:

```
lines = ["Line 1\n",
         "This is line 2\n",
         "That makes this line 3\n"]
```

Again, I inserted newline characters where I want them in the text file.

Next, I write the entire lists of strings to the file with the `writelines()` method:

```
text_file.writelines(lines)
```

Finally, I close the file:

```
text_file.close()
```

Lastly, I print out the contents of the file to show that the new file is exactly the same as the previous version:

```
print("\nReading the newly created file.")
text_file = open("write_it.txt", "r")
print(text_file.read())
text_file.close()

input("\n\nPress the enter key to exit.")
```

You've seen a lot of file object read and write methods. Take a look at Table 7.2 for a summary of them.

TABLE 7.2 SELECTED FILE OBJECT METHODS

Method	Description
close()	Closes the file. A closed file cannot be read from or written to until opened again.
read([*size*])	Reads *size* characters from a file and returns them as a string. If size is not specified, the method returns all of the characters from the current position to the end of the file.
readline([*size*])	Reads *size* characters from the current line in a file and returns them as a string. If size is not specified, the method returns all of the characters from the current position to the end of the line.
readlines()	Reads all of the lines in a file and returns them as elements in a list.
write(*output*)	Writes the string *output* to a file.
writelines(*output*)	Writes the strings in the list *output* to a file.

STORING COMPLEX DATA IN FILES

Text files are convenient because you can read and manipulate them with any text editor, but they're limited to storing a series of characters. Sometimes you may want to store more complex information, like a list or a dictionary, for example. You could try to convert the contents of these data structures to characters and save them to a text file, but Python offers a much better way. You can store more complex data in a file with a single line of code. You can even store a simple database of values in a single file that acts like a dictionary.

Introducing the Pickle It Program

Pickling means to preserve—and that's just what it means in Python. You can pickle a complex piece of data, like a list or dictionary, and save it in its entirety to a file. Best of all, your hands won't smell like vinegar when you're done.

The Pickle It program pickles, stores, and retrieves three lists of strings in a binary file. It does this twice. First, the program pickles, stores, and retrieves the three lists sequentially—much like you've seen with characters in a text file. Next, the program stores and retrieves the same three lists so that they can be randomly accessed. The results of the program are shown in Figure 7.4. You can find the code for the program on the companion website (www.courseptr.com/downloads) in the Chapter 7 folder; the file name is pickle_it.py.

```
C:\Python31\python.exe
Pickling lists.

Unpickling lists.
['sweet', 'hot', 'dill']
['whole', 'spear', 'chip']
['Claussen', 'Heinz', 'Vlassic']

Shelving lists.

Retrieving lists from a shelved file:
brand - ['Claussen', 'Heinz', 'Vlassic']
shape - ['whole', 'spear', 'chip']
variety - ['sweet', 'hot', 'dill']

Press the enter key to exit._
```

FIGURE 7.4

Each list is written to and read from a file in its entirety.

Pickling Data and Writing It to a File

The first thing I do in the program is import two new modules:

```
# Pickle It
# Demonstrates pickling and shelving data

import pickle, shelve
```

The `pickle` module allows you to pickle and store more complex data in a file. The `shelve` module allows you to store and randomly access pickled objects in a file.

Pickling is straightforward. Instead of writing characters to a file, you can write a pickled object to a file. Pickled objects are stored in files much like characters; you can store and retrieve them sequentially. First, I create the three lists that I plan to pickle and write to a file.

```
print("Pickling lists.")
variety = ["sweet", "hot", "dill"]
shape = ["whole", "spear", "chip"] brand = ["Claussen", "Heinz", "Vlassic"]
```

Next, I open the new file to store the pickled lists.

```
f = open("pickles1.dat", "wb")
```

Pickled objects must be stored in a binary file—they can't be stored in a text file. So, I open a new binary file named pickles1.dat for writing by passing `"wb"` as the file access mode. Table 7.3 lists useful binary file access modes.

TABLE 7.3 SELECTED BINARY FILE ACCESS MODES

Mode	Description
`"rb"`	Read from a binary file. If the file doesn't exist, Python will complain with an error.
`"wb"`	Write to a binary file. If the file exists, its contents are overwritten. If the file doesn't exist, it's created.
`"ab"`	Append a binary file. If the file exists, new data is appended to it. If the file doesn't exist, it's created.
`"rb+"`	Read from and write to a binary file. If the file doesn't exist, Python will complain with an error.
`"wb+"`	Write to and read from a binary file. If the file exists, its contents are overwritten. If the file doesn't exist, it's created.
`"ab+"`	Append and read from a binary file. If the file exists, new data is appended to it. If the file doesn't exist, it's created.

Next, I pickle and store the three lists `variety`, `shape`, and `brand` in the file pickles1.dat using the `pickle.dump()` function. The function requires two arguments: the data to pickle and the file in which to store it.

```
pickle.dump(variety, f)
pickle.dump(shape, f)
pickle.dump(brand, f)
f.close()
```

So, this code pickles the list referred to by variety and writes the whole thing as one object to the file pickles1.dat. Next, the program pickles the list referred to by shape and writes the whole thing as one object to the file. Then, the program pickles the list referred to by brand and writes the whole thing as one object to the file. Finally, the program closes the file.

You can pickle a variety of objects, including:

- Numbers
- Strings
- Tuples
- Lists
- Dictionaries

Reading Data from a File and Unpickling It

Next, I retrieve and unpickle the three lists with the pickle.load() function. The function takes one argument: the file from which to load the next pickled object.

```
print("\nUnpickling lists.")
f = open("pickles1.dat", "rb")
variety = pickle.load(f)
shape = pickle.load(f)
brand = pickle.load(f)
```

The program reads the first pickled object in the file, unpickles it to produce the list ["sweet", "hot", "dill"], and assigns the list to variety. Next, the program reads the next pickled object from the file, unpickles it to produce the list ["whole", "spear", "chip"], and assigns the list to shape. Finally, the program reads the last pickled object from the file, unpickles it to produce the list ["Claussen", "Heinz", "Vlassic"], and assigns the list to brand.

Finally, I print the unpickled lists to prove that the process worked:

```
print(variety)
print(shape)
print(brand)
f.close()
```

Table 7.4 describes selected `pickle` functions.

Function	Description
dump(object, file, [,bin])	Writes pickled version of object to file. If bin is True, object is written in binary format. If bin is False, object is written in less efficient, but more human-readable, text format. The default value of bin is equal to False.
load(file)	Unpickles and returns the next pickled object in file.

TABLE 7.4 · SELECTED PICKLE FUNCTIONS

Using a Shelf to Store Pickled Data

Next, I take the idea of pickling one step further by *shelving* the lists together in a single file. Using the `shelve` module, I create a *shelf* that acts like a dictionary, which provides random access to the lists.

First, I create a shelf, `s`:

```
print("\nShelving lists.")
s = shelve.open("pickles2.dat")
```

The `shelve.open()` function works a lot like the file `open()` function. However, the `shelve.open()` function works with a file that stores pickled objects and not characters. In this case, I assigned the resulting shelf to `s`, which now acts like a dictionary whose contents are stored in a file or group of files.

HINT When you call `shelve.open()`, Python may add an extension to the file name you specify. Python may also create additional files to support the newly created shelf.

The `shelve.open()` function requires one argument: a file name. It also takes an optional access mode. If you don't supply an access mode (like I didn't), it defaults to `"c"`. Table 7.5 details access modes for the function.

Next, I add three lists to the shelf:

```
s["variety"] = ["sweet", "hot", "dill"]
s["shape"] = ["whole", "spear", "chip"]
s["brand"] = ["Claussen", "Heinz", "Vlassic"]
```

Mode	Description
TABLE 7.5	**SHELVE ACCESS MODES**
"c"	Open a file for reading or writing. If the file doesn't exist, it's created.
"n"	Create a new file for reading or writing. If the file exists, its contents are overwritten.
"r"	Read from a file. If the file doesn't exist, Python will complain with an error.
"w"	Write to a file. If the file doesn't exist, Python will complain with an error.

pickles works like a dictionary. So, the key "variety" is paired with the value ["sweet", "hot", "dill"]. The key "shape" is paired with the value ["whole", "spear", "chip"]. And the key "brand" is paired with the value ["Claussen", "Heinz", "Vlassic"] One important thing to note is that a shelf key can only be a string.

Lastly, I invoke the shelf's sync() method:

```
s.sync()    # make sure data is written
```

Python writes changes to a shelf file to a buffer and then periodically writes the buffer to the file. To make sure the file reflects all the changes to a shelf, you can invoke a shelf's sync() method. A shelf file is also updated when you close it with its close() method.

While you could simulate a shelf by pickling a dictionary, the shelve module is more memory efficient. So, if you need random access to pickled objects, create a shelf.

Using a Shelf to Retrieve Pickled Data

Since a shelf acts like a dictionary, you can randomly access pickled objects from it by supplying a key. To prove this, I access the pickled lists in s in reverse order:

```
print("\nRetrieving lists from a shelved file:")
print("brand -", s["brand"])
print("shape -", s["shape"])
print("variety -", s["variety"])
```

Finally, I close the file:

```
s.close()

input("\n\nPress the enter key to exit.")
```

HANDLING EXCEPTIONS

When Python runs into an error, it stops the current program and displays an error message. More precisely, it raises an *exception*, indicating that, well, something exceptional has occurred. If nothing is done with the exception, Python halts what it's doing and displays an error message detailing the exception.

Here's a simple example of Python raising an exception:

```
>>> num = float("Hi!")
Traceback (most recent call last):
  File "<pyshell#1>", line 1, in <module>
    num = float("Hi!")
ValueError: could not convert string to float: Hi!
```

In this interactive session, Python tries to convert the string "Hi!" to a floating-point number. Since it can't, Python raises an exception and displays the details.

Using Python's exception handling functionality, you can intercept and handle exceptions so that your program doesn't end abruptly (even if a user enters "Hi!" when you ask for a number). At the very least, you can have your program exit gracefully instead of crashing awkwardly.

Introducing the Handle It Program

The Handle It program opens itself up to exceptions from user input and then purposely generates a few exceptions of its own. But instead of halting, the program runs to completion. That's because the program handles the exceptions that are raised. Figure 7.5 shows the program in action. You can find the code for the program on the companion website (www.courseptr.com/downloads) in the Chapter 7 folder; the file name is handle_it.py.

```
C:\Python31\python.exe                                              _ □ ×
Enter a number: Hi!
Something went wrong!

Enter a number: Hi!
That was not a number!

Attempting to convert None --> Something went wrong!
Attempting to convert Hi! --> Something went wrong!

Attempting to convert None --> I can only convert a string or a number!
Attempting to convert Hi! --> I can only convert a string of digits!

Enter a number: Hi!
That was not a number! Or as Python would say...
could not convert string to float: Hi!

Enter a number: 5.6
You entered the number 5.6


Press the enter key to exit._
```

FIGURE 7.5

Although the program can't convert "Hi!" to a number, it doesn't halt when exceptions are raised.

Using a try Statement with an except Clause

The most basic way to *handle* (or *trap*) exceptions is to use the try statement with an except clause. By using a try statement, you section off some code that could potentially raise an exception. Then, you write an except clause with a block of statements that are executed only if an exception is raised.

The first thing I do in the Handle It program is ask the user for a number. I get a string from the user and then attempt to convert the string to a floating-point number. I use try and except to handle any exceptions that might be raised in the process.

```
# Handle It
# Demonstrates handling exceptions

# try/except
try:
    num = float(input("Enter a number: "))
except:
    print("Something went wrong!")
```

If the call to float() raises an exception (as a result of the user entering an unconvertible string, like "Hi!", for example), the exception is caught and the user is informed that Something went wrong! If no exception is raised, num gets the number the user entered and the program skips the except clause, continuing with the rest of the code.

Specifying an Exception Type

Different kinds of errors result in different types of exceptions. For example, trying to convert the string "Hi!" with float() results in a ValueError exception because the characters in the string are of the wrong value (they're not digits). There are over two dozen exception types, but Table 7.6 lists a few of the most common ones.

TABLE 7.6	SELECTED EXCEPTION TYPES
Exception Type	**Description**
IOError	Raised when an I/O operation fails, such as when an attempt is made to open a nonexistent file in read mode.
IndexError	Raised when a sequence is indexed with a number of a nonexistent element.
KeyError	Raised when a dictionary key is not found.
NameError	Raised when a name (of a variable or function, for example) is not found.
SyntaxError	Raised when a syntax error is encountered.
TypeError	Raised when a built-in operation or function is applied to an object of inappropriate type.
ValueError	Raised when a built-in operation or function receives an argument that has the right type but an inappropriate value.
ZeroDivisionError	Raised when the second argument of a division or modulo operation is zero.

The except clause lets you specify exactly which type of exceptions it will handle. To specify a single exception type, you just list the specific type of exception after except.

I again ask the user for a number, but this time I specifically trap for a ValueError:

```
# specifying exception type
try:
    num = float(input("\nEnter a number: "))
except ValueError:
    print("That was not a number!")
```

Now, the print function will only execute if a ValueError is raised. As a result, I can be even more specific and display the message That was not a number! However, if any other type of exception is raised inside the try statement, the except clause will not catch it and the program will come to a halt.

It's good programming practice to specify exception types so that you handle each individual case. In fact, it's dangerous to catch all exceptions the way I did in the first `except` clause of the program. Generally, you should avoid that type of catchall.

When should you trap for exceptions? Any point of external interaction with your program is a good place to think about exceptions. It's a good idea to trap for exceptions when opening a file for reading, even if you believe the file already exists. You can also trap for exceptions when you attempt to convert data from an outside source, like the user.

So, let's say you know you want to trap for an exception, but you're not exactly sure what the exception type is called. Well, here's a shortcut for finding out: just create the exception. For example, if you know you want to trap for a division-by-zero exception, but can't remember exactly what the exception type is called, jump into the interpreter and divide a number by zero:

```
>>> 1/0
Traceback (most recent call last):
  File "<pyshell#0>", line 1, in <module>
    1/0
ZeroDivisionError: int division or modulo by zero
```

From this interactive session, I can see that the exception is called `ZeroDivisionError`. Fortunately, the interpreter isn't shy about telling you exactly which type of exception you raise.

Handling Multiple Exception Types

A single piece of code can result in different types of exceptions. Fortunately, you can trap for multiple exception types. One way to trap for multiple exception types is to list them in a single `except` clause as a comma-separated group enclosed in a set of parentheses:

```
# handle multiple exception types
print()
for value in (None, "Hi!"):
    try:
        print("Attempting to convert", value, "-->", end=" ")
        print(float(value))
    except (TypeError, ValueError):
        print("Something went wrong!")
```

This code tries to convert two different values to a floating-point number. Both fail, but each raises a different exception type. `float(None)` raises a `TypeError` because the function can only convert strings and numbers. `float("Hi!")` raises a `ValueError` because, while `"Hi!"` is a string, the characters in the string are of the wrong value (they're not digits). As a result of the `except` clause, each type of exception is handled.

Another way to catch multiple exceptions is with multiple `except` clauses. You can list as many `except` clauses as you like, following a single `try` statement:

```
print()
for value in (None, "Hi!"):
    try:
        print("Attempting to convert", value, "-->", end=" ")
        print(float(value))
    except TypeError:
        print("I can only convert a string or a number!")
    except ValueError:
        print("I can only convert a string of digits!")
```

Now, each exception type has its own block. So when `value` is `None`, a `TypeError` is raised and the string `"I can only convert a string or a number!"` is printed. When `value` is `"Hi!"`, a `ValueError` is raised and the string `"I can only convert a string of digits!"` is printed.

Using multiple `except` clauses allows you to define unique reactions to different types of exceptions from the same `try` block. In this case, I offer a more specific error message by trapping each exception type individually.

Getting an Exception's Argument

When an exception occurs, it may have an associated value, the exception's *argument*. The argument is usually an official message from Python describing the exception. You can receive the argument if you specify a variable after the exception type, preceded by the keyword `as`. Here, I receive the exception's argument in variable `e` and print it out along with my regular error message:

```
# get an exception's argument
try:
    num = float(input("\nEnter a number: "))
except ValueError as e:
    print("That was not a number! Or as Python would say...")
    print(e)
```

Adding an else Clause

You can add a single `else` clause after all the except clauses in a try statement. The `else` block executes only if no exception is raised in the `try` block.

```
# try/except/else
try:
    num = float(input("\nEnter a number: "))
except ValueError:
    print("That was not a number!")
else:
    print("You entered the number", num)

input("\n\nPress the enter key to exit.")
```

In this code, num is printed in the `else` block only if the assignment statement in the `try` block doesn't raise an exception. This is perfect because that means num will be printed only if the assignment statement was successful and the variable exists.

BACK TO THE TRIVIA CHALLENGE GAME

With the basics of files and exceptions under your belt, it's time to tackle the Trivia Challenge game presented at the beginning of the chapter. One of the cool things about the program is that it reads a plain text file, so you can create your own trivia game episodes with a text editor and a dash of creativity. As you'll see in the code, the text file the program reads, `trivia.txt`, needs to be in the same directory as the program file. To create your own episode full of questions, all you need to do is replace this file with one containing your own work.

Understanding the Data File Layout

Before I go over actual code from the game, you should understand exactly how the trivia.txt file is structured. The very first line in the file is the title of the episode. The rest of the file consists of blocks of seven lines for each question. You can have as many blocks (and thus questions) as you like. Here's a generic representation of a block:

```
<category>
<question>
<answer 1>
<answer 2>
<answer 3>
<answer 4>
<correct answer>
<explanation>
```

And here's the beginning of the file I created for the game:

```
An Episode You Can't Refuse
On the Run With a Mammal
Let's say you turn state's evidence and need to "get on the lamb. " If you ↵
  ↳ wait /too long, what will happen?
You'll end up on the sheep
You'll end up on the cow
You'll end up on the goat
You'll end up on the emu
1
A lamb is just a young sheep.
The Godfather Will Get Down With You Now
Let's say you have an audience with the Godfather of Soul. How would it be
/smart to address him?
Mr. Richard
Mr. Domino
Mr. Brown
Mr. Checker
3
James Brown is the Godfather of Soul.
```

To save space, I only show the first 15 lines of the file—two questions' worth. You can take a look at the complete file, trivia.txt, which is on the companion website (www.courseptr.com/downloads) in the Chapter 7 folder.

Remember, the very first line in the file, An Episode You Can't Refuse, is the episode title for this game. The next seven lines are for the first question. And the next seven lines are for the second question. So, the line On the Run With a Mammal is the category of the first question. The category is just a clever way to introduce the next question. The next line, Let's say you turn state's evidence and need to "get on the lamb." If you wait /too long, what will happen?, is the first question in the game. The next four lines, You'll end up on the sheep, You'll end up on the cow, You'll end up on the goat, and You'll end up on the emu, are the four possible answers from which the player will choose. The next line, 1, is the number of the correct answer. So in this case, the correct answer to the question is the first answer, You'll end up on the sheep. The next line, A lamb is just a young sheep., explains why the correct answer is correct. The rest of the questions follow the same pattern.

An important thing to note is that I included a forward slash (/) in two of the lines. I did this to represent a newline since Python does not automatically wrap text when it prints it. When the program reads a line from the file, it replaces all of the forward slashes with the newline character. You'll see exactly how the program does this when I go over the code.

The open_file() Function

The first thing I do in the program is define the function `open_file()`, which receives a file name and mode (both strings) and returns a corresponding file object. I use `try` and `except` to trap for an `IOError` exception for input-output errors, which would occur if the file doesn't exist, for example.

If I trap an exception, that means there was a problem opening the trivia file. If this happens, there's no point in continuing the program, so I print an appropriate message and call the `sys.exit()` function. This function raises an exception that results in the termination of the program. You should only use `sys.exit()` as a last resort, when you must end a program. Notice that I had to import the `sys` module to call `sys.exit()`.

```
# Trivia Challenge
# Trivia game that reads a plain text file

import sys

def open_file(file_name, mode):
    """Open a file."""
    try:
        the_file = open(file_name, mode)
    except IOError as e:
        print("Unable to open the file", file_name, "Ending program.\n", e)
        input("\n\nPress the enter key to exit.")
        sys.exit()
    else:
        return the_file
```

The next_line() Function

Next, I define the `next_line()` function, which receives a file object and returns the next line of text from it:

```
def next_line(the_file):
    """Return next line from the trivia file, formatted."""
    line = the_file.readline()
    line = line.replace("/", "\n")
    return line
```

However, I do one small bit of formatting to the line before I return it. I replace all forward slashes with newline characters. I do this because Python does not automatically word wrap printed text. My procedure gives the creator of a trivia text file some formatting control. He or she can indicate where newlines should go so that words don't get split across lines. Take a look at the triva.txt file and the output of the Trivia Challenge game to see this in action. Try removing the forward slashes from the text file and check out the results.

The next_block() Function

The next_block() function reads the next block of lines for one question. It takes a file object and returns four strings and a list of strings. It returns a string for the category, question, correct answer, and explanation as well as a list of four strings for the possible answers to the question.

```
def next_block(the_file):
    """Return the next block of data from the trivia file."""
    category = next_line(the_file)

    question = next_line(the_file)

    answers = []
    for i in range(4):
        answers.append(next_line(the_file))

    correct = next_line(the_file)
    if correct:
        correct = correct[0]

    explanation = next_line(the_file)

    return category, question, answers, correct, explanation
```

If the end of the file is reached, reading a line returns the empty string. So, when the program comes to the end of trivia.txt, category gets the empty string. I check category in the main() function of the program. When it becomes the empty string, the game is over.

The welcome() Function

The welcome() function welcomes the player to the game and announces the episode's title. The function gets the episode title as a string and prints it along with a welcome message.

```
def welcome(title):
    """Welcome the player and get his/her name."""
    print("\t\tWelcome to Trivia Challenge!\n")
    print("\t\t", title, "\n")
```

Setting Up the Game

Next, I create the `main()` function, which houses the main game loop. In the first part of the function, I set up the game by opening the trivia file, getting the title of the episode (the first line of the file), welcoming the player, and setting the player's score to 0.

```
def main():
    trivia_file = open_file("trivia.txt", "r")
    title = next_line(trivia_file)
    welcome(title)
    score = 0
```

Asking a Question

Next, I read the first block of lines for the first question into variables. Then, I start the `while` loop, which will continue to ask questions as long as `category` is not the empty string. If `category` is the empty string, that means the end of the trivia file has been reached and the loop won't be entered. I ask a question by printing the category of the question, the question itself, and the four possible answers.

```
    # get first block
    category, question, answers, correct, explanation = next_block(trivia_file)
    while category:
        # ask a question
        print(category)
        print(question)
        for i in range(4):
            print("\t", i + 1, "-", answers[i])
```

Getting an Answer

Next, I get the player's answer:

```
        # get answer
        answer = input("What's your answer?: ")
```

Checking an Answer

Then, I compare the player's answer to the correct answer. If they match, the player is congratulated and his or her score is increased by one. If they don't match, the player is told he or she is wrong. In either case, I then display the explanation, which describes why the correct answer is correct. Lastly, I display the player's current score.

```
# check answer
if answer == correct:
    print("\nRight!", end=" ")
    score += 1
else:
    print("\nWrong.", end=" ")
print(explanation)
print("Score:", score, "\n\n")
```

Getting the Next Question

Then, I call the next_block() function and get the block of strings for the next question. If there are no more questions, category will get the empty string and the loop won't continue.

```
# get next block
category, question, answers, correct, explanation = next_block(trivia_file)
```

Ending the Game

After the loop, I close the trivia file and display the player's score:

```
trivia_file.close()

print("That was the last question!")
print("You're final score is", score)
```

Starting the main() Function

The last lines of code start main() and kick off the game:

```
main()
input("\n\nPress the enter key to exit.")
```

SUMMARY

In this chapter, you learned about files and exceptions. You learned how to read from text files. You saw how to read a single character or an entire file at once. You learned several different ways to read one full line at a time, probably the most common way to read a text file. You also learned how to write to text files—everything from a single character to a list of strings. Next, you learned how to save more complex data to files through pickling and how to manage a group of pickled objects in a single binary file using a shelf. Then, you saw how to handle exceptions raised during the execution of a program. You saw how to trap for specific exceptions and how to write code to deal with them. Finally, you saw how to put files and exceptions together through the construction of a trivia game program that allows anyone with a text editor to create their very own trivia episodes.

CHALLENGES

1. Improve the Trivia Challenge game so that each question has a unique point value associated with it. The player's score should be the total of all the point values of the questions he or she answers correctly.

2. Improve the Trivia Challenge game so that it maintains a high-scores list in a file. The program should record the player's name and score if the player makes the list. Store the high scores using a pickled object.

3. Change the way the high-scores functionality you created in the last challenge is implemented. This time, use a plain text file to store the list.

4. Create a trivia game episode that tests a player's knowledge of Python files and exceptions.

Software Objects: The Critter Caretaker Program

Object-oriented programming (OOP) is a different way of thinking about programming. It's a modern methodology that's been embraced by the software industry and is used in the creation of the majority of new, commercial software. The basic building block in OOP is the *software object*—often just called an object. In this chapter, you'll take your first steps toward understanding OOP as you learn about objects. Specifically, you'll learn to do the following:

- Create classes to define objects
- Write methods and create attributes for objects
- Instantiate objects from classes
- Restrict access to an object's attributes

Introducing the Critter Caretaker Program

The Critter Caretaker program charges the user with the care of his or her own virtual pet. The user names the critter and is completely responsible for keeping it happy, which is no small task. The user must feed and play with the critter to keep it in a good mood. The user can listen to the critter to learn how the critter is feeling, which can range from happy to mad. Figures 8.1 through 8.3 show off the Critter program.

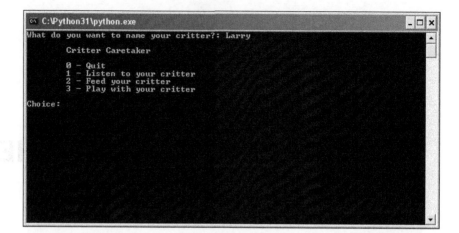

FIGURE 8.1

You get to name your very own critter.

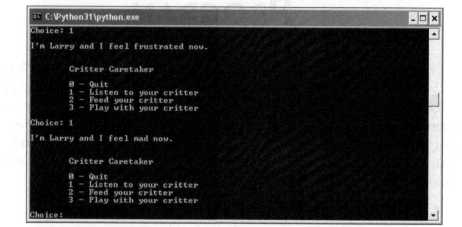

FIGURE 8.2

If you fail to feed or entertain your critter, it will have a mood change for the worse.

FIGURE 8.3

But with the proper care, your critter will come back to its original, sunny mood.

Though you could create this program without software objects, I created the critter as an object. Ultimately, this makes the program easier to work with and modify. Plus, it allows for painless scaling. Once you've created one critter, it's no sweat to create and manage a dozen. Could a critter farm be far off? (Not if you check the chapter challenges.)

UNDERSTANDING OBJECT-ORIENTED BASICS

OOP has a reputation for being complicated, but I think it's actually simpler than some of the concepts you've already learned. In fact, OOP allows you to represent things in your programs in a way that's more like the real world.

What you often want to represent in your programs—anything from a checking account to an alien spacecraft—are real-life objects. OOP lets you represent these real-life objects as software objects. Like real-life objects, software objects combine characteristics (called *attributes* in OOP-speak) and behaviors (called *methods* in OOP-speak). For example, if you were to create an alien spacecraft object, its attributes could include its location and energy level, while its methods could include its ability to move or fire its weapons.

Objects are created (or *instantiated* in OOP-speak) from a definition called a *class*—programming code that can define attributes and methods. Classes are like blueprints. A class isn't an object, it's a design for one. And just as a foreman can create many houses from the same blueprint, a programmer can create many objects from the same class. As a result, each object (also called an *instance*) instantiated from the same class will have a similar structure. So, if you have a checking account class, you could use it to create multiple checking account objects. And those different objects would each have the same basic structure. Each might have a balance attribute, for example.

But just as you can take two houses built from the same blueprint and decorate them differently, you can have two objects of the same class and give each its own unique set of attribute values. So, you could have one checking account object with a balance attribute of 100 and another with a balance attribute of 1,000,000.

 Don't worry if all this OOP talk isn't crystal clear yet. I just wanted to give you an overview of what objects are all about. Like all new programming concepts, reading about them isn't enough. But after seeing some real Python code that defines classes and creates objects (and coding some on your own), you'll soon "get" OOP.

CREATING CLASSES, METHODS, AND OBJECTS

To build an object, you first need a blueprint, or a class. Classes almost always include methods, things that an object can do. You can create a class without any methods, but that wouldn't be much fun.

Introducing the Simple Critter Program

The Simple Critter program includes your first example of a class written in Python. In it, I define an extremely simple type of critter that can only do one thing: say hi. While this kind of critter might be simple, at least it's polite. The results of the program are pictured in Figure 8.4.

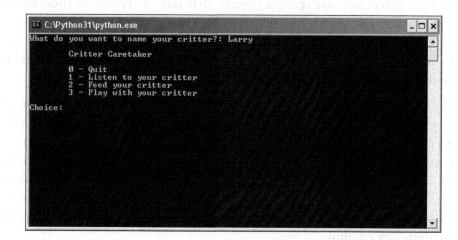

FIGURE 8.4

When the program invokes the Critter object's talk() method, the critter greets the world.

You can find the code for the program on the companion website (www.courseptr.com/downloads) in the Chapter 8 folder; the file name is simple_critter.py. The program itself is quite short.

```python
# Simple Critter
# Demonstrates a basic class and object

class Critter(object):
    """A virtual pet"""
    def talk(self):
        print("Hi.  I'm an instance of class Critter.")

# main
crit = Critter()
```

```
crit.talk()
```

```
input("\n\nPress the enter key to exit.")
```

Defining a Class

The program starts with a class definition, the blueprint of my first critter. The first line of the definition is the class header:

```
class Critter(object):
```

I used the keyword `class` followed by the class name I chose, `Critter`. You'll notice that my class name begins with a capital letter. Python doesn't require this, but it's the standard convention, so you should begin all your class names with a capital letter.

Next, I told Python to base my class on `object`, a fundamental, built-in type. You can base a new class on `object` or any previously defined class, but that's a topic for Chapter 9, "Object-Oriented Programming: The Blackjack Game." In this chapter, I base all of my classes on `object`.

The next line is a docstring, which documents the class. A good docstring describes the kind of objects a class can be used to create. My docstring is pretty straightforward:

```
    """A virtual pet"""
```

Defining a Method

The last part of the class defines a method. It looks very much like a function:

```
    def talk(self):
        print("Hi.  I'm an instance of class Critter.")
```

In fact, you can think of methods as functions associated with an object. (You've already seen this with string and list methods, for example.) The `talk()` method prints the string `"Hi. I'm an instance of class Critter."`

You'll notice that `talk()` has one parameter, `self` (which it doesn't happen to use). Every *instance method*—a method that every object of a class has—must have a special first parameter, called `self` by convention. This parameter provides a way for a method to refer to the object itself. For now, don't worry about `self`, you'll see it in action a little later in this chapter.

 TRAP If you create an instance method without any parameters, you'll generate an error when you invoke it. Remember, all instance methods must have a special first parameter, called `self` by convention.

Instantiating an Object

After I wrote my class, instantiating a new object took just one line:

```
crit = Critter()
```

This line creates a brand-new object of the `Critter` class and assigns it to the variable `crit`. Notice the parentheses after the class name `Critter` in the assignment statement. It's critical to use them if you want to create a new object.

You can assign a newly instantiated object to a variable with any name. The name doesn't have to be based on the class name. However, you should usually avoid using the same name in lowercase letters as the class name because it could lead to confusion.

Invoking a Method

My new object has a method called `talk()`. The method is like any other method you've already seen. It's basically a function that belongs to the object. I can invoke this method just like any other, using dot notation:

```
crit.talk()
```

The line invokes the `talk()` method of the `Critter` object assigned to `crit`. The method simply prints the string `"Hi. I'm an instance of class Critter."`

Using Constructors

You've seen how you can create methods, like `talk()`, but there's a special method you can write, called a *constructor,* that is automatically invoked right after a new object is created. A constructor method is extremely useful. In fact, you'll often write one for each class you create. The constructor method is usually used to set up the initial attribute values of an object, though I won't use it for that in this program.

Introducing the Constructor Critter Program

The Constructor Critter program defines a new `Critter` class that includes a simple constructor method. The program also shows how easy it is to create multiple objects from the same class. Figure 8.5 shows a sample run of the program.

FIGURE 8.5

Two separate
critters are
created. Each
says hi.

You can find the code for the program on the companion website (www.courseptr.com/downloads) in the Chapter 8 folder; the file name is constructor_critter.py.

```python
# Constructor Critter
# Demonstrates constructors

class Critter(object):
    """A virtual pet"""
    def __init__(self):
        print("A new critter has been born!")

    def talk(self):
        print("\nHi.  I'm an instance of class Critter.")

# main
crit1 = Critter()
crit2 = Critter()

crit1.talk()
crit2.talk()

input("\n\nPress the enter key to exit.")
```

Creating a Constructor

The first new piece of code in the class definition is the constructor method (also called the *initialization* method):

```
def __init__(self):
    print("A new critter has been born!")
```

Normally, you make up your own method names, but here I used a specific method name recognized by Python. By naming the method __init__, I told Python that this is my constructor method. As a constructor method, __init__() is automatically called by any newly created Critter object right after the object springs to life. As you can see from the second line in the method, that means any newly created Critter object automatically announces itself to the world by printing the string "A new critter has been born!".

 HINT Python has a collection of built-in "special methods" whose names begin and end with two underscores, like __init__, the constructor method.

Creating Multiple Objects

Once you've written a class, creating multiple objects is a snap. In the main part of the program, I create two:

```
# main
crit1 = Critter()
crit2 = Critter()
```

As a result, two objects are created. Just after each is instantiated, it prints "A new critter has been born!" through its constructor method.

Each object is its very own full-fledged critter. To prove the point, I invoke their talk() methods:

```
crit1.talk()
crit2.talk()
```

Even though these two lines of code print the exact same string, "\nHi. I'm an instance of class Critter.", each is the result of a different object.

USING ATTRIBUTES

You can have an object's attributes automatically created and initialized just after it's instantiated through its constructor method. This is a big convenience and something you'll do a lot.

Introducing the Attribute Critter Program

The Attribute Critter program creates a new type of object with an attribute, name. The Critter class has a constructor method that creates and initializes name. The program uses the new attribute so that the critter can offer a more personalized greeting. Figure 8.6 shows the program in action.

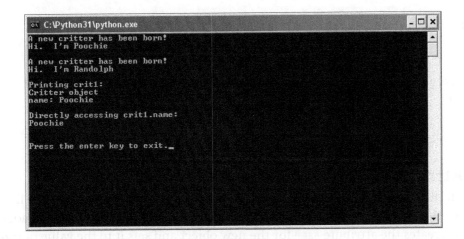

FIGURE 8.6

This time, each Critter object has an attribute name that it uses when it says hi.

The following is the code for the program:

```
# Attribute Critter
# Demonstrates creating and accessing object attributes

class Critter(object):
    """A virtual pet"""
    def __init__(self, name):
        print("A new critter has been born!")
        self.name = name

    def __str__(self):
        rep = "Critter object\n"
        rep += "name: " + self.name + "\n"
```

```
        return rep

    def talk(self):
        print("Hi.  I'm", self.name, "\n")

# main
crit1 = Critter("Poochie")
crit1.talk()

crit2 = Critter("Randolph")
crit2.talk()

print("Printing crit1:")
print(crit1)

print("Directly accessing crit1.name:")
print(crit1.name)

input("\n\nPress the enter key to exit.")
```

Initializing Attributes

The constructor in this program prints the message `"A new critter has been born!"` just like the constructor in the Constructor Critter program, but the next line of the method does something new. It creates the attribute `name` for the new object and sets it to the value of the parameter `name`. So, in the main part of the program, the line:

```
crit1 = Critter("Poochie")
```

results in the creation of a new `Critter` object with an attribute `name` set to `"Poochie"`. Finally, the object is assigned to `crit`.

So that you can understand exactly how this works, I'll reveal what the mysterious `self` parameter is all about. As the first parameter in every method, `self` automatically receives a reference to the object invoking the method. This means that, through `self`, a method can get at the object invoking it and access the object's attributes and methods (and even create new attributes for the object).

 You can name the first parameter in a method header something other than `self`, but you shouldn't. It's the "Pythonic" way to do things and other programmers will expect it.

So, back in the constructor method, the parameter self automatically receives a reference to the new Critter object while the parameter name receives "Poochie". Then, the line:

```
self.name = name
```

creates the attribute name for the object and sets it to the value of name, which is "Poochie".

Back in the main part of the program, the assignment statement assigns this new object to crit. This means that crit refers to a new object with its own attribute called name set to "Poochie". So, a critter has been created with its own name!

The line in the main program:

```
crit2 = Critter("Randolph")
```

kicks off the same basic chain of events. But this time, a new Critter object is created with its own attribute name set to "Randolph". And the object is assigned to crit2.

Accessing Attributes

Attributes aren't any good unless you can use them, so I wrote a more personal talk() method that uses a Critter object's name attribute. Now, when a critter says hi, it introduces itself with its name.

I got my first critter to say hi by invoking its talk() method with

```
crit1.talk()
```

The talk() method receives the automatically sent reference to the object into its self parameter:

```
def talk(self):
```

Then, the print function displays the text Hi. I'm Poochie by accessing the attribute name of the object through self.name:

```
print("Hi.  I'm", self.name, "\n")
```

The same basic events occur when I then call the method for my second object:

```
crit2.talk()
```

But this time, the talk() method displays the text Hi. I'm Randolph since the name attribute of crit2 is equal to "Randolph".

By default, you can access and modify an object's attributes outside of its class. In the main part of the program, I directly accessed the name attribute of crit1:

```
print(crit1.name)
```

The line prints the string `"Poochie"`. In general, to access an attribute of an object outside the object's class, you can use dot notation. Type the variable name, followed by a dot, followed by the attribute name.

 HINT Usually, you want to avoid directly accessing an object's attributes outside of its class definition. You'll learn more about this later in this chapter, in section "Understanding Object Encapsulation."

Printing an Object

Normally, if I were to print an object with the code `print(crit1)`, Python would come back with something like the cryptic:

```
<__main__.Critter object at 0x00A0BA90>
```

This tells me that I've printed a `Critter` object in the main part of my program, but doesn't give me any useful information about the object. However, there is a way to change this. By including the special method `__str__()` in a class definition, you can create a string representation for your objects that will be displayed whenever one is printed. Whatever string you return from the method will be the string that's printed for the object.

The `__str__()` method I wrote returns a string that includes the value of the object's `name` attribute. So, when the following line is executed:

```
print(crit1)
```

this, more useful, text appears:

```
Critter object
name: Poochie
```

 TRICK Even if you never plan to print an object in your program, creating a `__str__()` method is still not a bad idea. You may find that being able to see the values of an object's attributes helps you understand how a program is working (or not working).

USING CLASS ATTRIBUTES AND STATIC METHODS

Through attributes, different objects of the same class can each have their own, unique values. You could, for example, have 10 different critters running around, each with its own name. But you may have some information that relates not to individual objects, but the entire class. You might want to, say, keep track of the total number of critters you've created. You could give each `Critter` object an attribute called `total`. But then, whenever a new object is instantiated, you'd have to update every existing object's `total` attribute. This would be a real pain. Fortunately, Python offers a way to create a single value that's associated with a class itself, called a *class attribute*. If a class is like a blueprint, then a class attribute is like a Post-it note stuck to the blueprint. There's only one copy of it, no matter how many things you make from the blueprint.

You might also find that you want a method that's associated with the class; for this, Python offers the *static method*. Since static methods are associated with a class, they're often used to work with class attributes.

Introducing the Classy Critter Program

No, the Classy Critter program doesn't involve a critter that went to finishing school and scoffs at other critters who don't know which fork to use. Instead, the program involves attributes and methods that belong to a class rather than a specific object. The program defines a class attribute that keeps track of the total number of `Critter` objects instantiated. The class also has a static method that displays this number. Figure 8.7 shows the results of the program.

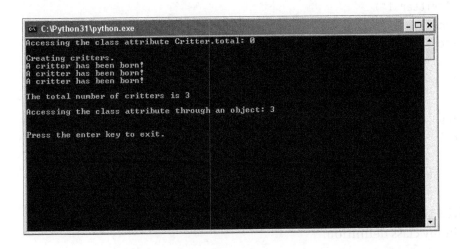

FIGURE 8.7

Critters are being born left and right! The program keeps track of all of them through a single class attribute, which it displays through a static method.

You can find the code for the program on the companion website (www.courseptr.com/downloads) in the Chapter 8 folder; the file name is classy_critter.py.

```
# Classy Critter
# Demonstrates class attributes and static methods
```

```
class Critter(object):
    """A virtual pet"""
    total = 0

    @staticmethod
    def status():
        print("\nThe total number of critters is", Critter.total)

    def __init__(self, name):
        print("A critter has been born!")
        self.name = name
        Critter.total += 1

#main
print("Accessing the class attribute Critter.total:", end=" ")
print(Critter.total)

print("\nCreating critters.")
crit1 = Critter("critter 1")
crit2 = Critter("critter 2")
crit3 = Critter("critter 3")

Critter.status()

print("\nAccessing the class attribute through an object:", end=" ")
print(crit1.total)

input("\n\nPress the enter key to exit.")
```

Creating a Class Attribute

The second line in my class definition:

```
    total = 0
```

creates a class attribute total and assigns 0 to it. Any assignment statement like this—a new variable assigned a value outside of a method—creates a class attribute. The assignment statement is executed only once, when Python first sees the class definition. This means that the class attribute exists even before a single object is created. So, you can use a class attribute without any objects of the class in existence.

Accessing a Class Attribute

Accessing a class attribute is simple. I access the new class attribute in several different places in the program. In the main part of the program, I print it with

```
print Critter.total
```

In the static method `status()`, I print the value of the `Critter` class attribute `total` with the line:

```
print("\nThe total number of critters is", Critter.total)
```

In the constructor method, I increment the value of this class attribute through the line:

```
Critter.total += 1
```

As a result of this line, every time a new object is instantiated, the value of the attribute is incremented by 1.

In general, to access a class attribute, use dot notation. Type the class name, followed by a dot, followed by the attribute name.

Finally, you can access a class attribute through an object of that class. That's just what I did in the main part of the program with the following line:

```
print(crit1.total)
```

This line prints the value of the class attribute `total` (and not an attribute of the object itself). You can read the value of a class attribute through any object that belongs to that class. So, I could have used `print(crit2.total)` or `print(crit3.total)` and gotten the same results in this case.

TRAP Although you can use an object of a class to access a class attribute, you can't assign a new value to a class attribute through an object. If you want to change the value of a class attribute, access it through its class name.

Creating a Static Method

The first method in the class is `status()`:

```
def status():
    print("\nThe total number of critters is", Critter.total)
```

I wrote the definition as part of creating a static method. Notice that the definition doesn't have `self` in its parameter list. That's because, like all static methods, it's designed to be invoked through a class and not an object. So, the method won't be passed a reference to an object and therefore won't need a parameter, like self, to receive such a reference. Static methods can certainly have parameters, but I just didn't need any for this one.

While the definition creates a method called status, I put a *decorator*—something you can imagine as decorating or modifying a function or method—right before the definition. This decorator ultimately creates a static method with the same name:

```
@staticmethod
```

As a result of these three lines of code, the class has a static method, status(), which displays the total number of Critter objects by printing the class attribute total.

To create your own static method, follow my example. Begin with @staticmethod decorator, followed by the class method definition. And since the method is for the entire class, you won't include the self parameter, necessary only for object methods.

Invoking a Static Method

Invoking a static method is simple. With the first line of the main part of the program, I invoke the static method:

```
Critter.status()
```

As you would guess, this displays 0 since no objects have been instantiated. But notice that I'm able to invoke the method without a single object in existence. Since static methods are invoked through a class, no objects of the class need to exist before you can invoke them.

Next, I create three objects. Then, I invoke status() again, which prints a message stating that three critters exist. This works because, during the execution of the constructor method for each object, the class attribute total is increased by 1.

UNDERSTANDING OBJECT ENCAPSULATION

You first learned about the concept of encapsulation with functions in the "Understanding Encapsulation" section in Chapter 6. You saw that functions are encapsulated and hide the details of their inner workings from the part of your program that calls it (called the *client* of the function). You learned that the client of a well-defined function communicates with the function only through its parameters and return values. In general, objects should be treated the same way. Clients should communicate with objects through method parameters and return values. In general, client code should avoid directly altering the value of an object's attribute.

As always, a concrete example helps. Say, for example, that you had a Checking_Account object with a balance attribute. Let's say your program needs to handle withdrawals from accounts, where a withdrawal decreases an object's `balance` attribute by some amount. To make a withdrawal, client code could simply subtract a number from the value of `balance`. This direct access is easy for the client, but can cause problems. The client code may subtract a number so that `balance` becomes negative, which might be considered unacceptable (especially by the bank). It's much better to have a method called `withdraw()` that allows a client to request a withdrawal by passing an amount to the method. Then, the object itself can handle the request. If the amount is too large, the object can deal with it, possibly rejecting the transaction. The object keeps itself safe by providing indirect access to its attributes through methods.

USING PRIVATE ATTRIBUTES AND PRIVATE METHODS

By default, all of an object's attributes and methods are *public*, meaning that they can be directly accessed or invoked by a client. To encourage encapsulation, you can define an attribute or method as *private*, meaning that only other methods of the object itself can easily access or invoke them.

Introducing the Private Critter Program

The Private Critter program instantiates an object that has both private and public attributes and methods. Figure 8.8 shows a sample run.

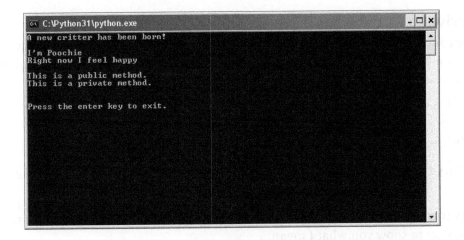

```
C:\Python31\python.exe
A new critter has been born!

I'm Poochie
Right now I feel happy

This is a public method.
This is a private method.

Press the enter key to exit.
```

FIGURE 8.8

The object's private attribute and private method are indirectly accessed.

I'll go through the code one section at a time, but you can find the entire program on the companion website (www.courseptr.com/downloads) in the Chapter 8 folder; the file name is private_critter.py.

Creating Private Attributes

To limit the direct access of object attributes by clients, you can use private attributes. In the constructor method, I create two attributes, one public and one private:

```
# Private Critter
# Demonstrates private variables and methods

class Critter(object):
    """A virtual pet"""
    def __init__(self, name, mood):
        print("A new critter has been born!")
        self.name = name          # public attribute
        self.__mood = mood        # private attribute
```

The two underscore characters that begin the second attribute name tell Python that this is a private attribute. To create a private attribute of your own, just begin the attribute name with two underscores.

 HINT You can create a private class attribute by beginning the attribute's name with two underscores.

Accessing Private Attributes

It's perfectly fine to access an object's private attribute inside the class definition of the object. (Remember, private attributes are meant to discourage client code from directly accessing the attribute.) I access a private attribute in the talk() method:

```
def talk(self):
    print("\nI'm", self.name)
    print("Right now I feel", self.__mood, "\n")
```

This method prints the value of the object's private attribute, which represents a critter's mood.

If I tried to access this attribute outside of the Critter class definition, I'd have trouble. Here's an interactive session to show you what I mean:

```
>>> crit = Critter(name = "Poochie", mood = "happy")
A new critter has been born!
>>> print(crit.mood)
Traceback (most recent call last):
```

```
  File "<pyshell#1>", line 1, in <module>
    print(crit.mood)
AttributeError: 'Critter' object has no attribute 'mood'
```

By raising an `AttributeError` exception, Python is saying that `crit` has no attribute `mood`. If you think you can outsmart Python by adding the two leading underscores, you'd be wrong. That's just what I tried in the next part of my interactive session:

```
>>> print(crit.__mood)
Traceback (most recent call last):
  File "<pyshell#2>", line 1, in <module>
    print(crit.__mood)
AttributeError: 'Critter' object has no attribute '__mood'
```

This also raises an `AttributeError` exception. Python is again saying that the attribute doesn't exist. So does this mean that the value of a private attribute is completely inaccessible outside of its class definition? Well, no. Python hides the attribute through a special naming convention, though it's still technically possible to access the attribute. That's what I did in the next part of my interactive session:

```
>>> print(crit._Critter__mood)
happy
```

This line prints the value of the elusive private attribute, which in this case is the string `"happy"`.

Since it's technically possible to access private attributes, you may be thinking: What good are they? Well, in Python, privacy is an indicator that the attribute or method is meant only for an object's internal use. In addition, it helps prevent inadvertent access to such an attribute or method.

 HINT You should never try to directly access the private attributes or methods of an object from outside of its class definition.

Creating Private Methods

You can create a private method in the same, simple way you create a private attribute: by adding two leading underscores to its name. That's just what I do in the next method definition in the class:

```
    def __private_method(self):
        print("This is a private method.")
```

This is a private method but it can easily be accessed by any other method in the class. Like private attributes, private methods are meant only to be accessed by an object's own methods.

Accessing Private Methods

Just as with private attributes, accessing an object's private methods within its class definition is simple. In the `public_method()` method, I access the class' private method:

```
def public_method(self):
    print("This is a public method.")
    self.__private_method()
```

This method prints the string `"This is a public method."` and then invokes the object's private method.

Like private attributes, private methods aren't meant to be directly accessed by clients. Back in my interactive session, I try to access `crit`'s private method:

```
>>> crit.private_method
Traceback (most recent call last):
  File "<pyshell#0>", line 1, in <module>
    crit.private_method
AttributeError: 'Critter' object has no attribute 'private_method'
```

This attempt raises the familiar `AttributeError` exception. Python is saying that `crit` has no method with this name. Python hides the method through the same, special naming convention. If I try again by adding the two leading underscores to the method name, I run into the same error message:

```
>>> crit.__private_method()
Traceback (most recent call last):
  File "<pyshell#1>", line 1, in <module>
    crit.__private_method()
AttributeError: 'Critter' object has no attribute '__private_method'
```

However, just as with private attributes, it is technically possible to access private methods from anywhere in a program. Here's the final part of my interactive session as proof:

```
>>> crit._Critter__private_method()
This is a private method.
```

But, as you probably know by now, a client should never attempt to directly access an object's private methods.

You can create a private static method by beginning the method's name with two underscores.

Respecting an Object's Privacy

In the main part of the program, I behave myself and don't go prodding into an object's private attributes or methods. Instead, I create an object and invoke its two public methods:

```
# main
crit = Critter(name = "Poochie", mood = "happy")
crit.talk()
crit.public_method()

input("\n\nPress the enter key to exit.")
```

The `Critter` object's __init__() method, which is automatically called right after the object is created, announces to the world that a new critter has been born. `crit`'s `talk()` method tells us how the critter is feeling. `crit`'s `public_method()` method prints the string "This is a public method." and then invokes `crit`'s private method, which prints the string "This is a private method." Finally, the program ends.

Understanding When to Implement Privacy

So now that you know how to use privacy, should you make every attribute in every class private to protect them from the evil, outside world? Well, no. Privacy is like a fine spice: used sparingly, it can greatly improve what you're making. Make private any method you don't want a client to invoke. If it's critical that an attribute never be directly accessed by a client, you can make it private. The philosophy among many Python programmers is to trust that clients will use an object's methods and not directly alter its attributes.

When you write a class:

* Create methods to reduce the need for clients to directly access an object's attributes.

* Use privacy for those attributes and methods that are completely internal to the operation of objects.

When you use an object:

* Minimize the direct reading of an object's attributes.

* Avoid directly altering an object's attributes.

* Never attempt to directly access an object's private attributes or methods.

CONTROLLING ATTRIBUTE ACCESS

Sometimes, instead of denying access to an attribute, you may want only to limit access to it. For example, you might have an attribute that you want client code to be able to read, but not change. Python provides a few tools to accomplish this kind of thing, including *properties*. Properties allow you to manage exactly how an attribute is accessed or changed.

Introducing the Property Critter

The Property Critter program allows client code to read a `Critter` object's attribute that refers to its name, but imposes restrictions when client code attempts to change the value that the attribute refers to. If client code tries to assign the empty string, the program complains and does not allow the change. Figure 8.9 shows the results of the program.

```
C:\Python31\python.exe

A new critter has been born!

Hi, I'm Poochie

My critter's name is: Poochie

Attempting to change my critter's name to Randolph...
Name change successful.
My critter's name is: Randolph

Attempting to change my critter's name to the empty string...
A critter's name can't be the empty string.
My critter's name is: Randolph

Press the enter key to exit._
```

FIGURE 8.9

A property controls access to the `Critter` object's attribute for its name.

I'll go through the code one section at a time, but you can find the entire program on the companion website (www.courseptr.com/downloads) in the Chapter 8 folder; the file name is property_critter.py.

Creating Properties

One way to control access to a private attribute is to create a *property*—an object with methods that allow indirect access to attributes and often impose some sort of restriction on that access. After the constructor of the `Critter` class, I create a property called `name` to allow indirect access to the private attribute __name:

```
# Property Critter
# Demonstrates properties
```

```
class Critter(object):
    """A virtual pet"""
    def __init__(self, name):
        print("A new critter has been born!")
        self.__name = name

    @property
    def name(self):
        return self.__name
```

I create the property by writing a method that returns the value I want to provide indirect access to (in this case, __name) and precede the method definition with the @property decorator. The property has the same name as the method—in this case, name. Now I can use the name property of any Critter object to get the value of the object's private __name attribute, inside or outside the class definition using the familiar dot notation. (You'll see examples of using this property in the next section, "Accessing Properties.")

To create a property of your own, write a method that returns the value you want to provide indirect access to and precede the method definition with the @property decorator. The property will have the same name as the method. If you're providing access to a private attribute, the convention is to give the property the same name as the private attribute without the leading underscores, just as I did here.

By creating a property, you can provide read access to a private attribute. However, a property can also provide write access—and even impose some limits on that access. I provide write access, with some limits, to the private attribute __name through the property name:

```
    @name.setter
    def name(self, new_name):
        if new_name == "":
            print("A critter's name can't be the empty string.")
        else:
            self.__name = new_name
            print("Name change successful.")
```

I begin the code with the decorator @name.setter. By accessing the setter attribute of the name property, I'm saying that the following method definition will provide a way to set the value of the property name. You can create your own decorator for setting a property value by following my example: start with the @ symbol, followed by the name of the property, followed by a dot (.), followed by setter.

After the decorator, I define a method called name that gets called when client code attempts to set a new value using the property. You'll notice that this method is called name just like the property; it has to be. When establishing a setter method in this way, the method must have the same name as the corresponding property.

In the method, the parameter new_name gets the value for the new critter name. If the value is the empty string, __name remains unchanged and a message saying that the attempted name change was unsuccessful is displayed. Otherwise, the method sets the private attribute __name to new_name and displays a message saying the name change was successful. And like this example, when you create a method for setting the value of a property, the method definition must have a parameter to receive the new value.

Accessing Properties

By creating the name property, I can get the name of a critter through dot notation. The next part of the program demonstrates this:

```
def talk(self):
    print("\nHi, I'm", self.name)

# main
crit = Critter("Poochie")
crit.talk()
```

The code self.name accesses the name property and indirectly calls the method that returns __name. In this case, it happens to return the string "Poochie". But not only can I use the name property of an object inside its class definition, but I can also use it outside the definition as I do next:

```
print("\nMy critter's name is:", end= " ")
print(crit.name)
```

Although this code is outside the Critter class, the same essential things happen—the code crit.name accesses the name property of the Critter object and indirectly calls the method that returns __name. In this case, it still returns the string "Poochie".

Next, I try to change the critter's name:

```
print("\nAttempting to change my critter's name to Randolph...")
crit.name = "Randolph"
```

The assignment statement crit.name = "Randolph" accesses the name property of the object and indirectly calls the method that attempts to set __name. In this case, a reference to the string "Randolph" is passed to the new_name parameter of the method—and since "Randolph" is not the empty string, the object's __name attribute becomes "Randolph" and the message Name change successful is displayed.

Next, I display the critter's name using the name property:

```
print("My critter's name is:", end= " ")
print(crit.name)
```

The program displays the message My critter's name is Randolph.

Next, I attempt to change the critter's name to the empty string:

```
print("\nAttempting to change my critter's name to the empty string...")
crit.name = ""
```

As before, the assignment accesses the name property of the object and indirectly calls the method that attempts to set __name. In this case, a reference to the empty string is passed to the new_name parameter of the method. As a result, the method displays the message A critter's name can't be the empty string and the object's __name attribute remains unchanged.

Finally, to prove that the critter's name hasn't been changed to the empty string, I display the name one last time:

```
print("My critter's name is:", end= " ")
print(crit.name)

input("\n\nPress the enter key to exit.")
```

The code displays a message indicating that the critter's name is still Randolph.

BACK TO THE CRITTER CARETAKER PROGRAM

The final Critter Caretaker program combines parts of classes you've seen throughout this chapter. It also includes the menu system you've worked with that allows the user to interact with his or her very own critter. I'll go through the code one section at a time, but you can find the entire program on the companion website (www.courseptr.com/downloads) in the Chapter 8 folder; the file name is critter_caretaker.py.

The Critter Class

The `Critter` class is the blueprint for the object that represents the user's critter. The class isn't complicated, and most of it should look quite familiar, but it's a long enough piece of code that attacking it in pieces makes sense.

The Constructor Method

The constructor method of the class initializes the three public attributes of a `Critter` object: `name`, `hunger`, and `boredom`. Notice that `hunger` and `boredom` both have default values of 0, allowing a critter to start off in a very good mood.

```
# Critter Caretaker
# A virtual pet to care for


class Critter(object):
    """A virtual pet"""
    def __init__(self, name, hunger = 0, boredom = 0):
        self.name = name
        self.hunger = hunger
        self.boredom = boredom
```

I take the more relaxed posture of a Python programmer with this method and leave the attributes at their default public status. I plan to provide all the methods I suspect a client will need, which should encourage the client to interact with a `Critter` object only through those methods.

The __pass_time() Method

The `__pass_time()` method is a private method that increases a critter's hunger and boredom levels. It's invoked at the end of each method where the critter does something (eats, plays, or talks) to simulate the passage of time. I made this method private because it should only be invoked by another method of the class. I only see time passing for a critter when it does something (like eat, play, or talk).

```
    def __pass_time(self):
        self.hunger += 1
        self.boredom += 1
```

The mood Property

The `mood` property represents a critter's mood. The following method calculates the mood. It adds the values of a `Critter` object's `hunger` and `boredom` attributes and, based on the total, returns a string for the mood—either `"happy"`, `"okay"`, `"frustrated"`, or `"mad"`.

The interesting thing about the mood property is that it doesn't provide access to a private attribute. That's because the string that represents a critter's mood is not stored as part of the Critter object, but is calculated on the fly. The mood property simply provides access to the string returned by the method.

```
@property
def mood(self):
    unhappiness = self.hunger + self.boredom
    if unhappiness < 5:
        m = "happy"
    elif 5 <= unhappiness <= 10:
        m = "okay"
    elif 11 <= unhappiness <= 15:
        m = "frustrated"
    else:
        m = "mad"
    return m
```

The talk() Method

The talk() method announces a critter's mood to the world by accessing the Critter object's mood property. Then it invokes __pass_time().

```
def talk(self):
    print("I'm", self.name, "and I feel", self.mood, "now.\n")
    self.__pass_time()
```

The eat() Method

The eat() method reduces a critter's hunger level by an amount passed to the parameter food. If no value is passed, food gets the default value of 4. The critter's hunger level is kept in check and not allowed to go below 0. Finally, the method invokes __pass_time().

```
def eat(self, food = 4):
    print("Brruppp.  Thank you.")
    self.hunger -= food
    if self.hunger < 0:
        self.hunger = 0
    self.__pass_time()
```

The play() Method

The play() method reduces the critter's boredom level by an amount passed to the parameter fun. If no value is passed, fun gets the default value of 4. The critter's boredom level is kept in check and not allowed to go below 0. Finally, the method invokes __pass_time().

```python
    def play(self, fun = 4):
        print("Wheee!")
        self.boredom -= fun
        if self.boredom < 0:
            self.boredom = 0
        self.__pass_time()
```

Creating the Critter

I put the main part of the program into its own function, main(). At the start of the program, I get the name of the critter from the user. Next, I instantiate a new Critter object. Since I don't supply values for hunger or boredom, the attributes start out at 0, and the critter begins life happy and content.

```python
def main():
    crit_name = input("What do you want to name your critter?: ")
    crit = Critter(crit_name)
```

Creating a Menu System

Next, I created the familiar menu system. If the user enters 0, the program ends. If the user enters 1, the object's talk() method is invoked. If the user enters 2, the object's eat() method is invoked. If the user enters 3, the object's play() method is invoked. If the user enters anything else, he or she is told the choice is invalid.

```python
    choice = None
    while choice != "0":
        print \
        ("""
        Critter Caretaker

        0 - Quit
        1 - Listen to your critter
        2 - Feed your critter
        3 - Play with your critter
        """)
```

```
    choice = input("Choice: ")
    print()

    # exit
    if choice == "0":
        print("Good-bye.")

    # listen to your critter
    elif choice == "1":
        crit.talk()

    # feed your critter
    elif choice == "2":
        crit.eat()

    # play with your critter
    elif choice == "3":
        crit.play()

    # some unknown choice
    else:
        print("\nSorry, but", choice, "isn't a valid choice.")
```

Starting the Program

The next line of code calls the `main()` function and begins the program. The last line waits for the user before ending.

```
main()
("\n\nPress the enter key to exit.")
```

SUMMARY

This chapter introduced you to a different way of programming by using the software object. You learned that software objects can combine functions and data (methods and attributes in OOP-speak) and in many ways mimic real-world objects. You saw how to write classes, the blueprints of objects. You learned about a special method called the constructor that is automatically invoked when a new object is instantiated. You saw how to create and initialize object attributes through a constructor. You learned how to create class-wide elements such as class attributes and static methods. Next, you learned about object encapsulation. You saw ways to help ensure encapsulation, including the use of private attributes and properties. You also learned that good object design goes a long way to help ensure encapsulation. Finally, you saw all of these ideas put to work to create a demanding virtual pet that requires constant attention.

CHALLENGES

1. Improve the Critter Caretaker program by allowing the user to specify how much food he or she feeds the critter and how long he or she plays with the critter. Have these values affect how quickly the critter's hunger and boredom levels drop.

2. Write a program that simulates a television by creating it as an object. The user should be able to enter a channel number and raise or lower the volume. Make sure that the channel number and volume level stay within valid ranges.

3. Create a "back door" in the Critter Caretaker program that shows the exact values of the object's attributes. Accomplish this by printing the object when a secret selection, not listed in the menu, is entered as the user's choice. (Hint: add the special method __str__() to the Critter class.)

4. Create a Critter Farm program by instantiating several Critter objects and keeping track of them through a list. Mimic the Critter Caretaker program, but instead of requiring the user to care for a single critter, require them to care for an entire farm. Each menu choice should allow the user to perform some action for all of the critters (feed all of the critters, play with all of the critters, or listen to all of the critters). To make the program interesting, give each critter random starting hunger and boredom levels.

OBJECT-ORIENTED PROGRAMMING: THE BLACKJACK GAME

In the last chapter, you learned about the software object. Almost every program you saw involved a single object. That's a great way to begin to understand how objects work, but the true power of OOP can only be appreciated by seeing a group of objects work together. In this chapter, you'll learn to create multiple objects and define relationships among them so that they can interact. Specifically, you'll learn to do the following:

- Create objects of different classes in the same program
- Allow objects to communicate with each other
- Create more complex objects by combining simpler ones
- Derive new classes from existing ones
- Extend the definition of existing classes
- Override method definitions of existing classes

INTRODUCING THE BLACKJACK GAME

The final project for this chapter is a simplified version of the card game blackjack. The game works like this: Players are dealt cards with point values. Each player tries to reach a total of 21 without going over. Numbered cards count as their face value. An ace counts as either 1 or 11 (whichever is best for the player) and any jack, queen, or king counts as 10.

The computer is the dealer and competes against one to seven players. At the opening of the round, the computer deals all participants (including itself) two cards. Players can see all of their cards, and the computer even displays their total. However, one of the dealer's cards is hidden for the time being.

Next, each player gets a chance to take additional cards. Each player can take one card at a time for as long as the player likes. But if the player's total goes over 21 (known as "busting"), the player loses. If all players bust, the computer reveals its first card and the round is over. Otherwise, play continues. The computer must take additional cards as long as its total is less than 17. If the computer busts, all players who have not themselves busted, win. Otherwise, each remaining player's total is compared with the computer's. If the player's total is greater, the player wins. If the player's total is less, the player loses. If the two totals are the same, the player ties the computer (also known as "pushing"). Figure 9.1 shows off the game.

```
C:\Python31\python.exe                                            _ □ x
                        Welcome to Blackjack!
How many players? (1 - 7): 2
Enter player name: Larry
Enter player name: Jerry

Larry:   4d      8h        (12)
Jerry:   10c     Jh        (20)
Dealer:  XX      5c

Larry, do you want a hit? (Y/N): y
Larry:   4d      8h        4h        (16)

Larry, do you want a hit? (Y/N): y
Larry:   4d      8h        4h        Qh        (26)
Larry busts.
Larry loses.

Jerry, do you want a hit? (Y/N): n
Dealer:  4c      5c        (9)
Dealer:  4c      5c        5h        (14)
Dealer:  4c      5c        5h        3s        (17)
Jerry wins.

Do you want to play again?: _
```

FIGURE 9.1

One player wins; the other is not so lucky.

SENDING AND RECEIVING MESSAGES

In a way, an object-oriented program is like an ecosystem and objects are like organisms. To maintain a thriving ecosystem, organisms must interact. The same is true in OOP. To have a useful program, objects must interact in well-defined ways. In OOP-speak, objects interact by *sending messages* to each other. What they do on a practical level is invoke each other's methods. That may sound a little impolite, but it's actually much more courteous than if an object were to access another object's attributes directly.

Introducing the Alien Blaster Program

The Alien Blaster program simulates an action game where a player blasts an alien. In the program, a hero blasts an invader and the invader dies (but not before giving a grand farewell speech). The program accomplishes this when one object sends another a message. Figure 9.2 shows the results of the program.

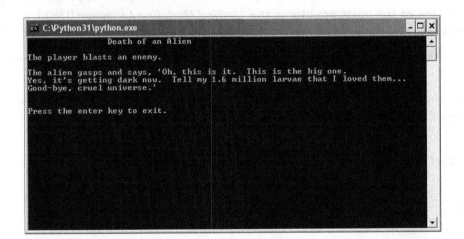

C:\Python31\python.exe

```
                Death of an Alien
The player blasts an enemy.

The alien gasps and says, 'Oh, this is it.  This is the big one.
Yes, it's getting dark now.  Tell my 1.6 million larvae that I loved them...
Good-bye, cruel universe.'

Press the enter key to exit.
```

FIGURE 9.2

The battle description is the result of objects exchanging a message.

Technically what happens is that the program instantiates a Player object, hero, and an Alien object, invader. When hero's blast() method is invoked with invader as its argument, hero invokes invader's die() method. In English, this means that when a player blasts an alien, the player sends a message to the alien telling it to die. Figure 9.3 provides a visual representation of the message exchange.

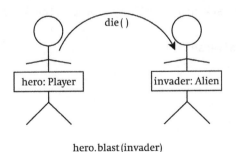

hero.blast(invader)

FIGURE 9.3

hero, a Player object, sends invader, an Alien object, a message.

IN THE REAL WORLD

The diagram I created to show two objects exchanging a message is a pretty simple one. But with many objects and many relationships among them, diagrams like this can become complex. In fact, there is a variety of formal methods for mapping software projects. One of the most popular is the *Unified Modeling Language* (UML), a notational language that is especially useful for visualizing object-oriented systems.

You can find the code for the program on the companion website (www.courseptr.com/downloads) in the Chapter 9 folder; the file name is alien_blaster.py:

```
# Alien Blaster
# Demonstrates object interaction

class Player(object):
    """ A player in a shooter game. """
    def blast(self, enemy):
        print("The player blasts an enemy.\n")
        enemy.die()

class Alien(object):
    """ An alien in a shooter game. """
    def die(self):
        print("The alien gasps and says, 'Oh, this is it.  This is the big one. \n" \
            "Yes, it's getting dark now.  Tell my 1.6 million larvae that ↵
 I loved them... \n" \
            "Good-bye, cruel universe.'")

# main
print("\t\tDeath of an Alien\n")

hero = Player()
invader = Alien()
hero.blast(invader)

input("\n\nPress the enter key to exit.")
```

Sending a Message

Before you can have one object send another object a message, you need two objects! So, I create two in the main part of the program. First, I create a Player object and assign it to hero. Then, I create an Alien object and assign it to invader.

The next line of code is where it gets interesting. Through hero.blast(invader), I invoke hero's blast() method and pass invader—the Alien object—as an argument. By examining the definition of blast(), you can see that the method accepts the object into its parameter enemy. So, when blast() executes, enemy refers to the Alien object. After displaying a message, blast() invokes the Alien object's die() method through enemy.die(). Essentially, the Player object is sending the Alien object a message by invoking its die() method.

Receiving a Message

The Alien object receives the message from the Player object in the form of its die() method being invoked. The Alien object's die() method then displays a melodramatic good-bye.

COMBINING OBJECTS

In the real world, interesting objects are usually made up of other, independent objects. For example, a drag racer can be seen as a single object that's composed of individual objects such as a body, tires, and an engine. Other times, you may see an object as a collection of other objects. For example, a zoo can be seen as a collection of animals. Well, you can mimic these kinds of relationships among objects in OOP. You could write a Drag_Racer class that has an attribute engine that references a Race_Engine object. Or, you could write a Zoo class that has an attribute, animals, which is a list of different Animal objects. Combining objects like this allows you to create more complex objects from simpler ones.

Introducing the Playing Cards Program

The Playing Cards program uses objects to represent individual playing cards that you might use in a game of Blackjack or Go Fish (depending upon your tastes ... and your tolerance for losing money). The program goes on to represent a hand of cards through an object that is a collection of card objects. Figure 9.4 shows the results of the program.

```
C:\Python31\python.exe                                          - □ ×
Printing a Card object:
Ac

Printing the rest of the objects individually:
2c
3c
4c
5c

Printing my hand before I add any cards:
<empty>

Printing my hand after adding 5 cards:
Ac  2c  3c  4c  5c

Gave the first two cards from my hand to your hand.
Your hand:
Ac  2c
My hand:
3c  4c  5c

My hand after clearing it:
<empty>

Press the enter key to exit.
```

FIGURE 9.4

Each Hand object is a collection of Card objects.

I'll go through the code one section at a time, but you can find the entire program on the companion website (www.courseptr.com/downloads) in the Chapter 9 folder; the file name is playing_cards.py.

Creating the Card Class

The first thing I do in the program is create a Card class for objects that represent playing cards.

```python
# Playing Cards
# Demonstrates combining objects

class Card(object):
    """ A playing card. """
    RANKS = ["A", "2", "3", "4", "5", "6", "7",
                       "8", "9", "10", "J", "Q", "K"]
    SUITS = ["c", "d", "h", "s"]

    def __init__(self, rank, suit):
        self.rank = rank
        self.suit = suit

    def __str__(self):
        rep = self.rank + self.suit
        return rep
```

Each Card object has a rank attribute, which represents the rank of the card. The possible values are listed in the class attribute RANKS. "A" represents an ace, "2" through "10" represent their corresponding numeric values, "J" represents a jack, "Q" represents a queen, and "K" represents a king.

Each card also has a suit attribute, which represents the suit of the card. The possible values for this attribute are listed in the class attribute SUITS. "c" represents clubs, "d" means diamonds, "h" stands for hearts, and "s" represents spades. So, an object with the rank attribute of "A" and a suit attribute of "d" represents the ace of diamonds.

The special method __str__() simply returns the concatenation of the rank and suit attributes so that an object can be printed.

Creating the Hand Class

The next thing I do in the program is create a Hand class for objects, which is a collection of Card objects:

```
class Hand(object):
    """ A hand of playing cards. """
    def __init__(self):
        self.cards = []

    def __str__(self):
        if self.cards:
            rep = ""
            for card in self.cards:
                rep += str(card) + "   "
        else:
            rep = "<empty>"
        return rep

    def clear(self):
        self.cards = []

    def add(self, card):
        self.cards.append(card)

    def give(self, card, other_hand):
        self.cards.remove(card)
        other_hand.add(card)
```

A new Hand object has an attribute cards that is intended to be a list of Card objects. So each single Hand object has an attribute that is a list of possibly many other objects.

The special method __str__() returns a string that represents the entire hand. The method iterates through each Card object in the Hand object and concatenates the Card object's string representation. If the Hand object has no Card objects, the string "<empty>" is returned.

The clear() method clears the list of cards by assigning an empty list to an object's cards attribute.

The add() method adds an object to the cards attribute.

The give() method removes an object from the Hand object and appends it to another Hand object by invoking the other Hand object's add() method. Another way to say this is that the first Hand object sends the second Hand object a message to add a Card object.

Using Card Objects

In the main part of the program, I create and print five Card objects:

```
# main
card1 = Card(rank = "A", suit = "c")
print("Printing a Card object:")
print(card1)

card2 = Card(rank = "2", suit = "c")
card3 = Card(rank = "3", suit = "c")
card4 = Card(rank = "4", suit = "c")
card5 = Card(rank = "5", suit = "c")
print("\nPrinting the rest of the objects individually:")
print(card2)
print(card3)
print(card4)
print(card5)
```

The first Card object created has a rank attribute equal to "A" and a suit attribute of "c". When I print the object, it's displayed on the screen as Ac. The remaining objects follow the same pattern.

Combining Card Objects Using a Hand Object

Next, I create a Hand object, assign it to my_hand, and print it:

```
my_hand = Hand()
print("\nPrinting my hand before I add any cards:")
print(my_hand)
```

Since the object's cards attribute is an empty list, printing the object displays the text <empty>.

Next, I add the five Card objects to my_hand and print it again:

```
my_hand.add(card1)
my_hand.add(card2)
my_hand.add(card3)
my_hand.add(card4)
my_hand.add(card5)
print("\nPrinting my hand after adding 5 cards:")
print(my_hand)
```

This time, the text Ac 2c 3c 4c 5c is displayed.

Then, I create another Hand object, your_hand. Using my_hand's give() method, I transfer the first two cards from my_hand to your_hand. Then, I print both hands:

```
your_hand = Hand()
my_hand.give(card1, your_hand)
my_hand.give(card2, your_hand)
print("\nGave the first two cards from my hand to your hand.")
print("Your hand:")
print(your_hand)
print("My hand:")
print(my_hand)
```

As you'd expect, your_hand is displayed as Ac 2c while my_hand appears as 3c 4c 5c.

Finally, I invoke my_hand's clear() method and print my_hand one last time:

```
my_hand.clear()
print("\nMy hand after clearing it:")
print(my_hand)

input("\n\nPress the enter key to exit.")
```

As it should, the text <empty> is displayed.

USING INHERITANCE TO CREATE NEW CLASSES

One of the key elements of OOP is *inheritance*, which allows you to base a new class on an existing one. By doing so, the new class automatically gets (or inherits) all of the methods and attributes of the existing class—it's like getting all of the work that went into writing the existing class for free!

TRAP   In Python, it's possible to create a new class that directly inherits from more than one class. This is called *multiple inheritance*. But the approach introduces a number of complications. So, as a beginning programmer, it's probably best to avoid multiple inheritance.

EXTENDING A CLASS THROUGH INHERITANCE

Inheritance is especially useful when you want to create a more specialized version of an existing class. As you just learned, by inheriting from an existing class, a new class gets all of the methods and attributes of the existing class. But you can also add methods and attributes to the new class to extend what objects of the new class can do.

For example, imagine that your Drag_Racer class defines a drag racer with methods stop() and go(). You could create a new class for a specialized type of drag racer that can clean its windshield (you get a lot of squashed bugs at 250 miles per hour) by basing it on the existing Drag_Racer class. Your new class would automatically inherit stop() and go() from Drag_Racer. So, all you'd have to do is define one new method for cleaning the windshield and the new class would be done.

Introducing the Playing Cards 2.0 Program

The Playing Cards 2.0 program is based on the Playing Cards program. The new version introduces the Deck class to describe a deck of playing cards. However, unlike any other class you've seen, Deck is based on an existing class, Hand. As a result, Deck automatically inherits all of Hand's methods. I create Deck this way because a deck of cards is really like a specialized hand of cards. It's a hand, but with extra behaviors. A deck can do anything that a hand can. It's a collection of cards. It can give a card to another hand, and so on. On top of that, a deck can do a few things that a hand can't. A deck can be shuffled and it can deal cards to multiple hands. The Playing Cards 2.0 program creates a deck that deals cards to two different hands. Figure 9.5 illustrates the results of the program. Your results when running the program will probably differ from those shown in the figure since the deck is randomly shuffled.

FIGURE 9.5

The Deck class inherits all of the methods of the Hand class.

I'll go through the code one section at a time, but you can find the entire program on the companion website (www.courseptr.com/downloads) in the Chapter 9 folder; the file name is playing_cards2.py.

Creating a Base Class

I begin the new program like the old version. The first two classes, Card and Hand, are the same as before:

```
# Playing Cards 2.0
# Demonstrates inheritance - class extension


class Card(object):
    """ A playing card. """
    RANKS = ["A", "2", "3", "4", "5", "6", "7",
             "8", "9", "10", "J", "Q", "K"]
    SUITS = ["c", "d", "h", "s"]

    def __init__(self, rank, suit):
        self.rank = rank
```

```
        self.suit = suit

    def __str__(self):
        rep = self.rank + self.suit
        return rep

class Hand(object):
    """ A hand of playing cards. """
    def __init__(self):
        self.cards = []

    def __str__(self):
        if self.cards:
            rep = ""
            for card in self.cards:
                rep += str(card) + "\t"
        else:
            rep = "<empty>"
        return rep

    def clear(self):
        self.cards = []

    def add(self, card):
        self.cards.append(card)

    def give(self, card, other_hand):
        self.cards.remove(card)
        other_hand.add(card)
```

Inheriting from a Base Class

The next thing I do is create the Deck class. You can see from the class header that Deck is based on Hand:

```
class Deck(Hand):
```

Hand is called a *base class* because Deck is based on it. Deck is considered a *derived class* because it derives part of its definition from Hand. As a result of this relationship, Deck inherits all of

Hand's methods. So, even if I didn't define a single new method in this class, Deck objects would still have all of the methods defined in Hand:

- __init__()
- __str__()
- clear()
- add()
- give()

If it helps, for this simple example, you can even imagine that you've copied and pasted all of Hand's methods right into Deck because of inheritance.

Extending a Derived Class

You can extend a derived class by defining additional methods in it. That's what I do in the class definition of Deck:

```
""" A deck of playing cards. """
def populate(self):
    for suit in Card.SUITS:
        for rank in Card.RANKS:
            self.add(Card(rank, suit))

def shuffle(self):
    import random
    random.shuffle(self.cards)

def deal(self, hands, per_hand = 1):
    for rounds in range(per_hand):
        for hand in hands:
            if self.cards:
                top_card = self.cards[0]
                self.give(top_card, hand)
            else:
                print("Can't continue deal. Out of cards!")
```

So, in addition to all of the methods that Deck inherits, it has the following new methods:

- populate()
- shuffle()
- deal()

As far as client code is concerned, any `Deck` method is as valid as any other—whether it's inherited from `Hand` or defined in `Deck`. And all of a `Deck` object's methods are invoked the same way, through dot notation.

Using the Derived Class

The first thing I do in the main part of the program is instantiate a new `Deck` object:

```
# main
deck1 = Deck()
```

Looking at the class, you'll notice that I don't define a constructor method in `Deck`. But `Deck` inherits the `Hand` constructor, so that method is automatically invoked with the newly created `Deck` object. As a result, the new `Deck` object gets a `cards` attribute that is initialized to an empty list, just as any newly created `Hand` object would get a similar `cards` attribute. Finally, the assignment statement assigns the new object to `deck1`.

Now armed with a new (but empty) deck, I print it:

```
print("Created a new deck.")
print("Deck:")
print(deck1)
```

I didn't define the special __str__() method in `Deck` either, but again, `Deck` inherits the method from `Hand`. Since the deck is empty, the code displays the text `<empty>`. So far, a deck seems just like a hand. That's because a deck is a specialized type of hand. Remember, a deck can do anything a hand can, plus more.

An empty deck is no fun, so I invoke the object's `populate()` method, which populates the deck with the traditional 52 cards:

```
deck1.populate()
```

Now the deck has finally done something a hand can't. That's because the `populate()` method is a new method that I define in the `Deck` class. The `populate()` method loops through all of the 52 possible combinations of values of `Card.SUITS` and `Card.RANKS` (one for each card in a real deck). For each combination, the method creates a new `Card` object that it adds to the deck.

Next, I print the deck:

```
print("\nPopulated the deck.")
print("Deck:")
print(deck1)
```

This time, all 52 cards are displayed! But if you look closely, you'll see that they're in an obvious order. To make things interesting, I shuffle the deck:

```
deck1.shuffle()
```

I define the `shuffle()` method in `Deck`. It imports the `random` module and then calls the `random.shuffle()` function with the object's `cards` attribute. As you might guess, the `random.shuffle()` method shuffles a list's elements into a random order. So, all of the elements of `cards` get shuffled. Perfect.

Now, with the cards in random order, I display the deck again:

```
print("\nShuffled the deck.")
print("Deck:")
print(deck1)
```

Next, I create two `Hand` objects and put them in a list that I assign to `hands`:

```
my_hand = Hand()
your_hand = Hand()
hands = [my_hand, your_hand]
```

Then, I deal each hand five cards:

```
deck1.deal(hands, per_hand = 5)
```

The `deal()` method is a new method I define in `Deck`. It takes two arguments: a list of hands and the number of cards to deal each hand. The method gives a card from the deck to each hand. If the deck is out of cards, the method prints the message `Can't continue deal. Out of cards!` The method repeats this process for the number of cards to be dealt each hand. So, the previous line of code deals five cards from `deck1` to each hand (`my_hand` and `your_hand`).

To see the results of the deal, I print each hand and the deck once more:

```
print("\nDealt 5 cards to my hand and your hand.")
print("My hand:")
print(my_hand)
print("Your hand:")
print(your_hand)
print("Deck:")
print(deck1)
```

By looking at the output, you can see that each hand has 5 cards and the deck now has only 42.

Finally, I put the deck back to its initial state by clearing it:

```
deck1.clear()
print("\nCleared the deck.")
```

And then I print the deck one last time:

```
print("Deck:", deck1)
input("\n\nPress the enter key to exit.")
```

ALTERING THE BEHAVIOR OF INHERITED METHODS

You've seen how you can extend a class by adding new methods to a derived class. But you can also redefine how an inherited method of a base class works in a derived class. This is known as *overriding* the method. When you override a base class method, you have two choices. You can create a method with completely new functionality, or you can incorporate the functionality of the base class method that you're overriding.

As an example, take your Drag_Racer class again. Let's say that its stop() method simply applies the racer's brakes. If you want to create a new drag racer class that can stop even more quickly (by releasing a parachute behind the racer), you could derive a new Parachute_Racer class from Drag_Racer and override its stop() method. You could write the new stop() method so that it invokes the stop() method of the original Drag_Racer class (which applies the racer's brakes) and then defines the action of the racer releasing a parachute.

Introducing the Playing Cards 3.0 Program

The Playing Cards 3.0 program derives two new classes of playing cards from the Card class you've been working with. The first new class defines cards that can't be printed. More precisely, when you print an object of this class, the text <unprintable> is displayed. The next class defines cards that can be either face up or face down. When you print an object of this class, there are two possible results. If the card is face up, it prints out just like an object of the Card class. But if the card is face down, the text XX is displayed. Figure 9.6 shows a sample run of the program.

FIGURE 9.6

By overriding
the inherited
__str__()
method, objects
of different
derived classes are
printed out
differently.

I'll go through the code one section at a time, but you can find the entire program on the companion website (www.courseptr.com/downloads) in the Chapter 9 folder; the file name is playing_cards3.py.

Creating a Base Class

To derive a new class, you need to start with a base class. For this program, I use the same Card class you've come to know and love:

```python
# Playing Cards 3.0
# Demonstrates inheritance - overriding methods

class Card(object):
    """ A playing card. """
    RANKS = ["A", "2", "3", "4", "5", "6", "7",
             "8", "9", "10", "J", "Q", "K"]
    SUITS = ["c", "d", "h", "s"]

    def __init__(self, rank, suit):
        self.rank = rank
        self.suit = suit

    def __str__(self):
        rep = self.rank + self.suit
        return rep
```

Overriding Base Class Methods

Next, I derive a new class for unprintable cards based on `Card`. The class header looks pretty standard:

```
class Unprintable_Card(Card):
```

From this header, you know that `Unprintable_Card` inherits all of the methods of `Card`. But I can change the behavior of an inherited method by defining it in a derived class. And that's just what I did in the remainder of the method definition:

```
""" A Card that won't reveal its rank or suit when printed. """
def __str__(self):
    return "<unprintable>"
```

The `Unprintable_Card` class inherits the `__str__()` method from `Card`. But I also define a new `__str__()` method in `Unprintable_Card` that overrides (or replaces) the inherited one. Any time you create a method in a derived class with the same name as an inherited method, you override the inherited method in the new class. So, when you print an `Unprintable_Card` object, the text `<unprintable>` is displayed.

A derived class has no effect on a base class. A base class doesn't care if you derive a new class from it, or if you override an inherited method in the new class. The base class still functions as it always has. This means that when you print a `Card` object, it will appear as it always does.

Invoking Base Class Methods

Sometimes when you override the method of a base class, you want to incorporate the inherited method's functionality. For example, I want to create a new type of playing card class based on `Card`. I want an object of this new class to have an attribute that indicates whether or not the card is face up. This means I need to override the inherited constructor method from `Card` with a new constructor that creates a face up attribute. However, I also want my new constructor to create and set `rank` and `suit` attributes, just like the `Card` constructor already does. Instead of retyping the code from the `Card` constructor, I could invoke it from inside my new constructor. Then, it would take care of creating and initializing `rank` and `suit` attributes for an object of my new class. Back in the constructor method of my new class, I could add the attribute that indicates whether or not the card is face up. Well, that's exactly the approach I take in the `Positionable_Card` class:

```
class Positionable_Card(Card):
    """ A Card that can be face up or face down. """
    def __init__(self, rank, suit, face_up = True):
        super(Positionable_Card, self).__init__(rank, suit)
        self.is_face_up = face_up
```

The new function in the constructor, super(), lets you invoke the method of a base class (also called a *superclass*). The line super(Positionable_Card, self).__init__(rank, suit) invokes the __init__() method of Card (the superclass of Positionable_Card). The first argument in the call to super(), Positionable_Card, says that I want to invoke a method of the superclass (or base class) of Positionable_Card, which is Card. The next argument, self, passes a reference to the newly instantiated Positionable_Card object so that code in the Card can get at the object to add the rank and suit attributes to it. The next part of the statement, __init__(rank, suit), tells Python that I want to invoke the constructor method of Card and I want to pass it the values of rank and suit.

The next method in Positionable_Card also overrides a method inherited from Card and invokes the overridden method:

```
def __str__(self):
    if self.is_face_up:
        rep = super(Positionable_Card, self).__str__()
    else:
        rep = "XX"
    return rep
```

This __str__() method first checks to see if an object's face_up attribute is True (which means that the card is face up). If so, the string representation for the card is set to the string returned from Card's __str__() method called with the Positionable_Card object. In other words, if the card is face up, the card prints out like any object of the Card class. However, if the card is not face up, the string representation returned is "XX".

The last method in the class doesn't override an inherited method. It simply extends the definition of this new class:

```
def flip(self):
    self.is_face_up = not self.is_face_up
```

The method flips a card over by toggling the value of an object's face_up attribute. If an object's face_up attribute is True, then invoking the object's flip() method sets the attribute to False. If an object's face_up attribute is False, then invoking the object's flip() method sets the attribute to True.

Using the Derived Classes

In the main part of the program, I create three objects: one from Card, another from Unprintable_Card, and the last from Positionable_Card:

```
#main
card1 = Card("A", "c")
card2 = Unprintable_Card("A", "d")
card3 = Positionable_Card("A", "h")
```

Next, I print the `Card` object:

```
print("Printing a Card object:")
print(card1)
```

This works just like in previous programs, and the text `Ac` is displayed.

The next thing I do is print an `Unprintable_Card` object:

```
print("\nPrinting an Unprintable_Card object:")
print(card2)
```

Even though the object has a `rank` attribute set to `"A"` and a `suit` attribute set to `"d"`, printing the object displays the text `<unprintable>` because the `Unprintable_Card` class overrides its inherited `__str__()` method with one that always returns the string `"<unprintable>"`.

The next two lines print a `Positionable_Card` object:

```
print("\nPrinting a Positionable_Card object:")
print(card3)
```

Since the object's `face_up` attribute is `True`, the object's `__str__()` method invokes `Card`'s `__str__()` method and the text `Ah` is displayed.

Next, I invoke the `Positionable_Card` object's `flip()` method:

```
print("Flipping the Positionable_Card object.")
card3.flip()
```

As a result, the object's `face_up` attribute is set to `False`.

The next two lines print the `Positionable_Card` object again:

```
print("Printing the Positionable_Card object:")
print(card3)

input("\n\nPress the enter key to exit.")
```

This time `XX` is displayed because the object's `face_up` attribute is `False`.

UNDERSTANDING POLYMORPHISM

Polymorphism is the quality of being able to treat different types of things the same and have those things each react in their own way. Used in the context of OOP, polymorphism means that you can send the same message to objects of different classes related by inheritance and achieve different and appropriate results. For example, Unprintable_Card is derived from Card, and when you invoke the __str__() method of an Unprintable_Card object, you get a different result than when you invoke the __str__() method of a Card object. The result of this polymorphic behavior is that you can print an object even if you don't know whether it's an Unprintable_Card or a Card object. Regardless of the class of the object, when printed, its __str__() method is invoked and the correct string representation of it is displayed.

CREATING MODULES

You first learned about modules in Chapter 3, in the section "Importing the random Module," where you met the random module. But a powerful aspect of Python programming is that you can create, use, and even share your own modules. Creating your own modules provides important benefits.

First, by creating your own modules, you can reuse code, which can save you time and effort. For example, you could reuse the Card, Hand, and Deck classes you've seen so far to create many different types of card games without having to reinvent basic card, deck, and hand functionality every time.

Second, by breaking up a program into logical modules, large programs become easier to manage. So far, the programs you've been working with have been contained in one file. Since they've been pretty short, this is no big deal. But imagine a program that's thousands (or even tens of thousands) of lines long. Working with a program of this size in one, massive file would be a real nightmare (professional projects, by the way, can easily get this large). Breaking up code into modules also makes it easier for members of a software engineering team to each tackle distinct parts of a project.

Third, by creating modules, you can share your genius. If you create a useful module, you can e-mail it to a friend, who then can use it much like any built-in Python module.

Introducing the Simple Game Program

The Simple Game program, as the name suggests, is simple. The program first asks how many players want to participate and then proceeds to get each player's name. Finally, the program assigns a random score to each player and displays the results. Not very thrilling, but the point of the program is not the game, but rather how the game works. The program uses a brand-new module with functions and a class that I created. Figure 9.7 displays the results of the program.

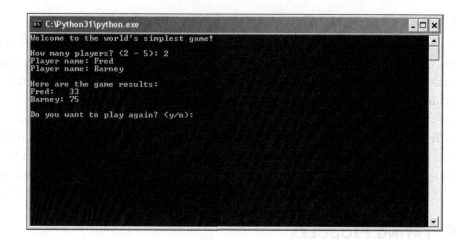

FIGURE 9.7

Several functions
and a class used in
the program are
from a
programmer-
created module.

Writing Modules

Normally, I'd show you the code for the next program, Simple Game, but in this section, I go over the module I've written that Simple Game uses.

You create a module the same way you write any other Python program. When you create a module, though, you should build a collection of related programming components, such as functions and classes, and store them in a single file to be imported into a new program.

I created a basic module, called games, that contains two functions and a class that might be useful in creating a game. You can find the code on the companion website (www.courseptr.com/downloads) in the Chapter 9 folder; the file name is games.py.

```
# Games
# Demonstrates module creation

class Player(object):
    """ A player for a game. """
    def __init__(self, name, score = 0):
        self.name = name
        self.score = score

    def __str__(self):
        rep = self.name + ":\t" + str(self.score)
        return rep

def ask_yes_no(question):
```

```
    """Ask a yes or no question."""
    response = None
    while response not in ("y", "n"):
        response = input(question).lower()
    return response

def ask_number(question, low, high):
    """Ask for a number within a range."""
    response = None
    while response not in range(low, high):
        response = int(input(question))
    return response


if __name__ == "__main__":
    print("You ran this module directly (and did not 'import' it).")
    input("\n\nPress the enter key to exit.")
```

This module is named games because I saved the file with the name games.py. Programmer-created modules are named (and imported) based on their file names.

The bulk of the module is straightforward. The Player class defines an object with two attributes, name and score, which are set in the constructor method. There's only one other method, __str__(), which returns a string representation so that objects can be printed.

You've seen the next two functions, ask_yes_no() and ask_number(), before in Chapter 6, in the "The ask_yes_no() Function" and the "The ask_number() Function" sections.

The next part of the program introduces a new idea, related to modules. The condition of the if statement, __name__ == "__main__", is true if the program is run directly. It's false if the file is imported as a module. So, if the games.py file is run directly, a message is displayed telling the user that the file is meant to be imported and not directly run.

Importing Modules

Now that you've seen the games module, I'll introduce the code of the Simple Game program. I'll go through the code one section at a time, but you can find the entire program on the companion website (www.courseptr.com/downloads) in the Chapter 9 folder; the file name is simple_game.py.

```
# Simple Game
# Demonstrates importing modules

import games, random
```

You import a programmer-created module the same way you import a built-in module, with the `import` statement. In fact, I import the `games` module along with the familiar `random` module in the same `import` statement.

TRAP

If a programmer-created module isn't in the same directory as the program that imports it, Python won't be able to find the module. There are ways around this. It's even possible to install a programmer-created module so that it's available system-wide, just like built-in modules, but this requires a special installation procedure that's beyond the scope of this book. So for now, make sure that any module you want to import is in the same directory as the programs that import it.

Using Imported Functions and Classes

I use the imported modules in the remainder of the Simple Game program. After welcoming the players and setting up a simple loop, I ask how many players there will be in the game:

```
print("Welcome to the world's simplest game!\n")

again = None
while again != "n":
    players = []
num = games.ask_number(question = "How many players? (2 - 5): ", low = 2, high = 5)
```

I get the number of players by calling the `ask_number()` function from the `games` module. Just as with other imported modules, to call a function I use dot notation, specifying first the module name, followed by the function name.

Next, for each player, I get the player's name and generate a random score between 1 and 100 by calling the `randrange()` function from the `random` module. Then, I create a player object using this name and score. Since the `Player` class is defined in the `games` module, again I use dot notation and include the module name before the class name. Then, I append this new player object to a list of players.

```
    for i in range(num):
        name = input("Player name: ")
```

```
        score = random.randrange(100) + 1
        player = games.Player(name, score)
        players.append(player)
```

Next, I print each player in the game:

```
    print("\nHere are the game results:")
    for player in players:
        print(player)
```

Finally, I ask if the players want to play another game. I use the ask_yes_no() function from the games module to obtain my answer:

```
    again = games.ask_yes_no("\nDo you want to play again? (y/n): ")
```

```
input("\n\nPress the enter key to exit.")
```

BACK TO THE BLACKJACK GAME

At this point, you're an expert in using Python classes to create playing cards, hands, and decks. So now it's time to build on that expertise and see how to combine these classes in a larger program to create a complete, casino-style card game (tacky green felt not included).

The cards Module

To write the Blackjack game, I created a final cards module based on the Playing Cards programs. The Hand and Deck classes are exactly the same as those in the Playing Cards 2.0 program. The new Card class represents the same functionality as the Positionable_Card from the Playing Cards 3.0 program. You can find the code for the program on the companion website (www.courseptr.com/downloads) in the Chapter 9 folder; the file name is cards.py.

```
# Cards Module
# Basic classes for a game with playing cards

class Card(object):
    """ A playing card. """
    RANKS = ["A", "2", "3", "4", "5", "6", "7",
             "8", "9", "10", "J", "Q", "K"]
    SUITS = ["c", "d", "h", "s"]

    def __init__(self, rank, suit, face_up = True):
        self.rank = rank
```

```python
        self.suit = suit
        self.is_face_up = face_up

    def __str__(self):
        if self.is_face_up:
            rep = self.rank + self.suit
        else:
            rep = "XX"
        return rep

    def flip(self):
        self.is_face_up = not self.is_face_up


class Hand(object):
    """ A hand of playing cards. """
    def __init__(self):
        self.cards = []

    def __str__(self):
        if self.cards:
            rep = ""
            for card in self.cards:
                rep += str(card) + "\t"
        else:
            rep = "<empty>"
        return rep

    def clear(self):
        self.cards = []

    def add(self, card):
        self.cards.append(card)

    def give(self, card, other_hand):
        self.cards.remove(card)
        other_hand.add(card)
```

```
class Deck(Hand):
    """ A deck of playing cards. """
    def populate(self):
        for suit in Card.SUITS:
            for rank in Card.RANKS:
                self.add(Card(rank, suit))

    def shuffle(self):
        import random
        random.shuffle(self.cards)

    def deal(self, hands, per_hand = 1):
        for rounds in range(per_hand):
            for hand in hands:
                if self.cards:
                    top_card = self.cards[0]
                    self.give(top_card, hand)
                else:
                    print("Can't continue deal. Out of cards!")



if __name__ == "__main__":
    print("This is a module with classes for playing cards.")
    input("\n\nPress the enter key to exit.")
```

Designing the Classes

Before you start coding a project with multiple classes, it can help to map them out on paper. You might make a list and include a brief description of each class. Table 9.1 shows my first pass at such a listing for the Blackjack game.

You should try to include all of the classes you think you'll need, but don't worry about making your class descriptions complete, because invariably they won't be (mine aren't). But making such a list should help you get a good overview of the types of objects you'll be working with in your project.

In addition to describing your classes in words, you might want to draw a family tree of sorts to visualize how your classes are related. That's what I did in Figure 9.8.

TABLE 9.1	BLACKJACK CLASSES	
Class	**Base Class**	**Description**
BJ_Card	cards.Card	A blackjack playing card. Define an attribute value to represent the point value of a card.
BJ_Deck	cards.Deck	A blackjack deck. A collection of BJ_Card objects.
BJ_Hand	cards.Hand	A blackjack hand. Define an attribute total to represent the point total of a hand. Define an attribute name to represent the owner of the hand.
BJ_Player	BJ_Hand	A blackjack player.
BJ_Dealer	BJ_Hand	A blackjack dealer.
BJ_Game	object	A blackjack game. Define an attribute deck for a BJ_Deck object. Define an attribute dealer for a BJ_Dealer object. Define an attribute players for a list of BJ_Player objects.

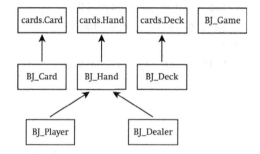

FIGURE 9.8

Inheritance hierarchy of classes for the Blackjack game.

A class hierarchy diagram, like the one in Figure 9.8, can give you a summary view of how you're using inheritance.

Writing Pseudocode for the Game Loop

The next thing I did in planning the game was write some pseudocode for the play of one round. I thought this would help me see how objects will interact. Here's the pseudocode I came up with:

```
Deal each player and dealer initial 2 cards
For each player
    While the player asks for a hit and the player is not busted
        Deal the player an additional card
If there are no players still playing
    Show the dealer's 2 cards
```

```
Otherwise
    While the dealer must hit and the dealer is not busted
        Deal the dealer an additional card
    If the dealer is busted
        For each player who is still playing
            The player wins
    Otherwise
        For each player who is still playing
            If the player's total is greater than the dealer's total
                The player wins
            Otherwise, if the player's total is less than the dealer's total
                The player loses
            Otherwise
                The player pushes
```

Importing the cards and games Modules

Now that you've seen the planning, it's time to check out the code. In the first part of the Blackjack program, I import the two modules, cards and games. I'll go through the code one section at a time, but you can find the entire program on the companion website (www.courseptr.com/downloads) in the Chapter 9 folder; the file name is blackjack.py.

```
# Blackjack
# From 1 to 7 players compete against a dealer


import cards, games
```

I created the games module, you'll remember, in the Simple Game program, earlier in this chapter.

The BJ_Card Class

The BJ_Card class extends the definition of what a card is by inheriting from cards.Card. In BJ_Card, I create a new property, value, for the point value of a card:

```
class BJ_Card(cards.Card):
    """ A Blackjack Card. """
    ACE_VALUE = 1

    @property
    def value(self):
```

```
if self.is_face_up:
    v = BJ_Card.RANKS.index(self.rank) + 1
    if v > 10:
        v = 10
else:
    v = None
return v
```

The method returns a number between 1 and 10, which represents the value of a blackjack card. The first part of the calculation is computed through the expression BJ_Card.RANKS.index (self.rank) + 1. This expression takes the rank attribute of an object (say "6") and finds its corresponding index number in BJ_Card.RANKS through the list method index() (for "6" this would be 5). Finally, 1 is added to the result since the computer starts counting at 0 (this makes the value calculated from "6" the correct 6). However, since rank attributes of "J", "Q", and "K" result in numbers larger than 10, any value greater than 10 is set to 10. If an object's face_up attribute is False, this whole process is skipped and a value of None is returned.

The BJ_Deck Class

The BJ_Deck class is used to create a deck of blackjack cards. The class is almost exactly the same as its base class, cards.Deck. The only difference is that I override cards.Deck's populate() method so that a new BJ_Deck object gets populated with BJ_Card objects:

```
class BJ_Deck(cards.Deck):
    """ A Blackjack Deck. """
    def populate(self):
        for suit in BJ_Card.SUITS:
            for rank in BJ_Card.RANKS:
                self.cards.append(BJ_Card(rank, suit))
```

The BJ_Hand Class

The BJ_Hand class, based on cards.Hand, is used for blackjack hands. I override the cards.Hand constructor and add a name attribute to represent the name of the hand owner:

```
class BJ_Hand(cards.Hand):
    """ A Blackjack Hand. """
    def __init__(self, name):
        super(BJ_Hand, self).__init__()
        self.name = name
```

Next, I override the inherited __str__() method to display the total point value of the hand:

```
def __str__(self):
    rep = self.name + ":\t" + super(BJ_Hand, self).__str__()
    if self.total:
        rep += "(" + str(self.total) + ")"
    return rep
```

I concatenate the object's name attribute with the string returned from the cards.Hand __str__() method for the object. Then, if the object's total property isn't None, I concatenate the string representation of the value of total. Finally, I return that string.

Next, I create a property called total, which represents the total point value of a blackjack hand. If a blackjack hand has a facedown card in it, then its total property is None. Otherwise, the value is calculated by adding the point values of all the cards in the hand.

```
@property
def total(self):
    # if a card in the hand has value of None, then total is None
    for card in self.cards:
        if not card.value:
            return None

    # add up card values, treat each Ace as 1
    t = 0
    for card in self.cards:
        t += card.value

    # determine if hand contains an Ace
    contains_ace = False
    for card in self.cards:
        if card.value == BJ_Card.ACE_VALUE:
            contains_ace = True

    # if hand contains Ace and total is low enough, treat Ace as 11
    if contains_ace and t <= 11:
        # add only 10 since we've already added 1 for the Ace
        t += 10

    return t
```

The first part of this method checks to see if any card in the blackjack hand has a value property equal to None (which would mean that the card is face down). If so, the method returns None. The next part of the method simply sums the point values of all the cards in the hand. The next part determines if the hand contains an ace. If so, the last part of the method determines if the card's point value should be 11 or 1.

The last method in BJ_Hand is is_busted(). It returns True if the object's total property is greater than 21. Otherwise, it returns False.

```
def is_busted(self):
    return self.total > 21
```

Notice that in this method, I return the result of the condition self.total > 21 instead of assigning the result to a variable and then returning that variable. You can create this kind of return statement with any condition (any expression actually) and it often results in a more elegant method.

This kind of method, which returns either True or False, is pretty common. It's often used (like here) to represent a condition of an object with two possibilities, such as "on" or "off," for example. This type of method almost always has a name that starts with the word "is," as in is_on().

The BJ_Player Class

The BJ_Player class, derived from BJ_Hand, is used for blackjack players:

```
class BJ_Player(BJ_Hand):
    """ A Blackjack Player. """
    def is_hitting(self):
        response = games.ask_yes_no("\n" + self.name + ", do you want a hit? (Y/N): ")
        return response == "y"

    def bust(self):
        print(self.name, "busts.")
        self.lose()

    def lose(self):
        print(self.name, "loses.")

    def win(self):
        print(self.name, "wins.")
```

```
def push(self):
    print(self.name, "pushes.")
```

The first method, is_hitting(), returns True if the player wants another hit and returns False if the player doesn't. The bust() method announces that a player busts and invokes the object's lose() method. The lose() method announces that a player loses. The win() method announces that a player wins. And the push() method announces that a player pushes. The bust(), lose(), win(), and push() methods are so simple that you may wonder why they exist. I put them in the class because they form a great skeleton structure to handle the more complex issues that arise when players are allowed to bet (which they will, when you complete one of the chapter challenges at the end of the chapter).

The BJ_Dealer Class

The BJ_Dealer class, derived from BJ_Hand, is used for the game's blackjack dealer:

```
class BJ_Dealer(BJ_Hand):
    """ A Blackjack Dealer. """
    def is_hitting(self):
        return self.total < 17

    def bust(self):
        print(self.name, "busts.")

    def flip_first_card(self):
        first_card = self.cards[0]
        first_card.flip()
```

The first method, is_hitting(), represents whether or not the dealer is taking additional cards. Since a dealer must hit on any hand totaling 17 or less, the method returns True if the object's total property is less than 17; otherwise, it returns False. The bust() method announces that the dealer busts. The flip_first_card() method turns over the dealer's first card.

The BJ_Game Class

The BJ_Game class is used to create a single object that represents a blackjack game. The class contains the code for the main game loop in its play() method. However, the mechanics of the game are complex enough that I create a few elements outside the method, including an __additional_cards() method that takes care of dealing additional cards to a player and a still_playing property that returns a list of all players still playing in the round.

The __init__() Method

The constructor receives a list of names and creates a player for each name. The method also creates a dealer and a deck.

```python
class BJ_Game(object):
    """ A Blackjack Game. """
    def __init__(self, names):
        self.players = []
        for name in names:
            player = BJ_Player(name)
            self.players.append(player)

        self.dealer = BJ_Dealer("Dealer")

        self.deck = BJ_Deck()
        self.deck.populate()
        self.deck.shuffle()
```

The still_playing Property

The `still_playing` property returns a list of all the players that are still playing (those that haven't busted this round):

```python
    @property
    def still_playing(self):
        sp = []
        for player in self.players:
            if not player.is_busted():
                sp.append(player)
        return sp
```

The __additional_cards() Method

The `__additional_cards()` method deals additional cards to either a player or the dealer. The method receives an object into its `player` parameter, which can be either a `BJ_Player` or `BJ_Dealer` object. The method continues while the object's `is_busted()` method returns `False` and its `is_hitting()` method returns `True`. If the object's `is_busted()` method returns `True`, then the object's `bust()` method is invoked.

```python
    def __additional_cards(self, player):
        while not player.is_busted() and player.is_hitting():
            self.deck.deal([player])
```

```
        print(player)
        if player.is_busted():
            player.bust()
```

Polymorphism is at work here in two method calls. The `player.is_hitting()` method call works equally well whether `player` refers to a `BJ_Player` object or a `BJ_Dealer` object. The `__additional_cards()` method never has to know which type of object it's working with. The same is true in the line `player.bust()`. Since both classes, `BJ_Player` and `BJ_Dealer`, each defines its own `bust()` method, the line creates the desired result in either case.

The play() Method

The `play()` method is where the game loop is defined and bears a striking resemblance to the pseudocode I introduced earlier:

```
def play(self):
    # deal initial 2 cards to everyone
    self.deck.deal(self.players + [self.dealer], per_hand = 2)
    self.dealer.flip_first_card()    # hide dealer's first card
    for player in self.players:
        print(player)
    print(self.dealer)

    # deal additional cards to players
    for player in self.players:
        self.__additional_cards(player)

    self.dealer.flip_first_card()    # reveal dealer's first

    if not self.still_playing:
        # since all players have busted, just show the dealer's hand
        print(self.dealer)
    else:
        # deal additional cards to dealer
        print(self.dealer)
        self.__additional_cards(self.dealer)

        if self.dealer.is_busted():
            # everyone still playing wins
            for player in self.still_playing:
```

```
                    player.win()
        else:
            # compare each player still playing to dealer
            for player in self.still_playing:
                if player.total > self.dealer.total:
                    player.win()
                elif player.total < self.dealer.total:
                    player.lose()
                else:
                    player.push()

    # remove everyone's cards
    for player in self.players:
        player.clear()
    self.dealer.clear()
```

Each player and dealer is dealt the initial two cards. The dealer's first card is flipped to hide its value. Next, all of the hands are displayed. Then, each player is given cards as long as the player requests additional cards and hasn't busted. If all players have busted, the dealer's first card is flipped and the dealer's hand is printed. Otherwise, play continues. The dealer gets cards as long as the dealer's hand total is less than 17. If the dealer busts, all remaining players win. Otherwise, each remaining player's hand is compared with the dealer's. If the player's total is greater than the dealer's, the player wins. If the player's total is less, the player loses. If the two totals are equal, the player pushes.

The main() Function

The main() function gets the names of all the players, puts them in a list, and creates a BJ_Game object, using the list as an argument. Next, the function invokes the object's play() method and will continue to do so until the players no longer want to play.

```
def main():
    print("\t\tWelcome to Blackjack!\n")

    names = []
    number = games.ask_number("How many players? (1 - 7): ", low = 1, high = 8)
    for i in range(number):
        name = input("Enter player name: ")
        names.append(name)
```

```
    print()

    game = BJ_Game(names)

    again = None
    while again != "n":
        game.play()
        again = games.ask_yes_no("\nDo you want to play again?: ")


main()
input("\n\nPress the enter key to exit.")
```

SUMMARY

This chapter introduced you to the world of OOP. You saw how to send messages between objects. You learned how to combine objects together to form more complex objects. You were introduced to inheritance, the process of creating new classes based on existing ones. You saw how to extend a derived class by adding new methods. You also saw how to override inherited methods. You learned how to write and import your own modules. You were shown an example of how to sketch out your classes before you begin a project. And finally, you saw all of these concepts come together in the creation of a multiplayer, casino-style card game.

CHALLENGES

1. Add some much-needed error checking to the Blackjack game. Before a new round begins, make sure that the deck has enough cards. If not, repopulate and reshuffle it. Find other places where you could add error checking and create the necessary safeguards.
2. Write a one-card version of the game war, where each player gets a single card and the player with the highest card wins.
3. Improve the Blackjack project by allowing players to bet. Keep track of each player's bankroll and remove any player who runs out of money.
4. Create a simple adventure game using objects, where a player can travel between various, connected locations.

GUI Development: The Mad Lib Program

So far, all the programs you've seen have used plain old text to interact with the user. But there are more sophisticated ways to present and accept information. A graphical user interface (GUI) provides a visual way for a user to interact with the computer. The most popular home operating systems all employ a GUI, making user interactions simpler and more consistent. In this chapter, you'll learn to create GUIs. Specifically, you'll learn to do the following:

- Work with a GUI toolkit
- Create and fill frames
- Create and use buttons
- Create and use text entries and text boxes
- Create and use check buttons
- Create and use radio buttons

Introducing the Mad Lib Program

The chapter project, the Mad Lib program, asks for the user's help in creating a story. The user supplies the name of a person, a plural noun, and a verb. The user can also choose from several adjectives and may select one body part. The program takes all of this information and uses it to create a story. Figures 10.1 through 10.3 show off the program. As you can see, the Mad Lib program uses a GUI to interact with the user.

FIGURE 10.1

A nicely laid-out
GUI awaits the
user's creativity.

FIGURE 10.2

The user has
entered all of the
necessary
information.

FIGURE 10.3

After clicking the
Click for story
button, the text
box displays the
literary
masterpiece.

EXAMINING A GUI

Before I describe how to program a GUI, I want to define all of the GUI elements you'll meet in this chapter. Figure 10.4 shows off the Mad Lib program, though this time the various elements are labeled.

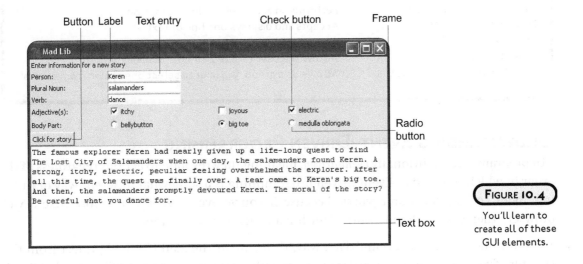

FIGURE 10.4

You'll learn to create all of these GUI elements.

To create a GUI with Python, you need to use a GUI toolkit. There are many to pick from, but I use Tkinter, a popular cross-platform toolkit, in this chapter.

If you're running an operating system other than Windows, you may need to download and install additional software to use the Tkinter toolkit. To find out more, visit the Python website's Tkinter page at http://www.python.org/topics/tkinter.

You create GUI elements by instantiating objects from classes of the tkinter module, which is part of the Tkinter toolkit. Table 10.1 describes each GUI element from Figure 10.4 and lists its corresponding tkinter class.

There's no need to memorize all of these tkinter classes. I just want to give you an overview of the classes that you learn about in this chapter.

TABLE 10.1		SELECTED GUI ELEMENTS
Element	**tkinter**	**Class Description**
Frame	Frame	Holds other GUI elements
Label	Label	Displays uneditable text or icons
Button	Button	Performs an action when the user activates it
Text entry	Entry	Accepts and displays one line of text
Text box	Text	Accepts and displays multiple lines of text
Check button	Checkbutton	Allows the user to select or not select an option
Radio button	Radiobutton	Allows, as a group, the user to select one option from several

UNDERSTANDING EVENT-DRIVEN PROGRAMMING

GUI programs are traditionally *event-driven*, meaning they respond to actions regardless of the order in which they occur. Event-driven programming is a somewhat different way of thinking about coding. But don't worry, because if you've ever used a GUI before (like a web browser), then you've already worked within an event-driven system.

To better understand the event-driven way, think about the Mad Lib final project from this chapter. If you were to write a similar program with your current Python skills, you'd probably ask the user a series of questions with the input() function. You might ask for the name of a person, followed by a plural noun, followed by a verb, and so on. As a result, the user would have to provide each piece of information, in order. But, if you were to write the program in an event-driven way, say with a GUI, the user could enter the information in any order. Also, the timing of when the program actually generates the story would be up to the user as well.

When you write an event-driven program, you *bind* (associate) *events* (things that can happen involving the program's objects) with *event handlers* (code that runs when the events occur). As a concrete example, think about the Mad Lib chapter project again. When the user clicks the Click for story button (the event), the program invokes a method that displays the story (the event handler). In order for this to happen, I have to associate the button click with the story-telling method (I bind the two with each other).

By defining all of your objects, events, and event handlers, you establish how your program works. Then, you kick off the program by entering an *event loop*, where the program waits for the events that you've described to occur. When any of those events do occur, the program handles them, just as you've laid out.

Don't worry if this somewhat different way of thinking about programming isn't completely clear yet. After seeing a few working examples, you'll understand how to devise event-driven programs of your own.

USING A ROOT WINDOW

The foundation of your GUI program is its root window, upon which you add all other GUI elements. If you think of your GUI as a tree, then the root window is, well, the root. Your tree can branch out in all directions, but every part of it is, directly or indirectly, anchored by the root.

Introducing the Simple GUI Program

The Simple GUI program creates about the simplest GUI possible: a single window. Figure 10.5 shows the results of the program.

FIGURE 10.5

The program creates only a lone window. Hey, you have to start somewhere.

Running a Tkinter program directly from IDLE will cause either your program or IDLE to lock up. The simplest solution is to run your Tkinter program directly. In Windows, you can do this simply by double-clicking your program's icon.

Although you can run a Tkinter program by double-clicking its icon, you'll have a problem if the program contains an error—your console window will close before you can read the error message. Under Windows, you can create a batch file that runs your program and pauses once the program ends, keeping the console window open so you can see any error messages. For example, if your program is simple_gui.py, just create a batch file comprised of the two lines:

```
simple_gui.py
pause
```

Then run the batch file by double-clicking its icon.

To create a batch file:

1. Open a text editor like Notepad (not Word or WordPad)
2. Type your text
3. Save the file with a .bat extension (such as simple_gui.bat) and make sure there is no .txt extension after the .bat

I've created batch files for all of the programs in this chapter. You can find them on the companion website (www.courseptr.com/downloads) in the Chapter 10 folder, along with the chapter programs.

In addition to the window pictured in Figure 10.5, Simple GUI may generate another window (depending upon your operating system): the familiar console window, pictured in Figure 10.6.

FIGURE 10.6

A GUI program can generate a console window too.

Although you may think that this console window is just an eyesore, marring your otherwise perfect GUI, don't be so quick to dismiss it. The console window can provide valuable feedback if (and when) your Tkinter program produces errors. Also, don't close the console window, because that will close your GUI program along with it.

Once you get your GUI programming running perfectly, you may want to suppress its accompanying console window. On a Windows machine, the easiest way to do this is to change the extension of your program from py to pyw.

You can find the code for the program on the companion website (www.courseptr.com/ downloads) in the Chapter 10 folder; the file name is simple_gui.py.

Importing the tkinter Module

Finally, it's time to get your hands dirty with some code! The first thing I do in the Simple GUI program is import the `tkinter` module:

```
# Simple GUI
# Demonstrates creating a window

from tkinter import *
```

The previous code imports all of `tkinter` directly into the program's global scope. Normally, you want to avoid doing something like this; however, a few modules, like `tkinter`, are designed to be imported in this way. You'll see just how this helps in the next line of code.

Creating a Root Window

To create a root window, I instantiate an object of the `tkinter` class `Tk`:

```
# create the root window
root = Tk()
```

Notice, though, that I didn't have to prefix the module name, `tkinter`, to the class name, `Tk`. In fact, I can now directly access any part of the `tkinter` module, without having to use the module name. Since most `tkinter` programs involve many references to classes and constants in the module, this saves a lot of typing and makes code easier to read.

 TRAP   You can have only one root window in a Tkinter program. If you create more than one, you're bound to freeze up your program as both root windows fight for control.

Modifying a Root Window

Next, I modify the root window using a few of its methods:

```
# modify the window
root.title("Simple GUI")
root.geometry("200x100")
```

The `title()` method sets the title of the root window. All you have to do is pass the title you want displayed as a string. I set the title so that the text `Simple GUI` appears in the window's title bar.

The `geometry()` method sets the size of the root window, in pixels. The method takes a string (and not integers) that represents the window's width and height, separated by the "x" character. I set the window's width to 200 and its height to 100.

Entering a Root Window's Event Loop

Finally, I start up the window's event loop by invoking `root`'s `mainloop()` method:

```
# kick off the window's event loop
root.mainloop()
```

As a result, the window stays open, waiting to handle events. Since I haven't defined any events, the window doesn't do much. But it is a full-fledged window that you can resize, minimize, and close. Feel free to give it a test drive by double-clicking the batch file's icon.

USING LABELS

GUI elements are called *widgets* (short for "window gadgets"). Probably the simplest widget is the `Label` widget, which is uneditable text or icons (or both). A `Label` widget labels part of a GUI. It's often used to label other widgets. Unlike most other widgets, labels aren't interactive. A user can't click on a label (alright, a user can, but the label won't do anything). Still, labels are important and you'll probably use at least one every time you create a GUI.

Introducing the Labeler Program

The Labeler program creates a root window and adds a label to it. The `Label` widget simply declares that it is a label. Figure 10.7 illustrates the program.

FIGURE 10.7

A label can provide information about a GUI.

You can find the code for the program on the companion website (www.courseptr.com/downloads) in the Chapter 10 folder; the file name is labeler.py.

Setting Up the Program

First, I set up the Labeler program by importing `tkinter` and creating a root window:

```
# Labeler
# Demonstrates a label
```

```
from tkinter import *

# create the root window
root = Tk()
root.title("Labeler")
root.geometry("200x50")
```

Creating a Frame

A `Frame` is a widget that can hold other widgets (such as `Label` widgets). A frame is like the cork in a corkboard; you use it as a base on which to place other things. So, I create a new frame:

```
# create a frame in the window to hold other widgets
app = Frame(root)
```

Any time you create a new widget, you must pass its *master* (the thing that will contain the widget) to the constructor of the new object. Here, I pass `root` to the `Frame` constructor. As a result, the new frame is placed inside the root window.

Next, I invoke the `grid()` method of the new object:

```
app.grid()
```

`grid()` is a method that all widgets have. It's associated with a *layout manager,* which lets you arrange widgets. To keep things simple, I save the discussion of layout managers for a bit later in this chapter.

Creating a Label

I create a `Label` widget by instantiating an object of the `Label` class:

```
# create a label in the frame
lbl = Label(app, text = "I'm a label!")
```

By passing `app` to the `Label` object's constructor, I make the frame that `app` refers to the master of the `Label` widget. As a result, the label is placed in the frame.

Widgets have options that you can set. Many of these options affect how the widget appears. By passing the string `"I'm a label!"` to the `text` parameter, I set the widget's `text` option to that string. As a result, the text `I'm a label!` appears when the label is displayed.

Next, I invoke the object's `grid()` method:

```
lbl.grid()
```

This ensures that the label will be visible.

Entering the Root Window's Event Loop

Last, but not least, I invoke the root window's event loop to start up the GUI:

```
# kick off the window's event loop
root.mainloop()
```

USING BUTTONS

A `Button` widget can be activated by the user to perform some action. Since you already know how to create labels, learning how to create buttons will be pretty easy.

Introducing the Lazy Buttons Program

In the Lazy Buttons program, I create several buttons that don't do anything when activated. This is sort of like installing a new light fixture before wiring it. The fixture is put into place, but not yet functional. Figure 10.8 illustrates the program.

FIGURE 10.8

You can click these lazy buttons all you want; they won't do a thing.

You can find the code for the program on the companion website (www.courseptr.com/downloads) in the Chapter 10 folder; the file name is lazy_buttons.py.

Setting Up the Program

First, I set up the program by importing `tkinter` and creating a root window and a frame:

```
# Lazy Buttons
# Demonstrates creating buttons

from tkinter import *

# create a root window
root = Tk()
root.title("Lazy Buttons")
root.geometry("200x85")
```

```
# create a frame in the window to hold other widgets
app = Frame(root)
app.grid()
```

Creating Buttons

You create a Button widget by instantiating an object of the Button class. That's what I did in the next lines:

```
# create a button in the frame
bttn1 = Button(app, text = "I do nothing!")
bttn1.grid()
```

These lines create a new button with the text I do nothing! The button's master is the frame I created earlier, which means that the button is placed in the frame.

The tkinter module offers flexibility when it comes to creating, defining, and altering widgets. You can create a widget and set all of its options in one line (like I've been doing), or you can create a widget and set or alter its options later. I'll show you what I mean with the next button. First, I create a new button:

```
# create a second button in the frame
bttn2 = Button(app)
bttn2.grid()
```

Notice though that the only value I pass to the object's constructor is app, the button's master. So, all I've done is add a blank button to the frame. However, I can fix that. I can modify a widget after I create it, using the object's configure() method:

```
bttn2.configure(text = "Me too!")
```

This line sets the text option of the button to the string "Me too!", which puts the text Me too! on the button.

You can use a widget's configure() method for any widget option (and any type of widget). You can even use the method to change an option that you've already set.

Next, I create a third button:

```
# create a third button in the frame
bttn3 = Button(app)
bttn3.grid()
```

Then, I set the button's text option, using a different interface:

```
bttn3["text"] = "Same here!"
```

I access the button's text option through a dictionary-like interface. I set the text option to the string "Same here!", which puts the text Same here! on the button. When you set the value of an option using this type of dictionary-style access, the key for the option is the name of the option as a string.

Entering the Root Window's Event Loop

As always, I invoke the root window's event loop to start up the GUI:

```
# kick off the window's event loop
root.mainloop()
```

CREATING A GUI USING A CLASS

As you've learned in other chapters, organizing your code into classes can make your programming life a lot easier. It's often beneficial to write larger GUI programs by defining your own classes. So next, I show you how to write a GUI program by organizing the code with a class.

Introducing the Lazy Buttons 2 Program

The Lazy Buttons 2 program is simply the Lazy Buttons program rewritten using a class. The program appears exactly the same to the user, but behind the scenes I've done some restructuring. Figure 10.9 shows the ever-so-familiar program in action.

FIGURE 10.9

It's déjà vu all over again. The program looks the same as its predecessor even though there are significant changes under the hood.

You can find the code for the program on the companion website (www.courseptr.com/downloads) in the Chapter 10 folder; the file name is lazy_buttons2.py.

Importing the tkinter Module

Though there are significant structural changes to the program, importing the GUI module is still the same:

```
# Lazy Buttons 2
# Demonstrates using a class with tkinter

from tkinter import *
```

Defining the Application Class

Next, I create a new class, Application, based on Frame:

```
class Application(Frame):
    """ A GUI application with three buttons. """
```

Instead of instantiating a Frame object, I'll end up instantiating an Application object to hold all of the buttons. This works since an Application object is just a specialized type of Frame object.

Defining a Constructor Method

Next, I define Application's constructor:

```
    def __init__(self, master):
        """ Initialize the Frame. """
        super(Application, self).__init__(master)
        self.grid()
        self.create_widgets()
```

The first thing I do is call the superclass constructor. I pass along the Application object's master, so it gets properly set as the master. Finally, I invoke the Application object's create_widgets() method, which I define next.

Defining a Method to Create the Widgets

I define a method that creates all three buttons, create_widgets():

```
    def create_widgets(self):
        """ Create three buttons that do nothing. """
        # create first button
        self.bttn1 = Button(self, text = "I do nothing! ")
        self.bttn1.grid()

        # create second button
        self.bttn2 = Button(self)
        self.bttn2.grid()
```

```
    self.bttn2.configure(text = "Me too!")

    # create third button
    self.bttn3 = Button(self)
    self.bttn3.grid()
    self.bttn3["text"] =  "Same here! "
```

The code looks pretty similar to the code that creates the buttons in the original Lazy Buttons program. An important difference is that `bttn1`, `bttn2`, and `bttn3` are attributes of an `Application` object. Another important difference is that I use `self` as the master for the buttons so that the `Application` object is their master.

Creating the Application Object

In the main section of code, I create a root window and give it a title and a proper size:

```
# main
root = Tk()
root.title("Lazy Buttons 2")
root.geometry("200x85")
```

Then, I instantiate an `Application` object with the root window as its master:

```
app = Application(root)
```

This code creates an `Application` object with the root window as its master. The `Application` object's constructor invokes the object's `create_widgets()` method. This method then creates the three buttons, with the `Application` object as their master.

Finally, I invoke the root window's event loop to kick off the GUI and keep it running:

```
root.mainloop()
```

BINDING WIDGETS AND EVENT HANDLERS

So far, the GUI programs you've seen don't do a whole lot. That's because there's no code associated with the activation of their widgets. Again, these widgets are like light fixtures that have been installed, but not connected to electrical wiring. Well, now it's time to get the electricity flowing; or in the case of GUI programming, it's time to write event handlers and bind them with events.

Introducing the Click Counter Program

The Click Counter program has a button that does something: it displays the number of times the user has clicked it. Technically, the button's event handler takes care of updating the click count and changing the text on the button. Figure 10.10 shows off the program.

FIGURE 10.10

The button's event handler updates the number of times the button is clicked.

You can find the code for the program on the companion website (www.courseptr.com/downloads) in the Chapter 10 folder; the file name is click_counter.py.

Setting Up the Program

As my traditional first step, I import the GUI module:

```
# Click Counter
# Demonstrates binding an event with an event handler

from tkinter import *
```

Next, I start the `Application` class definition:

```
class Application(Frame):
    """ GUI application which counts button clicks. """
    def __init__(self, master):
        """ Initialize the frame. """
        super(Application, self).__init__(master)
        self.grid()
        self.bttn_clicks = 0      # the number of button clicks
        self.create_widget()
```

You've seen most of this code before. The new line is `self.bttn_clicks = 0`, which creates an `object` attribute to keep track of the number of times the user clicks the button.

Binding the Event Handler

In the `create_widget()` method, I create a single button:

```
def create_widget(self):
    """ Create button which displays number of clicks. """
    self.bttn = Button(self)
    self.bttn["text"]= "Total Clicks: 0"
    self.bttn["command"] = self.update_count
    self.bttn.grid()
```

I set the Button widget's command option to the update_count() method. As a result, when the user clicks the button, the method is invoked. Technically, what I've done is bind an event (the clicking of Button widget) to an event handler (the update_count() method).

In general, you set a widget's command option to bind the activation of the widget with an event handler.

Creating the Event Handler

Next, I write the update_count() method, which handles the event of the button being clicked:

```
def update_count(self):
    """ Increase click count and display new total. """
    self.bttn_clicks += 1
    self.bttn["text"] = "Total Clicks: " + str(self.bttn_clicks)
```

This method increments the total number of button clicks and then changes the text of the button to reflect the new total. That's all it takes to get a button to do something useful (or almost useful).

Wrapping Up the Program

The main part of the code should be pretty familiar to you by now:

```
# main
root = Tk()
root.title("Click Counter")
root.geometry("200x50")

app = Application(root)

root.mainloop()
```

I create a root window and set its title and dimensions. Then I instantiate a new Application object with the root window as its master. Lastly, I start up the root window's event loop to bring the GUI to life on the screen.

Using Text and Entry Widgets and the Grid Layout Manager

In GUI programming, there will be times where you'll want a user to enter some text. Other times, you may want to display text to the user. For both of these occasions, you can use text-based widgets. I introduce you to two kinds. The Entry widget is good for one line of text, while the Text widget is great for multiline blocks of text. You can read the contents of either of these widget types to get user input. You can also insert text into them to provide the user with feedback.

Once you start throwing a bunch of widgets into a frame, you need a way to organize them. So far, I've used the Grid layout manager, but in only the most limited way. The Grid layout manager offers you a lot more control over the way your GUI looks. The manager lets you place widgets at specific locations by treating a frame as a grid.

Introducing the Longevity Program

The Longevity program reveals the secret to living to the ripe old age of 100, if the user enters the secret password (the highly secure "secret"). The user enters the password in the text entry and then clicks the Submit button. If the password is correct, the program displays the key to longevity in the text box. Figures 10.11 and 10.12 show off the program.

FIGURE 10.11

If the user fails to enter the correct password, the program politely refuses to divulge its secret.

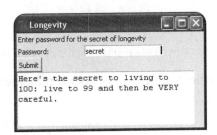

FIGURE 10.12

Given the correct password, the program shares its invaluable knowledge to long life.

You can find the code for the program on the companion website (www.courseptr.com/downloads) in the Chapter 10 folder; the file name is longevity.py.

Setting Up the Program

I set up the program just like the last few:

```
# Longevity
# Demonstrates text and entry widgets, and the Grid layout manager

from tkinter import *

class Application(Frame):
    """ GUI application which can reveal the secret of longevity. """
    def __init__(self, master):
        """ Initialize the frame. """
        super(Application, self).__init__(master)
        self.grid()
        self.create_widgets()
```

I import the `tkinter` module and start to define the `Application` class. In the constructor method, I initialize the new `Application` object, make sure it will be visible, and invoke the object's `create_widgets()` method.

Placing a Widget with the Grid Layout Manager

Next, I start the `create_widgets()` method and create a label that provides instructions to the user:

```
    def create_widgets(self):
        """ Create button, text, and entry widgets. """
        # create instruction label
        self.inst_lbl = Label(self, text = "Enter password for the secret of longevity")
```

So far, nothing new. But in the next line, I use the `Grid` layout manager to be specific about the placement of this label:

```
        self.inst_lbl.grid(row = 0, column = 0, columnspan = 2, sticky = W)
```

A widget object's `grid()` method can take values for many different parameters, but I only use four of them: `row`, `column`, `columnspan`, and `sticky`.

The `row` and `column` parameters take integers and define where an object is placed within its master widget. In this program, you can imagine the frame in the root window as a grid, divided into rows and columns. At each row and column intersection is a cell, where you can place a widget. Figure 10.13 illustrates the placement of nine `Button` widgets, in nine different cells, using row and column numbers.

FIGURE 10.13

Each button is located in a unique cell, based on a row and a column number.

For my `Label` widget, I pass 0 to `row` and 0 to `column`, which puts the label in the upper-left corner of the frame.

If a widget is very wide (like the long instruction `Label` widget I have in this program), you may want to allow the widget to span more than one cell so that your other widgets are correctly spaced. The `columnspan` parameter lets you span a widget over more than one column. I pass 2 to this parameter to allow the long label to span two columns. This means that the label takes up two cells, the one at row 0, column 0, and the other at row 0, column 1. (You can also use the `rowspan` parameter to allow a widget to span more than one row.)

Even after you've established which cell (or cells) a widget occupies, you have the flexibility to justify the widget within the cell (or cells) by using the parameter `sticky`, which takes directions as values, including `N`, `S`, `E`, and `W`. A widget is moved to the quadrant of the cell (or cells) that corresponds to the direction. Since I pass `W` to `sticky` for the `Label` object, the label is forced to the west (left). Another way to say this is that the label is left-justified in its cells.

Next, I create a label that appears in the next row, left-justified:

```
# create label for password
self.pw_lbl = Label(self, text = "Password: ")
self.pw_lbl.grid(row = 1, column = 0, sticky = W)
```

Creating an Entry Widget

Next, I create a new type of widget, an `Entry` widget:

```
# create entry widget to accept password
self.pw_ent = Entry(self)
```

This code creates a text entry where the user can enter a password.

I position the Entry widget so that it's in the cell next to the password label:

```
self.pw_ent.grid(row = 1, column = 1, sticky = W)
```

Then, I create a button that lets the user submit his or her password:

```
# create submit button
self.submit_bttn = Button(self, text = "Submit", command = self.reveal)
```

I bind the activation of the button with the reveal() method, which reveals the longevity secret, if the user has entered the correct password.

I place the button in the next row, all the way to the left:

```
self.submit_bttn.grid(row = 2, column = 0, sticky = W)
```

Creating a Text Widget

Next, I create a new type of widget, a Text widget:

```
# create text widget to display message
self.secret_txt = Text(self, width = 35, height = 5, wrap = WORD)
```

I pass values to width and height to set the dimensions of the text box. Then I pass a value to the parameter wrap, which determines how text in the box is wrapped. Possible values for the parameter are WORD, CHAR, and NONE. WORD, the value I use for this Text widget, wraps entire words when you reach the right edge of the text box. CHAR wraps characters, meaning that when you get to the right edge of the text box, the next character simply appears on the following line. NONE means no wrapping. As a result, you can only write text on the first line of the text box.

Next, I set the text box so that it's on the next row and spans two columns:

```
self.secret_txt.grid(row = 3, column = 0, columnspan = 2, sticky = W)
```

Getting and Inserting Text with Text-Based Widgets

Next, I write the reveal() method, which tests to see if the user has entered the correct password. If so, the method displays the secret to a long life. Otherwise, the user is told that the password is incorrect.

The first thing I do is get the text in the Entry widget by invoking its get() method:

```
def reveal(self):
    """ Display message based on password. """
    contents = self.pw_ent.get()
```

The get() method returns the text in the widget. Both Entry and Text objects have a get() method.

I check to see if the text is equal to "secret". If so, I set message to the string describing the secret to living to 100. Otherwise, I set message to the string that tells the user that he or she entered the wrong password.

```
if contents == "secret":
    message = "Here's the secret to living to 100: live to 99 " \
              "and then be VERY careful. "
else:
    message = "That's not the correct password, so I can't share " \
              "the secret with you."
```

Now that I have the string that I want to show to the user, I need to insert it into the Text widget. First, I delete any text already in the Text widget by invoking its delete() method:

```
self.secret_txt.delete(0.0, END)
```

The delete() method can delete text from text-based widgets. The method can take a single index, or a beginning and an ending point. You pass floating-point numbers to represent a row and column number pair where the digit to the left of the decimal point is the row number and the digit to the right of the decimal point is the column number. For example, in the previous line of code, I pass 0.0 as the starting point, meaning that the method should delete text starting at row 0, column 0 (the absolute beginning) of the text box.

tkinter provides several constants to help out with this type of method, such as END, which means the end of the text. So, this previous line of code deletes everything from the first position in the text box to the end. Both Text and Entry widgets have a delete() method.

Next, I insert the string I want to display into the Text widget:

```
self.secret_txt.insert(0.0, message)
```

The insert() method can insert a string into a text-based widget. The method takes an insertion position and a string. In the previous line of code, I pass 0.0 as the insertion position, meaning the method should start inserting at row 0, column 0. I pass message as the second value, so that the appropriate message shows up in the text box. Both Text and Entry widgets have an insert() method.

The insert() method doesn't replace the text in a text-based widget—it simply inserts it. If you want to replace the existing text with new text, first call the text-based widget's delete() method.

Wrapping Up the Program

To wrap up the program, I create a root window and set its title and dimensions. Then I create a new Application object with the root window as its master. Finally, I begin the application by starting the window's event loop.

```
# main
root = Tk()
root.title("Longevity")
root.geometry("300x150")

app = Application(root)

root.mainloop()
```

USING CHECK BUTTONS

Check buttons allow a user to select any number of choices from a group. While this gives the user a lot of flexibility, it actually gives the programmer greater control by limiting to a specific list what the user can choose.

Introducing the Movie Chooser Program

The Movie Chooser program lets the user choose his or her favorite movie types from a list of three: comedy, drama, and romance. Since the program uses check buttons, the user can select as many (or as few) as he or she wants. The program displays the results of the user's selections in a text box. Figure 10.14 shows off the program.

FIGURE 10.14

The results of the user's selections show up in the text box.

You can find the code for the program on the companion website (www.courseptr.com/down-loads) in the Chapter 10 folder; the file name is movie_chooser.py.

Setting Up the Program

I set up the Movie Chooser program by importing `tkinter` and starting my `Application` class definition:

```
# Movie Chooser
# Demonstrates check buttons

from tkinter import *

class Application(Frame):
    """ GUI Application for favorite movie types. """
    def __init__(self, master):
        super(Application, self).__init__(master)
        self.grid()
        self.create_widgets()
```

Allowing a Widget's Master to Be Its Only Reference

Next, I create a label that describes the program:

```
    def create_widgets(self):
        """ Create widgets for movie type choices. """
        # create description label
        Label(self,
              text = "Choose your favorite movie types"
              ).grid(row = 0, column = 0, sticky = W)
```

There's one important difference between this label and others I've created: I don't assign the resulting `Label` object to a variable. Normally, this would be a big mistake, rendering the object useless because it wouldn't be connected to the program in any way. But with `tkinter`, a `Label` object is connected to the program, like all GUI elements, by its master. What this means is that if I know I won't need to directly access a widget, then I don't need to assign the object to a variable. The main benefit of this approach is shorter, cleaner code.

So far, I've been pretty conservative, always assigning each new widget to a variable. But in this case, I know that I'm not going to need to access this label, so I don't assign the `Label` object to a variable. Instead, I let its master maintain the only reference to it.

Next, I create another label in much the same way:

```
# create instruction label
Label(self,
      text = "Select all that apply: "
      ).grid(row = 1, column = 0, sticky = W)
```

This label provides instructions, telling the user that he or she can select as many movie types as apply.

Creating Check Buttons

Next, I create the check buttons, one for each movie type. I first tackle the Comedy check button.

Every check button needs a special object associated with it that automatically reflects the check button's status. The special object must be an instance of the `BooleanVar` class from the `tkinter` module. So, before I create the Comedy check button, I instantiate a `BooleanVar` object and assign it to a new object attribute, `likes_comedy`:

```
# create Comedy check button
self.likes_comedy = BooleanVar()
```

IN THE REAL WORLD

A *Boolean variable* is a special kind of variable that can be only true or false. Programmers often call such a variable simply a "Boolean." The term is always capitalized because it's derived from the name of the English mathematician George Boole.

Next, I create the check button itself:

```
Checkbutton(self,
            text = "Comedy",
            variable = self.likes_comedy,
            command = self.update_text
            ).grid(row = 2, column = 0, sticky = W)
```

This code creates a new check button with the text Comedy. By passing `self.likes_comedy` to the parameter `variable`, I associate the check button's status (selected or unchecked) with the likes_comedy attribute. By passing self.update_text() to the parameter command, I bind the activation of the check button with the update_text() method. This means that whenever the user selects or clears the check button, the update_text() method is invoked. Finally, I place the check button on the next row, all the way to the left.

Notice that I don't assign the resulting Checkbutton object to a variable. This is fine, because what I really care about is the status of the button, which I can access from the likes_comedy attribute.

I create the next two check buttons in the same way:

```
# create Drama check button
self.likes_drama = BooleanVar()
Checkbutton(self,
            text = "Drama",
            variable = self.likes_drama,
            command = self.update_text
            ).grid(row = 3, column = 0, sticky = W)

# create Romance check button
self.likes_romance = BooleanVar()
Checkbutton(self,
            text = "Romance",
            variable = self.likes_romance,
            command = self.update_text
            ).grid(row = 4, column = 0, sticky = W)
```

So, whenever the user selects or clears the Drama or Romance check buttons, the update_text() method is invoked. And even though I don't assign the resulting Checkbutton objects to any variables, I can always see the status of the Drama check button through the likes_drama attribute, and I can always see the status of the Romance check button through the likes_romance attribute.

Finally, I create the text box that I use to show the results of the user's selections:

```
# create text field to display results
self.results_txt = Text(self, width = 40, height = 5, wrap = WORD)
self.results_txt.grid(row = 5, column = 0, columnspan = 3)
```

Getting the Status of a Check Button

Next, I write the `update_text()` method, which updates the text box to reflect the check buttons the user has selected:

```
def update_text(self):
    """ Update text widget and display user's favorite movie types. """
    likes = ""

    if self.likes_comedy.get():
        likes += "You like comedic movies.\n"

    if self.likes_drama.get():
        likes += "You like dramatic movies.\n"

    if self.likes_romance.get():
        likes += "You like romantic movies."

    self.results_txt.delete(0.0, END)
    self.results_txt.insert(0.0, likes)
```

You can't access the value of a `BooleanVar` object directly. Instead, you must invoke the object's `get()` method. In the previous code, I use the `get()` method of the `BooleanVar` object referenced by `likes_comedy` to get the object's value. If the value evaluates to true, that means the Comedy check button is selected, and I add the string `"You like comedic movies.\n"` to the string I'm building to display in the text box. I perform similar operations based on the status of the Drama and Romance check buttons. Finally, I delete all of the text in the text box and then insert the new string, `likes`, which I just built.

Wrapping Up the Program

I finish the program with the familiar main section. I create a root window and a new `Application` object with the root window as its master. Then, I start the window's event loop.

```
# main
root = Tk()
root.title("Movie Chooser")
app = Application(root)
root.mainloop()
```

USING RADIO BUTTONS

Radio buttons are a lot like check buttons, except that radio buttons only allow one button in a group to be selected at once. This is great if you want the user to make a single selection from a group of choices. Since radio buttons have so much in common with check buttons, learning to use them is pretty straightforward.

Introducing the Movie Chooser 2 Program

The Movie Chooser 2 program is like the Movie Chooser program. The user is presented with three different movie types from which to select. The difference is that the Movie Chooser 2 program uses radio buttons instead of check buttons, so the user can select only one movie type. This is perfect since the program asks the user for his or her favorite type of movie. Figure 10.15 shows off the program.

FIGURE 10.15

The user can select only a single movie type.

You can find the code for the program on the companion website (www.courseptr.com/downloads) in the Chapter 10 folder; the file name is movie_chooser2.py.

Setting Up the Program

I start the program by importing the tkinter module:

```
# Movie Chooser 2
# Demonstrates radio buttons

from tkinter import *
```

Next, I write the Application class. I define its constructor, which initializes a new Application object:

```
class Application(Frame):
    """ GUI Application for favorite movie type. """
    def __init__(self, master):
```

```
    """ Initialize Frame. """
    super(Application, self).__init__(master)
    self.grid()
    self.create_widgets()
```

Then, I create labels that give the user instructions:

```
def create_widgets(self):
    """ Create widgets for movie type choices. """
    # create description label
    Label(self,
          text = "Choose your favorite type of movie"
          ).grid(row = 0, column = 0, sticky = W)

    # create instruction label
    Label(self,
          text = "Select one:"
          ).grid(row = 1, column = 0, sticky = W)
```

Creating Radio Buttons

Since only one radio button in a group can be selected at one time, there's no need for each radio button to have its own status variable, as required for check buttons. Instead, a group of radio buttons share one, special object that reflects which of the radio buttons is selected. This object can be an instance of the StringVar class from the tkinter module, which allows a string to be stored and retrieved. So, before I create the radio buttons themselves, I create a single StringVar object for all of the radio buttons to share, assign it to the attribute favorite, and set its initial value to None using the object's set() method:

```
# create variable for single, favorite type of movie
self.favorite = StringVar()
self.favorite.set(None)
```

Next, I create the Comedy radio button:

```
# create Comedy radio button
Radiobutton(self,
            text = "Comedy",
            variable = self.favorite,
            value = "comedy.",
            command = self.update_text
            ).grid(row = 2, column = 0, sticky = W)
```

A radio button's `variable` option defines the special variable associated with the radio button, while a radio button's `value` option defines the value to be stored by the special variable when the radio button is selected. So, by setting this radio button's `variable` option to `self.favorite` and its `value` option to `"comedy."`, I'm saying that when the Comedy radio button is selected, the `StringVar` referenced by `self.favorite` should store the string `"comedy."`

Next, I create the other two radio buttons:

```
# create Drama radio button
Radiobutton(self,
            text = "Drama",
            variable = self.favorite,
            value = "drama.",
            command = self.update_text
            ).grid(row = 3, column = 0, sticky = W)

# create Romance radio button
Radiobutton(self,
            text = "Romance",
            variable = self.favorite,
            value = "romance.",
            command = self.update_text
            ).grid(row = 4, column = 0, sticky = W)
```

By setting the Drama radio button's `variable` option to `self.favorite` and its `value` option to `"drama."`, I'm saying that when the Drama radio button is selected, the `StringVar` referenced by `self.favorite` should store the string `"drama."`

And by setting the Romance radio button's `variable` option to `self.favorite` and its `value` option to `"romance."`, I'm saying that when the Romance radio button is selected, the `StringVar` referenced by `self.favorite` should store the string `"romance."`.

Next, I create the text box to display the results of the user's selection:

```
# create text field to display result
self.results_txt = Text(self, width = 40, height = 5, wrap = WORD)
self.results_txt.grid(row = 5, column = 0, columnspan = 3)
```

Getting a Value from a Group of Radio Buttons

Getting a value from a group of radio buttons is as simple as invoking the `get()` method of the `StringVar` object that they all share:

```
def update_text(self):
    """ Update text area and display user's favorite movie type. """
    message = "Your favorite type of movie is "
    message += self.favorite.get()
```

When the Comedy radio button is selected, `self.favorite.get()` returns `"comedy."`; when the Drama radio button is selected, `self.favorite.get()` returns `"drama."`; and when the Romance radio button is selected, `self.favorite.get()` returns `"romance."`.

Next, I delete any text that may be in the text box and insert the string I just created, which declares the user's favorite movie type:

```
self.results_txt.delete(0.0, END)
self.results_txt.insert(0.0, message)
```

Wrapping Up the Program

I wrap up the program by creating a root window and a new `Application` object. Then, I begin the root window's event loop to start up the GUI.

```
# main
root = Tk()
root.title("Movie Chooser 2")
app = Application(root)
root.mainloop()
```

BACK TO THE MAD LIB PROGRAM

Now that you've seen a nice variety of widgets used in isolation, it's time to combine them in one, larger GUI. I don't introduce any new concepts in the Mad Lib program, so I don't comment too much on the code. You can find the code for the program on the companion website (www.courseptr.com/downloads) in the Chapter 10 folder; the file name is mad_lib.py.py.

Importing the tkinter Module

As you probably know by now, you have to import the `tkinter` module before you can use it:

```
# Mad Lib
# Create a story based on user input

from tkinter import *
```

The Application Class's Constructor Method

Like all other Application class constructors before it, this one initializes the newly created Application object and invokes its create_widgets() method:

```
class Application(Frame):
    """ GUI application that creates a story based on user input. """
    def __init__(self, master):
        """ Initialize Frame. """
        super(Application, self).__init__(master)
        self.grid()
        self.create_widgets()
```

The Application Class's create_widgets() Method

This class creates all of the widgets in the GUI. The only new thing I do is create all three radio buttons in a loop by moving through a list of strings for each radio button's text and value options:

```
    def create_widgets(self):
        """ Create widgets to get story information and to display story. """
        # create instruction label
        Label(self,
              text = "Enter information for a new story"
              ).grid(row = 0, column = 0, columnspan = 2, sticky = W)

        # create a label and text entry for the name of a person
        Label(self,
              text = "Person: "
              ).grid(row = 1, column = 0, sticky = W)
        self.person_ent = Entry(self)
        self.person_ent.grid(row = 1, column = 1, sticky = W)

        # create a label and text entry for a plural noun
        Label(self,
              text = "Plural Noun:"
              ).grid(row = 2, column = 0, sticky = W)
        self.noun_ent = Entry(self)
        self.noun_ent.grid(row = 2, column = 1, sticky = W)

        # create a label and text entry for a verb
```

```
Label(self,
      text = "Verb:"
      ).grid(row = 3, column = 0, sticky = W)
self.verb_ent = Entry(self)
self.verb_ent.grid(row = 3, column = 1, sticky = W)

# create a label for adjectives check buttons
Label(self,
      text = "Adjective(s):"
      ).grid(row = 4, column = 0, sticky = W)

# create itchy check button
self.is_itchy = BooleanVar()
Checkbutton(self,
            text = "itchy",
            variable = self.is_itchy
            ).grid(row = 4, column = 1, sticky = W)

# create joyous check button
self.is_joyous = BooleanVar()
Checkbutton(self,
            text = "joyous",
            variable = self.is_joyous
            ).grid(row = 4, column = 2, sticky = W)

# create electric check button
self.is_electric = BooleanVar()
Checkbutton(self,
            text = "electric",
            variable = self.is_electric
            ).grid(row = 4, column = 3, sticky = W)

# create a label for body parts radio buttons
Label(self,
      text = "Body Part:"
      ).grid(row = 5, column = 0, sticky = W)

# create variable for single body part
```

```
self.body_part = StringVar()
self.body_part.set(None)

# create body part radio buttons
body_parts = ["bellybutton", "big toe", "medulla oblongata"]
column = 1
for part in body_parts:
    Radiobutton(self,
                text = part,
                variable = self.body_part,
                value = part
                ).grid(row = 5, column = column, sticky = W)
    column += 1

# create a submit button
Button(self,
        text = "Click for story",
        command = self.tell_story
        ).grid(row = 6, column = 0, sticky = W)

self.story_txt = Text(self, width = 75, height = 10, wrap = WORD)
self.story_txt.grid(row = 7, column = 0, columnspan = 4)
```

The Application Class's tell_story() Method

In this method, I get the values the user has entered and use them to create the one, long string for the story. Then, I delete any text in the text box and insert the new string to show the user the story he or she created.

```
def tell_story(self):
    """ Fill text box with new story based on user input. """
    # get values from the GUI
    person = self.person_ent.get()
    noun = self.noun_ent.get()
    verb = self.verb_ent.get()
    adjectives = ""
    if self.is_itchy.get():
        adjectives += "itchy, "
    if self.is_joyous.get():
```

```
        adjectives += "joyous, "
    if self.is_electric.get():
        adjectives += "electric, "
    body_part = self.body_part.get()

    # create the story
    story = "The famous explorer "
    story += person
    story += " had nearly given up a life-long quest to find The Lost City of "
    story += noun.title()
    story += " when one day, the "
    story += noun
    story += " found "
    story += person + "."
    story += "A strong, "
    story += adjectives
    story += "peculiar feeling overwhelmed the explorer. "
    story += "After all this time, the quest was finally over. A tear came to "
    story += person + "'s "
    story += body_part + ". "
    story += "And then, the "
    story += noun
    story += " promptly devoured "
    story += person + "."
    story += "The moral of the story? Be careful what you "
    story += verb
    story += " for."

    # display the story
    self.story_txt.delete(0.0, END)
    self.story_txt.insert(0.0, story)
```

The Main Part of the Program

You've seen this code more than a few times before. I create a root window and an Application instance. Then, I start the whole GUI up by invoking root's mainloop() method.

```
# main
root = Tk()
root.title("Mad Lib")
app = Application(root)
root.mainloop()
```

Summary

In this chapter, you learned about creating GUIs. First, you learned about event-driven programming, a new way to think about writing code. Then, you learned about a number of GUI widgets, including frames, buttons, text entries, text boxes, check buttons, and radio buttons. You saw how to customize widgets. You also saw how to organize them in a frame, using the Grid layout manager. You learned how to bind events to event handlers so that widgets do something when activated. Finally, you saw how to put together a fairly complex GUI to create a fun Mad Lib program.

CHALLENGES

1. Write your own version of the Mad Lib program using a different arrangement of widgets.
2. Write a version of the Guess My Number game, the Chapter 3 project, using a GUI.
3. Create a GUI program, Order Up!, that presents the user with a simple restaurant menu, which lists items and prices. Let the user select different items and then show the user the total bill.

11

GRAPHICS: THE PIZZA PANIC GAME

The majority of programs you've seen so far have focused on presenting text, but today people expect rich, visual content from their programs, regardless of the application. In this chapter, you'll learn how to use graphics with the help of a few multimedia modules designed for writing games in Python. Specifically, you'll learn to do the following:

- Create a graphics window
- Create and manipulate sprites
- Display text in a graphics window
- Test for collisions between sprites
- Handle mouse input
- Control a computer opponent

INTRODUCING THE PIZZA PANIC GAME

The project for this chapter, the Pizza Panic game, involves a crazy chef, a deep-dish pan, and a bunch of flying pizzas. Here's the scenario: After being pushed over the edge by one-too-many finicky diners, the chef at the local pizza parlor has taken to the rooftop and is madly flinging pizzas to their doom. Of course, the pizzas must be saved. Using the mouse, the player controls a pan that he or she maneuvers to catch the falling pizzas. The player's score increases with every pizza caught, but, once a pie hits the ground, the game is over. Figures 11.1 and 11.2 show the game in action.

FIGURE 11.1

The player must catch the falling pizzas.

FIGURE 11.2

Once the player misses a pizza, the game is over.

INTRODUCING THE PYGAME AND LIVEWIRES PACKAGES

pygame and livewires are sets of modules (called *packages*) that give Python programmers access to a wide range of multimedia classes. With these classes, you can create programs with graphics, sound effects, music, and animation. The packages also allow input from a variety of devices, including the mouse and keyboard. With these packages, you won't have to worry about the low-level hardware details, like what kind of graphics card the player has—or whether he or she has a graphics card at all. Instead, you can concentrate on the program logic and get to writing games fast.

pygame is the secret weapon in your media arsenal. Written by Pete Shinners, the package allows you to write impressive multimedia programs in Python. Because the package is so powerful, however, it can be a bit overwhelming for the new programmer.

livewires, written by a group of educators in the United Kingdom, was designed to take advantage of the power of pygame while reducing the complexity for the programmer. livewires provides a simpler way to get started programming games with graphics and sound. And even though you won't directly access pygame, it will still be there, working hard behind the scenes.

You need to install both pygame and livewires before you can run the programs presented in this chapter. Fortunately, versions of both are on the companion website (www.courseptr.com/downloads) in the Software folder. Just follow the installation instructions that accompany the packages.

 Although you're welcome to visit the website of the LiveWires organization at http://www.livewires.org.uk, be aware that the livewires package included on the companion website (www.courseptr.com/downloads) is a modified version of the package that LiveWires created. I updated the package to make it even easier for new programmers to use. And don't worry—I've included a modified version of the documentation in Appendix B.

If you want to learn more about pygame, visit its website at http://www.pygame.org.

CREATING A GRAPHICS WINDOW

Before you can display any graphics, you must first create a graphics window—your blank canvas on which to display text and images.

Introducing the New Graphics Window Program

Creating a graphics window with the `livewires` package is a snap. The New Graphics Window program creates an empty graphics window in just a few lines of code. Figure 11.3 shows the results of the program.

FIGURE 11.3

My first graphics window. Not much, but it's mine.

TRAP   Just as with a program that uses Tkinter to create a new window, you shouldn't run a `livewires` program from IDLE. If you're using Windows, create a batch file that runs your Python program and then pauses. To review writing such a batch file, see "Introducing the Simple GUI Program" in Chapter 10.

You can find the code for the program on the companion website (www.courseptr.com/downloads) in the Chapter 11 folder; the file name is new_graphics_window.py.

Importing the games Module

The `livewires` package is made up of several important modules, including `games`, which contains a group of objects and classes for game programming. You can import a specific module of a package by using the `from` statement. To import a module, use `from`, followed by a package name, followed by `import`, followed by a module name (or a list of module names separated by commas).

The first thing I do in the program is import the games module of the livewires package:

```
# New Graphics Window
# Demonstrates creating a graphics window

from livewires import games
```

As a result, I can use games like any other module I import. To get an overview of the games module, check out Table 11.1, which lists useful games objects, and Table 11.2, which lists useful games classes.

TABLE 11.1 USEFUL GAMES MODULE OBJECTS

Object	Description
screen	Provides access to the graphics screen—the region on which graphics objects may exist, move, and interact.
mouse	Provides access to the mouse.
keyboard	Provides access to the keyboard.

TABLE 11.2 USEFUL GAMES MODULE CLASSES

Class	Description
Sprite	For graphics objects that can be displayed on the graphics screen.
Text	A subclass of Sprite. For text objects displayed on the graphics screen.
Message	A subclass of Text. For text objects displayed on the graphics screen that disappear after a set period of time.

Initializing the Graphics Screen

Next, I initialize the graphics screen:

```
games.init(screen_width = 640, screen_height = 480, fps = 50)
```

When you call the games init() function, you create a new graphics screen. The width of the screen is determined by the value you pass screen_width, while (drumroll, please) the height of the screen is determined by the value you pass screen_height. The screen dimensions are measured in *pixels*—a single point in a graphics area. The value you pass fps (short for "frames per second") is the number of times the screen will update itself every second.

Starting the Main Loop

The final line in the program is

```
games.screen.mainloop()
```

`screen` is the `games` object that represents the graphics screen. `mainloop()` is the workhorse of `screen` and updates the graphics window, redrawing everything `fps` times per second. So, this last line keeps the graphics window open and updates the screen 50 times per second. Check out Table 11.3 for a few `screen` properties. For a list of useful `screen` methods, see Table 11.4.

TABLE 11.3   USEFUL SCREEN PROPERTIES

Property	Description
width	Width of screen.
height	Height of screen.
fps	Frames per second screen is updated.
background	Background image of screen.
all objects	List of all the sprites on the screen.
event_grab	Boolean that determines if input is grabbed to screen. `True` for input grabbed to screen. `False` for input not grabbed to screen.

TABLE 11.4   USEFUL SCREEN METHODS

Method	Description
add(*sprite*)	Adds *sprite*, a `Sprite` object (or an object of a `Sprite` subclass), to the graphics screen.
clear()	Removes all sprites from the graphics screen.
mainloop()	Starts the graphics screen's main loop.
quit()	Closes the graphics window.

SETTING A BACKGROUND IMAGE

A blank screen is all well and good, if your goal is to create the world's most boring program. Fortunately, the `screen` object has a property for its background image.

Introducing the Background Image Program

The Background Image program is just a modification of the New Graphics Window program. I add a background image to the graphics screen, shown in Figure 11.4.

FIGURE 11.4

By using the background property of the screen object, I apply a background image to the graphics window.

To create the Background Image program, I add two lines to the New Graphics Window program, just before invoking `mainloop()`. You can find the code for the program on the companion website (www.courseptr.com/downloads) in the Chapter 11 folder; the file name is background_image.py.

```
# Background Image
# Demonstrates setting the background image of a graphics screen

from livewires import games

games.init(screen_width = 640, screen_height = 480, fps = 50)

wall_image = games.load_image("wall.jpg", transparent = False)
games.screen.background = wall_image

games.screen.mainloop()
```

Loading an Image

Before you can do anything with an image, like set it as the background of a graphics screen, you have to load the image into memory to create an image object. I load an image by adding the following line right after I initialize the graphics window:

```
wall_image = games.load_image("wall.jpg", transparent = False)
```

This calls the `games load_image()` function, which loads the image stored in the file `wall.jpg` into memory and assigns the resulting image object to `wall_image`.

 TRAP Make sure that any file you want your Python program to access is associated with the correct path information, as you learned in Chapter 7, in the section "Opening and Closing a File." The simplest file management solution, and the one I use here, is to store image files in the same folder with the program that loads them. If you follow this method, you won't need to worry about path information at all.

The `load_image()` function takes two arguments: a string for the file name of the image and `True` or `False` for `transparent`. I'll go over exactly what `transparent` means a bit later in this chapter. For now, just remember this rule: Always load a background image with `transparent = False`.

You'll notice that I load a JPEG image for the background in this program. However, you're not restricted to JPEGs when using the `load_image()` function. It works just as well with many other image file types, including BMP, GIF, PNG, PCX, and TGA.

Setting the Background

In order to set an image object as the screen background, you just need to use the `screen` background property. I add the following line right after I load the image:

```
games.screen.background = wall_image
```

This sets the background of the screen to the image object `wall_image`.

When the program encounters `mainloop()`, it keeps the graphics window open, with its new background image, for all to see.

UNDERSTANDING THE GRAPHICS COORDINATE SYSTEM

So far, I've created several graphics screens, each time with a width of 640 and a height of 480, but I haven't said much about them beyond that. Now we'll take a closer look at the screen and its coordinate system.

You can think of a graphics screen as a grid, 640 columns across by 480 rows down. Each intersection of a column and a row is a location on the screen, a single point or pixel. When you talk about a specific point on the screen, you give two coordinates: an x, which represents the column, and a y, which represents the row. You start counting coordinates from the upper-left corner of the screen. So, the upper-leftmost point is where the x-coordinate is 0 and the y-coordinate is 0, which you write as the pair (0,0). As you move to the right, the x values increase. As you move down the screen, the y values increase. That makes the point in the lower-right corner (639,479). Figure 11.5 gives a visual representation of the graphics screen coordinate system.

FIGURE 11.5

You specify points on a graphics screen with x- and y-coordinate pairs.

You can place graphics objects, like the image of a pizza or the red-colored text "Game Over," on the screen using the coordinate system. The center of a graphics object is placed at the specified coordinates. You'll see exactly how this works in the next program.

DISPLAYING A SPRITE

Background images can spruce up a plain graphics screen, but even a breathtaking background is still just a static image. A graphics screen with only a background image is like an empty stage. What you need are some actors. Enter the sprite.

A *sprite* is a graphics object with an image that can make programs really come alive. Sprites are used in games, entertainment software, presentations, and all over the web. In fact, you've already seen examples of sprites in the Pizza Panic game. The crazy chef, pan, and pizzas are all sprites.

IN THE REAL WORLD

Sprites aren't just for games. There are plenty of places in non-entertainment software where they're used…or misused. In fact, you probably know the most infamous sprite in application software history, Clippy the Office Assistant—the animated paperclip meant to give helpful suggestions in Microsoft Office. However, many people found Clippy obtrusive and irritating. One major online publication even ran an article entitled "Kill Clippy!" Well, Microsoft finally saw the light. Starting with Office 2007, Clippy is no longer available. So, while graphics can make a program more interesting, remember: Use your sprite powers for good instead of evil.

While it would be cool to see a bunch of sprites flying around and crashing into each other, I start with the first step: displaying a single, nonmoving sprite.

Introducing the Pizza Sprite Program

In the Pizza Sprite program, I create a graphics window and set a background image, just like before. Following this step, however, I create a pizza sprite right in the middle of the screen. Figure 11.6 shows the results of the program.

The Pizza Sprite program is just a modification of the Background Image program. I add only three lines to get the new sprite on the screen, just before invoking `mainloop()`. You can find the code for the program on the companion website (www.courseptr.com/downloads) in the Chapter 11 folder; the file name is pizza_sprite.py.

FIGURE 11.6

The pizza image is not part of the background, but an independent object of the Sprite class.

```
# Pizza Sprite
# Demonstrates creating a sprite

from livewires import games

games.init(screen_width = 640, screen_height = 480, fps = 50)

wall_image = games.load_image("wall.jpg", transparent = False)
games.screen.background = wall_image

pizza_image = games.load_image("pizza.bmp")
pizza = games.Sprite(image = pizza_image, x = 320, y = 240)
games.screen.add(pizza)

games.screen.mainloop()
```

Loading an Image for a Sprite

First, I load a pizza image into memory to create an image object:

```
pizza_image = games.load_image("pizza.bmp")
```

You'll notice one small difference in the way I load a background image. This time, I didn't include a value for `transparent`. The default value is `True`, so the image is loaded with transparency on.

When an image is loaded with transparency on, it's displayed on a graphics screen so that the background image shows through its transparent parts. This is great for irregular sprites that aren't perfect rectangles and sprites with "holes" in them, like, say, a Swiss cheese sprite.

The parts of an image that are transparent are defined by their color. If an image is loaded with transparency on, then the color of the point at the upper-left corner of the image is its transparent color. All parts of the image that are this transparent color will allow the background of the screen to show through. Figure 11.7 shows a Swiss cheese sprite on a solid, white background, ready to take advantage of transparency.

FIGURE 11.7

A cheesy sprite drawn on a solid-color background to take advantage of transparency.

If I load this Swiss cheese image with transparency on, every part that is pure white (the color taken from the pixel in the image's upper-left corner) will be transparent when the sprite is displayed on a graphics screen. The background image will show through these transparent parts. Figure 11.8 shows how the image looks when loaded with transparency on and off.

As a general rule, you'll want to create your sprite image on a solid color that is not used in any other part of the image.

TRAP

Make sure your sprite image doesn't also contain the color you're using for transparency. Otherwise, those parts of the sprite will become transparent too, making your sprite look like it has small holes or tears in it as the background image of the graphics screen shows through.

FIGURE 11.8

On the left, the image is loaded with transparency on. On the right, the same image is loaded with transparency off.

Creating a Sprite

Next, I create a pizza sprite:

```
pizza = games.Sprite(image = pizza_image, x = 320, y = 240)
```

A new `Sprite` object is created with the image of a pizza and x- and y-coordinates of (320,240), which puts it right in the middle of the screen. The new object is then assigned to `pizza`. When you create a `Sprite` object, you should pass at least an image, an x-coordinate, and a y-coordinate to the class constructor.

Adding a Sprite to the Screen

After you create a sprite, you need to add it to the screen so it can be seen and updated, which is exactly what I do in the next line:

```
games.screen.add(pizza)
```

The `add()` method simply adds a sprite to the graphics screen.

TRICK

You don't need to be an artist to create graphics for your games. As you see in this chapter, I make up for my utter lack of artistic ability with a modern piece of technology: my digital camera. If you have access to a digital camera, you can create some great images for your projects. In fact, that's how I created all of the graphics for the Pizza Panic game. The brick wall is the back of a friend's house. For the pizza, I ordered delivery one night. And the chef is my brave, brave friend, Dave.

While this is a great technique, an important thing to remember is that, if you take a picture of a person or object, you don't necessarily own the image—obviously, some things are trademarked or copyrighted. Using a digital camera, however, is a great way to capture generic images while infusing your programs with a unique, photorealistic style.

Table 11.5 lists useful Sprite properties while Table 11.6 lists useful Sprite methods.

TABLE 11.5 USEFUL SPRITE PROPERTIES

Property	Description
angle	Facing in degrees.
x	x-coordinate.
y	y-coordinate.
dx	x velocity.
dy	y velocity.
left	x-coordinate of left sprite edge.
right	x-coordinate of right sprite edge.
top	y-coordinate of top sprite edge.
bottom	y-coordinate of bottom sprite edge.
image	Image object of sprite.
overlapping_sprites	List of other objects that overlap sprite.
is_collideable	Whether or not sprite is collideable. True means sprite will register in collisions. False means sprite will not show up in collisions.

TABLE 11.6 USEFUL SPRITE METHODS

Method	Description
update()	Updates sprite. Automatically called every mainloop() cycle.
destroy()	Removes sprite from the screen.

DISPLAYING TEXT

Whether you need to show off the numbers for a sales presentation or the number of aliens obliterated, there are times when you'll want to display text on a graphics screen. The games module contains a class that allows you to do just that, aptly named Text.

Introducing the Big Score Program

Displaying text on the graphics screen is just a matter of creating an object of the Text class. The Big Score program is a modification of the Background Image program. I display a score in the upper-right corner of the screen, just like in many classic arcade games. Figure 11.9 shows the results.

FIGURE 11.9

The impressively high score is displayed after a Text object is instantiated.

You can find the code for the program on the companion website (www.courseptr.com/downloads) in the Chapter 11 folder; the file name is big_score.py.

```
# Big Score
# Demonstrates displaying text on a graphics screen

from livewires import games, color
```

```
games.init(screen_width = 640, screen_height = 480, fps = 50)

wall_image = games.load_image("wall.jpg", transparent = False)
games.screen.background = wall_image

score = games.Text(value = 1756521,
                    size = 60,
                    color = color.black,
                    x = 550,
                    y = 30)
games.screen.add(score)

games.screen.mainloop()
```

Importing the color Module

The livewires package contains another module, color, which defines a set of constants that represent different colors. These colors can be used with certain graphics objects, including any Text or Message object. For a complete list of predefined colors, see the livewires documentation in Appendix B.

To choose from a group of possible colors, I import the color module by replacing the import line at the top of the program with:

```
from livewires import games, color
```

Both the color and games modules are loaded from the livewires package.

Creating a Text Object

A Text object represents text on the graphics screen. Just before I invoke mainloop(), I create a Text object and assign it to score:

```
score = games.Text(value = 1756521,
                    size = 60,
                    color = color.black,
                    x = 550,
                    y = 30)
```

At a minimum, you should pass the constructor method for a Text object, a value to be displayed as text, a font size, a color, an x-coordinate, and a y-coordinate.

I pass the integer 1756521 to text so that the characters that make up the number will be displayed. (A Text object will be displayed as the string representation of whatever you pass value.) Then I pass 60 to size, which represents the height of the text in pixels, so the font is nice and big, to match the score. I pass color the constant color.black from the color module to make the text—you guessed it—black. I pass 550 to x and 30 to y, placing the center of the object at the coordinates (550,30). This puts the text in the upper-right corner of the graphics window.

Adding a Text Object to the Screen

In the next line of code, I add the new object to the screen so it will be displayed:

```
games.screen.add(score)
```

Once mainloop() is invoked, the graphics window is displayed along with score.

Since Text is a subclass of Sprite, Text inherits all of Sprite's properties, attributes, and methods. Table 11.7 lists two additional Text properties that the class defines.

TABLE 11.7	ADDITIONAL TEXT PROPERTIES
Property	**Description**
value	Value to be displayed as text.
color	Color of text.

DISPLAYING A MESSAGE

You may want to display some text on the screen for only a brief period of time. You might want to show a message saying "All records have been updated" or "Attack Wave Seven Complete!" The games class Message is perfect for creating temporary messages just like these.

Introducing the You Won Program

The You Won program is a modified version of the Background Image program. I instantiate a Message object right before invoking mainloop() to display the text "You won!" in big, red letters. The message is displayed for about five seconds and then the program ends. Figure 11.10 illustrates the program.

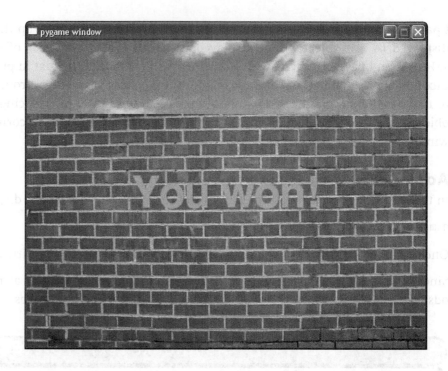

FIGURE 11.10

Ah, the thrill of
victory.

You can find the code for the program on the companion website (www.courseptr.com/down-loads) in the Chapter 11 folder; the file name is you_won.py.

```
# You Won
# Demonstrates displaying a message

from livewires import games, color

games.init(screen_width = 640, screen_height = 480, fps = 50)

wall_image = games.load_image("wall.jpg", transparent = False)
games.screen.background = wall_image

won_message = games.Message(value = "You won!",
                            size = 100,
                            color = color.red,
                            x = games.screen.width/2,
                            y = games.screen.height/2,
                            lifetime = 250,
```

```
                              after_death = games.screen.quit)
games.screen.add(won_message)

games.screen.mainloop()
```

Importing the color Module

Message objects, like Text objects, have a color property. To choose from a group of possible colors, I import the color module by replacing the import line at the top of the program with.

```
from livewires import games, color
```

Creating a Message Object

Messages are created from the games class Message. A message is a special kind of Text object that destroys itself after a set period of time. A message can also specify a method or a function to be executed after the object destroys itself.

The constructor method for Message takes all of the values you saw with Text, but adds two more: lifetime and after_death. lifetime takes an integer value that represents how long the message should be displayed, measured in mainloop() cycles. after_death can be passed a method or function to be executed after the Message object destroys itself. The default value for after_death is None, so a value isn't required.

I create this Message object right before I invoke mainloop():

```
won_message = games.Message(value = "You won!",
                            size = 100,
                            color = color.red,
                            x = games.screen.width/2,
                            y = games.screen.height/2,
                            lifetime = 250,
                            after_death = games.screen.quit)
```

This creates the message "You Won!" in big, red letters at the center of the screen for about five seconds, after which the program ends.

This code instantiates a new Message object with a lifetime attribute set to 250. This means that the object will live for about five seconds, because mainloop() runs at 50 frames per second. After the five seconds, games.screen.quit() is called, since I pass that method's name to after_death. At that point, the screen and all of its associated objects are destroyed and the program ends.

> **HINT** Make sure to pass after_death just the name of the function or method you want called after the Message object disappears. Don't include a set of parentheses after the name.

Using the Screen's Width and Height

The screen object has a width property, which represents the width of the graphics screen, and a height property, which represents the height of the graphics screen. Sometimes it's clearer to use these properties rather than literal integers when you specify a location on the screen.

I use these properties when I pass values for the location of the new Message object, with x = games.screen.width/2, and y = games.screen.height/2. By setting the x-coordinate to half of the screen width and the y-coordinate to half of the screen height, I put the object right in the middle of the screen. You can use this technique to put an object in the middle of the graphics screen, independent of the actual screen width and height.

Adding a Message Object to the Screen

In the next line of code, I add the new object to the screen so it will be displayed:

```
games.screen.add(won_message)
```

Message is a subclass of Text. This means that Message inherits all of Text's properties, attributes, and methods. Table 11.8 lists two additional Message attributes.

TABLE 11.8 ADDITIONAL MESSAGE ATTRIBUTES

Attributes	Description
lifetime	Number of mainloop() cycles before object destroys itself. 0 means never destroy itself. The default value is 0.
after_death	Function or method to be run after object destroys itself. The default value is None.

MOVING SPRITES

Moving images are the essence of most games—most forms of entertainment, for that matter. With sprites, going from stationary to moving is easy. Sprite objects have properties that allow them to move around a graphics screen.

Introducing the Moving Pizza Program

This new program is a modification of the Pizza Sprite program. In this program, the pizza moves down and to the right. All I need to do is change a few lines of code to get the pizza to move. That's the power of sprites. Figure 11.11 illustrates the program.

FIGURE 11.11

The pizza moves down and to the right in the direction of the arrow.

You can find the code for the program on the companion website (www.courseptr.com/downloads) in the Chapter 11 folder; the file name is moving_pizza.py.

```
# Moving Pizza
# Demonstrates sprite velocities

from livewires import games

games.init(screen_width = 640, screen_height = 480, fps = 50)

wall_image = games.load_image("wall.jpg", transparent = False)
games.screen.background = wall_image

pizza_image = games.load_image("pizza.bmp")
```

```
the_pizza = games.Sprite(image = pizza_image,
                         x = games.screen.width/2,
                         y = games.screen.height/2,
                         dx = 1,
                         dy = 1)
games.screen.add(the_pizza)

games.screen.mainloop()
```

Setting a Sprite's Velocity Values

All I have to do is modify the code that creates a new sprite by providing additional values for dx and dy to the constructor method:

```
the_pizza = games.Sprite(image = pizza_image,
                         x = games.screen.width/2,
                         y = games.screen.height/2,
                         dx = 1,
                         dy = 1)
```

Every object based on Sprite has dx and dy properties for the object's velocity along the x and y axes, respectively. ("d," by the way, stands for "delta," which means a change.) So, dx is the change in the object's x-coordinate and dy is the change in the object's y-coordinate each time screen is updated by mainloop(). A positive value for dx moves the sprite to the right, while a negative value moves it to the left. A positive value for dy moves the sprite down, while a negative value moves it up.

Back in the Pizza Sprite program, I didn't pass any values for dx or dy. Although the sprite in that program did have dx and dy properties, they both had the default value of 0.

Since I pass 1 to dx and 1 to dy, every time the graphics window is updated by mainloop(), the pizza's x-coordinate is increased by 1 and its y-coordinate is increased by 1, moving the sprite right and down.

DEALING WITH SCREEN BOUNDARIES

If you watch the Moving Pizza program run for any length of time, you may notice that once the pizza hits a screen boundary, it keeps going. In fact, it disappears out of sight.

Whenever you set a sprite in motion, you should create a mechanism to deal with the graphics window's boundaries. You have a few choices. A moving sprite could simply stop when it reaches the edge of the screen. It could die in, say, a fiery explosion. It could bounce, like a giant rubber ball. It could even wrap around the screen so that, just as it disappears off one edge, it reappears on the opposite. What seems to make the most sense for a pizza? Bouncing, of course.

The Bouncing Pizza Program

When I say that a sprite "bounces" off the edges of the graphics window, I mean that when it reaches a screen boundary, it should reverse the velocity component that was moving it toward that boundary. So, if the bouncing pizza sprite reaches the top or bottom screen edge, it should reverse its `dy` property. When it reaches the sides of the screen, it should reverse its `dx`. Figure 11.12 illustrates the Bouncing Pizza program.

FIGURE 11.12

Though you can't tell from the screen shot, the pizza bounces around, following the path of the arrow.

You can find the code for the program on the companion website (www.courseptr.com/downloads) in the Chapter 11 folder; the file name is bouncing_pizza.py.

Setting Up the Program

I begin as I would with any other graphics program:

```
# Bouncing Pizza
# Demonstrates dealing with screen boundaries
```

```
from livewires import games
```

```
games.init(screen_width = 640, screen_height = 480, fps = 50)
```

As before, the previous lines give me access to the games module and create the graphics screen.

Deriving a New Class from Sprite

For the first time, I want a sprite to do something it isn't programmed to do: bounce. So, I need to derive a new class from Sprite. Since I want a bouncing pizza, I call the new class Pizza:

```
class Pizza(games.Sprite):
    """ A bouncing pizza. """
```

Overriding the update() Method

I need to add just a single method to the Pizza class to turn a moving pizza into a bouncing one. Every time the graphics window is updated by mainloop(), the following two things happen:

- Each sprite's position is updated based on its dx and dy properties
- Each sprite's update() method is called

Every Sprite object has an update() method; it just does nothing by default. So, by overriding update() in Pizza, I get the perfect place to put code that will handle screen boundary checking.

```
    def update(self):
        """ Reverse a velocity component if edge of screen reached. """
        if self.right > games.screen.width or self.left < 0:
            self.dx = -self.dx

        if self.bottom > games.screen.height or self.top < 0:
            self.dy = -self.dy
```

In the method, I check to see if the sprite is about to go beyond the screen limits in any direction. If so, I reverse the responsible velocity.

If the object's right property, which represents the x-coordinate of its right edge, is greater than games.screen.width, then the pizza is about to go off the right edge into oblivion. If the object's left property, which represents the x-coordinate of its left edge, is less than 0, then the pizza is headed off the screen to the left. In either case, I simply reverse dx, the pizza's horizontal velocity, to "bounce" the pizza off the screen boundary.

If the object's `bottom` property, which represents the y-coordinate of its bottom edge, is greater than `games.screen.height`, then the pizza is about to go off the bottom edge into oblivion. If the object's `top` property, which represents the y-coordinate of its top edge, is less than 0, then the pizza is headed off the top of the screen. In either case, I simply reverse `dy`, the pizza's vertical velocity, to "bounce" the pizza off the screen boundary.

Wrapping Up the Program

Since I define a class in the program, I thought I'd organize the rest of the code into a function:

```
def main():
    wall_image = games.load_image("wall.jpg", transparent = False)
    games.screen.background = wall_image

    pizza_image = games.load_image("pizza.bmp")
    the_pizza = Pizza(image = pizza_image,
                      x = games.screen.width/2,
                      y = games.screen.height/2,
                      dx = 1,
                      dy = 1)
    games.screen.add(the_pizza)

    games.screen.mainloop()

# kick it off!
main()
```

You've seen the bulk of this code before. One important difference is that I created an object from my new `Pizza` class instead of `Sprite`. Because of this, the object's `update()` method checks for screen boundaries and reverses the velocities when necessary for a pizza that bounces!

HANDLING MOUSE INPUT

Although you've seen a lot of what the `livewires` package has to offer, you haven't seen the main ingredient of interactivity: user input. One of the most common ways to get input from a user is through the mouse. `livewires` offers an object to let you do just that.

Introducing the Moving Pan Program

The mouse object from the games module gives you access to the mouse. The object has properties that make reading the mouse position on the graphics screen a piece of cake. With these properties, I create the Moving Pan program that allows a user to drag a pan sprite across the screen as he or she moves the mouse. The results of the program are displayed in Figure 11.13.

FIGURE 11.13

The pan sprite follows the mouse around the graphics screen.

You can find the code for the program on the companion website (www.courseptr.com/downloads) in the Chapter 11 folder; the file name is moving_pan.py.

Setting Up the Program

The following code should look remarkably familiar:

```
# Moving Pan
# Demonstrates mouse input

from livewires import games

games.init(screen_width = 640, screen_height = 480, fps = 50)
```

As before, I import games and initialize the graphics screen. The init() also creates the mouse object I'll use to read the mouse position.

Reading Mouse x- and y-coordinates

Next, I create Pan for the pan sprite:

```
class Pan(games.Sprite):
    """ A pan controlled by the mouse. """
    def update(self):
        """ Move to mouse coordinates. """
        self.x = games.mouse.x
        self.y = games.mouse.y
```

Like a Sprite object, the mouse object has an x property for its x-coordinate and a y property for its y-coordinate. With them, I can read the current mouse location on the graphics screen.

In the update() method, I assign the Pan object's x property the value of the mouse object's x property. Then I assign the Pan object's y property the value of the mouse object's y property. This moves the pan to the current location of the mouse pointer.

Next, I write a main() function that contains the type of code you've seen before that sets the background image and creates sprite objects:

```
def main():
    wall_image = games.load_image("wall.jpg", transparent = False)
    games.screen.background = wall_image

    pan_image = games.load_image("pan.bmp")
    the_pan = Pan(image = pan_image,
                  x = games.mouse.x,
                  y = games.mouse.y)
    games.screen.add(the_pan)
```

By passing games.mouse.x to x and games.mouse.y to y, the Pan object starts off at the mouse coordinates.

Setting Mouse Pointer Visibility

Next in main(), I use the mouse object's is_visible property to set the visibility of the mouse pointer.

```
    games.mouse.is_visible = False
```

Setting the property to True means the mouse pointer will be visible, while setting it to False means the pointer will not be visible. Since I don't want the pointer sitting on top of the pan image, I set the property to False.

Grabbing Input to the Graphics Window

Next in main(), I use the screen object's event_grab property to grab all of the input to the graphics screen:

```
games.screen.event_grab = True
```

Setting the property to True means that all input will be focused on the graphics screen. The benefit of this is that the mouse won't leave the graphics window. Setting the property to False means that all input is not focused on the graphics screen and that the mouse pointer can leave the graphics window.

 If you grab all of the input to the graphics screen, you won't be able to close the graphics window with the mouse. However, you can always close the window by pressing the Escape key.

Wrapping up the Program

Finally, I wrap up main() as before and invoke mainloop() to make sure everything on the screen is updated.

```
games.screen.mainloop()

# kick it off!
main()
```

Check out Table 11.9 for a summary of a few useful mouse properties.

TABLE 11.9   USEFUL MOUSE PROPERTIES

Property	Description
x	x-coordinate of mouse pointer.
y	y-coordinate of mouse pointer.
is_visible	Boolean value for setting visibility of mouse pointer. True is visible while False is not visible. Default value is True.

DETECTING COLLISIONS

In most games, when two things collide, there's a clear result. It can be as simple as a 2D character running into a boundary that won't let him pass, or as spectacular as a 3D scene where an asteroid tears through the hull of a massive mother ship. Either way, there's a need to detect when objects collide.

Introducing the Slippery Pizza Program

The Slippery Pizza program is an extension of the Moving Pan program. In the Slippery Pizza program, the user controls a pan with the mouse, just like in the Moving Pan program. This time, however, there's a pizza sprite on the screen. The user can move the pan toward the pizza, but as soon as he or she reaches it, the slippery pizza moves to a new, random screen location. Figures 11.14 and 11.15 show the program in action.

FIGURE 11.14

The player almost reaches the pizza.

FIGURE 11.15

The slippery pizza
gets away again.

You can find the code for the program on the companion website (www.courseptr.com/downloads) in the Chapter 11 folder; the file name is slippery_pizza.py.

Setting Up the Program

The initial code is taken from the Moving Pan program, with one minor addition:

```
# Slippery Pizza Program
# Demonstrates testing for sprite collisions

from livewires import games
import random

games.init(screen_width = 640, screen_height = 480, fps = 50)
```

The one new thing I do is import our old friend the random module. This allows me to generate a new, random location for the pizza sprite after the collision.

Detecting Collisions

I create a new Pan class by adding some code for the collision detection:

```
class Pan(games.Sprite):
    """ A pan controlled by the mouse. """
    def update(self):
        """ Move to mouse position. """
        self.x = games.mouse.x
        self.y = games.mouse.y
        self.check_collide()

    def check_collide(self):
        """ Check for collision with pizza. """
        for pizza in self.overlapping_sprites:
            pizza.handle_collide()
```

In the last line of update(), I invoke the Pan method check_collide(). The check_collide() method loops through the Pan object's overlapping_sprites property—a list of all of the objects that overlap it. Each object that overlaps the pan has its handle_collide() method called. Basically, the pan is telling any object that overlaps it to handle the collision.

Handling Collisions

Next, I create a new Pizza class:

```
class Pizza(games.Sprite):
    """ A slippery pizza. """
    def handle_collide(self):
        """ Move to a random screen location. """
        self.x = random.randrange(games.screen.width)
        self.y = random.randrange(games.screen.height)
```

I write just one method, handle_collide(), which generates random screen coordinates and moves the Pizza object to this new location.

Wrapping Up the Program

Here's the main() function:

```
def main():
    wall_image = games.load_image("wall.jpg", transparent = False)
    games.screen.background = wall_image

    pizza_image = games.load_image("pizza.bmp")
    pizza_x = random.randrange(games.screen.width)
```

```
pizza_y = random.randrange(games.screen.height)
the_pizza = Pizza(image = pizza_image, x = pizza_x, y = pizza_y)
games.screen.add(the_pizza)

pan_image = games.load_image("pan.bmp")
the_pan = Pan(image = pan_image,
              x = games.mouse.x,
              y = games.mouse.y)
games.screen.add(the_pan)

games.mouse.is_visible = False

games.screen.event_grab = True

games.screen.mainloop()
```

```
# kick it off!
main()
```

As always, I set a background image. Then, I create two objects: a `Pizza` object and a `Pan` object. I generate a random set of screen coordinates for the pizza and place the pan at the mouse coordinates. I set the mouse pointer to invisible and grab all input to the game window. Then, I invoke `mainloop()`. Finally, I kick everything off by calling `main()`.

BACK TO THE PIZZA PANIC GAME

Now that you've gotten a taste of what the `livewires` multimedia package can do, it's time to create the Pizza Panic game introduced at the beginning of the chapter. Much of the code for the game can be taken directly from the example programs. However, I'll also introduce a few new concepts. You can find the code for the program on the companion website (www.courseptr.com/downloads) in the Chapter 11 folder; the file name is pizza_panic.py.

Setting Up the Program

As in all of the programs in this chapter, I begin by importing modules and initializing the graphics screen:

```
# Pizza Panic
# Player must catch falling pizzas before they hit the ground

from livewires import games, color
```

```
import random

games.init(screen_width = 640, screen_height = 480, fps = 50)
```

To do any graphics work, I need to import games, while color gives me access to the set of predefined colors. I import random so that the crazy chef seems more life-like when he makes his choices. Finally, I call games init() to initialize the graphics screen and to give me access to the games mouse object.

The Pan Class

The Pan class is a blueprint for the pan sprite that the player controls with the mouse. However, the pan will only move left and right. I'll go through the class, one section at a time.

Loading the Pan Image

I do something a little different in the beginning of this class: I load a sprite image and assign it to a class variable, image. I do this because Pizza Panic has several classes, and loading an image in its corresponding class definition is cleaner than loading all of the images in the program's main() function.

```
class Pan(games.Sprite):
    """
    A pan controlled by player to catch falling pizzas.
    """
    image = games.load_image("pan.bmp")
```

The __init__() Method

Next, I write the constructor to initialize a new Pan object:

```
    def __init__(self):
        """ Initialize Pan object and create Text object for score. """
        super(Pan, self).__init__(image = Pan.image,
                                  x = games.mouse.x,
                                  bottom = games.screen.height)

        self.score = games.Text(value = 0, size = 25, color = color.black,
                                top = 5, right = games.screen.width - 10)
        games.screen.add(self.score)
```

I use the super() function to make sure that the Sprite init() method is called. Then, I define an attribute score—a Text object—for the player's score, which begins at 0. Of course, I remember to add the new Text object to the screen so it's displayed.

The update() Method

This method moves the player's pan:

```
def update(self):
    """ Move to mouse x position. """
    self.x = games.mouse.x

    if self.left < 0:
        self.left = 0

    if self.right > games.screen.width:
        self.right = games.screen.width

    self.check_catch()
```

The method assigns the mouse x-coordinate to the Pan object's x-coordinate, allowing the player to move the pan left and right with the mouse.

Next, I use the object's left property to check if its left edge is less than 0—meaning that part of the pan is beyond the left edge of the graphics window. If it is, I set the left edge to 0 so that the pan is displayed at the left edge of the window.

Then, I use the object's right property to check if its right edge is greater than games.screen.width—meaning that part of the pan is beyond the right edge of the graphics window. If it is, I set the right edge to games.screen.width so that the pan is displayed at the right edge of the window.

Finally, I invoke the object's check_catch() method.

The check_catch() Method

This method checks if the player has caught any of the falling pizzas:

```
def check_catch(self):
    """ Check if catch pizzas. """
    for pizza in self.overlapping_sprites:
        self.score.value += 10
        self.score.right = games.screen.width - 10
        pizza.handle_caught()
```

For each object that overlaps the pan, the method increases the player's score by 10. Then it ensures that the right edge of the Text object for the score is always 10 pixels from the right edge of the screen, no matter how many digits long the score gets. Lastly, the method invokes the handle_caught() method of the overlapping sprite.

The Pizza Class

This class is for the falling pizzas that the player must catch:

```
class Pizza(games.Sprite):
    """
    A pizza which falls to the ground.
    """
    image = games.load_image("pizza.bmp")
    speed = 1
```

I define two class variables: image for the pizza image and speed for the pizzas' falling speed. I set speed to 1 so that the pizzas fall at a fairly slow speed. I use both class variables in the Pizza constructor method, as you'll soon see.

The __init__() Method

This method initializes a new Pizza object:

```
    def __init__(self, x, y = 90):
        """ Initialize a Pizza object. """
        super(Pizza, self).__init__(image = Pizza.image,
                                    x = x, y = y,
                                    dy = Pizza.speed)
```

All I do in this method is call the constructor of the super class of Pizza. Note that I set the default value for y to 90, which puts each new pizza right at the chef's chest level.

The update() Method

This method handles screen boundary checking:

```
    def update(self):
        """ Check if bottom edge has reached screen bottom. """
        if self.bottom > games.screen.height:
            self.end_game()
            self.destroy()
```

All this method does is check if a pizza has reached the bottom of the screen. If it has, the method invokes the object's `end_game()` method and then the object removes itself from the screen.

The handle_caught() Method

Remember, this method is invoked by the `Pan` object when the `Pizza` object collides with it:

```python
def handle_caught(self):
    """ Destroy self if caught. """
    self.destroy()
```

When a pizza collides with a pan, the pizza is considered "caught" and simply ceases to exist. So, the `Pizza` object invokes its own `destroy()` method and the pizza literally disappears.

The end_game() Method

This method ends the game. It's invoked when a pizza reaches the bottom of the screen.

```python
def end_game(self):
    """ End the game. """
    end_message = games.Message(value = "Game Over",
                                size = 90,
                                color = color.red,
                                x = games.screen.width/2,
                                y = games.screen.height/2,
                                lifetime = 5 * games.screen.fps,
                                after_death = games.screen.quit)
    games.screen.add(end_message)
```

The code creates a `Message` object that declares that the game is over. After about five seconds, the message disappears and the graphics window closes, ending the game.

The `end_game()` method is called whenever a pizza reaches the bottom of the screen. However, since the "Game Over" message lasts about five seconds, it's possible for another pizza to reach the bottom of the screen before the graphics window closes—resulting in multiple "Game Over" messages.

In Chapter 12, you'll see how to create an object to represent the game itself, which could keep track of whether or not the game is over and prevent something like multiple "Game Over" messages from being created.

The Chef Class

The `Chef` class is used to create the crazy chef who throws the pizzas off the restaurant rooftop.

```
class Chef(games.Sprite):
    """
    A chef which moves left and right, dropping pizzas.
    """
    image = games.load_image("chef.bmp")
```

I define a class attribute, image, for the chef image.

The __init__() Method

Here's the constructor method:

```
def __init__(self, y = 55, speed = 2, odds_change = 200):
    """ Initialize the Chef object. """
    super(Chef, self).__init__(image = Chef.image,
                               x = games.screen.width / 2,
                               y = y,
                               dx = speed)

    self.odds_change = odds_change
    self.time_til_drop = 0
```

First, I call the constructor of the super class of Chef. I pass image the class attribute Chef.image. I pass x a value that puts the chef right in the middle of the screen. For y, the default value of 55 puts the chef right on top of the brick wall. dx is passed speed, which determines the chef's horizontal velocity as he moves along the rooftop. The default value is 2.

The method also creates two object attributes: odds_change and time_til_drop. odds_change is an integer that represents the odds that the chef will change his direction. For example, if odds_change is 200, then there's a 1 in 200 chance that every time the chef moves, he'll reverse direction. You'll see how this works in the update() method of the class.

time_til_drop is an integer that represents the amount of time, in mainloop() cycles, until the chef drops his next pizza. I set it to 0 initially, meaning that when a Chef object springs to life, it should immediately drop a pizza. You'll see how time_til_drop works in the check_drop() method.

The update() Method

This method defines the rules for how the chef decides to slide back and forth along the rooftop:

```
def update(self):
    """ Determine if direction needs to be reversed. """
    if self.left < 0 or self.right > games.screen.width:
        self.dx = -self.dx
    elif random.randrange(self.odds_change) == 0:
        self.dx = -self.dx

    self.check_drop()
```

A chef slides along the rooftop in one direction until he either reaches the edge of the screen or "decides," at random, to switch directions. The beginning of this method checks to see if the chef has moved beyond the left or right edge of the graphics window. If he has, then he reverses direction with the code `self.dx = -self.dx`. Otherwise, the chef has a 1 in `odds_change` chance of changing direction.

Regardless of whether or not the chef changes direction, the last thing the method does is invoke the `Chef` object's `check_drop()` method.

The check_drop() Method

This method is invoked every `mainloop()` cycle, but that doesn't mean a new pizza is dropped 50 times a second!

```
def check_drop(self):
    """ Decrease countdown or drop pizza and reset countdown. """
    if self.time_til_drop > 0:
        self.time_til_drop -= 1
    else:
        new_pizza = Pizza(x = self.x)
        games.screen.add(new_pizza)

        # set buffer to approx 30% of pizza height, regardless of pizza speed
        self.time_til_drop = int(new_pizza.height * 1.3 / Pizza.speed) + 1
```

`time_til_drop` represents a countdown for our chef. If `time_til_drop` is greater than 0, then 1 is subtracted from it. Otherwise, a new `Pizza` object is created and `time_til_drop` is reset.

In creating a new pizza, I pass the `Chef` object's x-coordinate to the `Pizza` constructor so that the new pizza sprite begins at the same location as the chef sprite.

The new value of `time_til_drop` is calculated so that the next pizza will be dropped when the distance from the previous one is about 30% of the pizza height, independent of how fast the pizzas are falling.

The main() Function

The `main()` function creates objects and starts up the game:

```
def main():
    """ Play the game. """
    wall_image = games.load_image("wall.jpg", transparent = False)
    games.screen.background = wall_image

    the_chef = Chef()
    games.screen.add(the_chef)

    the_pan = Pan()
    games.screen.add(the_pan)

    games.mouse.is_visible = False

    games.screen.event_grab = True
    games.screen.mainloop()

# start it up!
main()
```

First, I set the brick wall as the background. I create a chef and a pan. Then, I set the mouse pointer to invisible and grab all of the input so the mouse pointer can't leave the graphics window. I invoke `mainloop()` to begin the game. Finally, I call `main()` to kick it all off!

SUMMARY

In this chapter, you saw how to use the `livewires` multimedia package to add graphics to your programs. You learned how to create a new graphics window and how to set a background image for it. You saw how to display text on a graphics window. You learned about the sprite, a special graphics object with an image. Specifically, you saw how to place and move a sprite on a graphics screen. You also saw how to test for collisions between sprites. You learned how to get input from the mouse. Finally, you saw how to put everything together in a fast-paced video game, complete with a computer-controlled opponent.

CHALLENGES

1. Improve the Pizza Panic game by increasing its difficulty as the game progresses. Think of different ways to accomplish this. You could increase the speed of the pizzas and the speed of the chef. You could raise the player's pan to a higher position on the screen. You could even increase the number of crazy chefs flinging pizzas.

2. Write a game where the player controls a character that must avoid falling debris. The player controls the character with the mouse and objects fall from the sky.

3. Create a simple, one-player game of pong, where a player controls a paddle and the ball bounces off three walls. If the ball gets by the player's paddle, the game is over.

Sound, Animation, and Program Development: The Astrocrash Game

I n this chapter, you'll expand your multimedia programming skills to include sound and moving images. You'll also see how to write a large program in stages. Specifically, you'll learn to do the following:

- Read the keyboard
- Play sound files
- Play music files
- Create animations
- Develop a program by writing progressively more complete versions of it

Introducing the Astrocrash Game

The project for this chapter, the Astrocrash game, is my version of the classic arcade game *Asteroids*. In Astrocrash, the player controls a ship in a moving field of deadly asteroids. The ship can rotate and thrust forward—most importantly, though, it can fire missiles at the asteroids to destroy them. The player, however, has some work cut out for him or her as large- and medium sized asteroids break apart into two smaller asteroids when destroyed. And just when the player manages to obliterate all of the asteroids, a new, larger wave appears. The player's score increases with every asteroid he or she destroys, but once the player's ship collides with a floating space rock, the game is over. Figures 12.1 and 12.2 show the game in action.

FIGURE 12.1

The player controls a spaceship and blasts asteroids to increase his or her score. (Nebula image is in the public domain. Credit: NASA, The Hubble Heritage Team—AURA/ STScI)

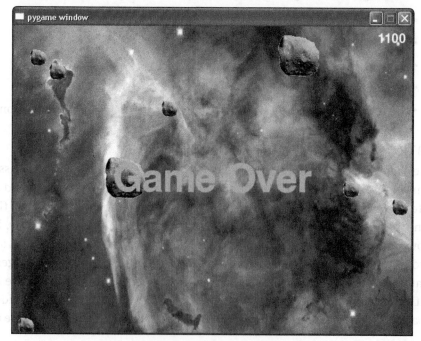

FIGURE 12.2

If an asteroid hits the player's ship, the game is over.

READING THE KEYBOARD

You already know how to get strings from the user through the input() function, but reading the keyboard for individual keystrokes is another matter. Fortunately, there's a new object from the games module that lets you do just this.

Introducing the Read Key Program

The Read Key program displays the ship on the nebula background. The user can move the ship around with different keystrokes. When the user presses the W key, the ship moves up. When the user presses the S key, the ship moves down. When the user presses the A key, the ship moves left. When the user presses the D key, the ship moves right. The user can also press multiple keys simultaneously for a combined effect. For example, when the user presses the W and D keys simultaneously, the ship moves diagonally, up and to the right. The program is illustrated in Figure 12.3.

FIGURE 12.3

The ship moves around the screen based on keystrokes.

You can find the code for the program on the companion website (www.courseptr.com/downloads) in the Chapter 12 folder; the file name is read_key.py.

Setting Up the Program

As I do with all programs that use the livewires package, I start by importing the modules I need and calling the initialization method:

```
# Read Key
# Demonstrates reading the keyboard

from livewires import games

games.init(screen_width = 640, screen_height = 480, fps = 50)
```

Testing for Keystrokes

Next, I write a class for the ship. In the update() method, I check for keystrokes and change the position of the ship accordingly.

```
class Ship(games.Sprite):
    """ A moving ship. """
    def update(self):
        """ Move ship based on keys pressed. """
        if games.keyboard.is_pressed(games.K_w):
            self.y -= 1
        if games.keyboard.is_pressed(games.K_s):
            self.y += 1
        if games.keyboard.is_pressed(games.K_a):
            self.x -= 1
        if games.keyboard.is_pressed(games.K_d):
            self.x += 1
```

I use the new keyboard object from the games module. You can use the object to test for specific keypresses. I invoke the object's is_pressed() method, which returns True if the key being tested for is pressed, and False if not.

I use the is_pressed() method in a series of if statements to test if any of the four keys—W, S, A, or D—is being pressed. If the W key is pressed, I decrease the object's y property by 1, moving the sprite up the screen by one pixel. If the S key is pressed, I increase the object's y property by 1, moving the sprite down the screen. If the A key is pressed, I decrease the object's x property by 1, moving the sprite left. If the D key is pressed, I increase the object's x property by 1, moving the sprite right.

Since multiple calls to is_pressed() can read simultaneous keypresses, the user can hold down multiple keys for a combined effect. For example, if a user holds down the D and S keys at the same time, the ship moves down and to the right because each time update() executes, the Ship object adds one to its x-coordinate and one to its y-coordinate.

The games module has a set of constants that represent keys that you can use as an argument in is_pressed(). In this program, I use the games.K_w constant for the W key; games.K_s for the S key; games.K_a for the A key; and games.K_d for the D key. The naming of these constants is pretty intuitive. Here's a quick way to figure out the name of most key constants:

- All keyboard constants begin with games.K_.
- For alphabetic keys, add the key letter, in lowercase, to the end of the constant name. For example, the constant for the A key is games.K_a.
- For numeric keys, add the key number to the end of the constant name. For example, the constant for the 1 key is games.K_1.
- For other keys, you can often add their name, in all capital letters, to the end of the constant name. For example, the constant for the spacebar is games.K_SPACE.

For a complete list of keyboard constants, see the livewires documentation in Appendix B.

Wrapping Up the Program

Finally, I write the familiar main() function. I load the nebula background image, create a ship in the middle of the screen, and kick everything off by invoking mainloop().

```
def main():
    nebula_image = games.load_image("nebula.jpg", transparent = False)
    games.screen.background = nebula_image

    ship_image = games.load_image("ship.bmp")
    the_ship = Ship(image = ship_image,
                    x = games.screen.width/2,
                    y = games.screen.height/2)
    games.screen.add(the_ship)

    games.screen.mainloop()

main()
```

ROTATING A SPRITE

In Chapter 11, you learned how to move sprites around the screen, but livewires lets you rotate them as well. You rotate a sprite through one of its properties.

Introducing the Rotate Sprite Program

In the Rotate Sprite program, the user can rotate the spacecraft using the keyboard. If the user presses the right arrow key, the ship rotates clockwise. If the user presses the left arrow key, the ship rotates counterclockwise. If the user presses the 1 key, the ship jumps to a rotation of 0 degrees. If the user presses the 2 key, the ship jumps to a rotation of 90 degrees. If the user presses the 3 key, the ship jumps to a rotation of 180 degrees. If the user presses the 4 key, the ship jumps to a rotation of 270 degrees. Figure 12.4 displays the program.

> The Rotate Sprite program checks for keypresses of the numeric keys above the letter keys on the keyboard, not the numeric keys on the keypad.

FIGURE 12.4

The ship can rotate clockwise, rotate counterclockwise, or jump to a predetermined angle.

You can find the code for the program on the companion website (www.courseptr.com/downloads) in the Chapter 12 folder; the file name is rotate_sprite.py.

```python
# Rotate Sprite
# Demonstrates rotating a sprite

from livewires import games

games.init(screen_width = 640, screen_height = 480, fps = 50)

class Ship(games.Sprite):
    """ A rotating ship. """
    def update(self):
        """ Rotate based on keys pressed. """
        if games.keyboard.is_pressed(games.K_RIGHT):
            self.angle += 1
        if games.keyboard.is_pressed(games.K_LEFT):
            self.angle -= 1

        if games.keyboard.is_pressed(games.K_1):
            self.angle = 0
        if games.keyboard.is_pressed(games.K_2):
            self.angle = 90
        if games.keyboard.is_pressed(games.K_3):
            self.angle = 180
        if games.keyboard.is_pressed(games.K_4):
            self.angle = 270

def main():
    nebula_image = games.load_image("nebula.jpg", transparent = False)
    games.screen.background = nebula_image

    ship_image = games.load_image("ship.bmp")
    the_ship = Ship(image = ship_image,
                    x = games.screen.width/2,
                    y = games.screen.height/2)
    games.screen.add(the_ship)

    games.screen.mainloop()

main()
```

Using a Sprite's angle Property

The new element in the program is the `angle` property, which represents a sprite's facing in degrees. You can add to or subtract from the property, or you can simply assign a new value to it to change the facing of a sprite.

In the `update()` method, I first check if the right arrow key is pressed. If it is, I add one to the object's `angle` property, which rotates the sprite by one degree clockwise. Next, I check if the left arrow key is pressed. If it is, I subtract one from the property, rotating the sprite one degree counterclockwise.

The next set of lines rotates the ship directly to a specific angle by assigning a new value to the `angle` property. When the user presses the 1 key, the code assigns 0 to `angle` and the sprite jumps to a rotation of 0 degrees (its starting orientation). When the user presses the 2 key, the code assigns `90` to `angle` and the sprite jumps to a rotation of 90 degrees. When the user presses the 3 key, the code assigns `180` to `angle` and the sprite jumps to a rotation of 180 degrees. Finally, when the user presses the 4 key, the code assigns `270` to `angle` and the sprite jumps to a rotation of 270 degrees.

CREATING AN ANIMATION

Moving and rotating sprites adds excitement to a game, but animation really makes a game come to life. Fortunately, the `games` module contains a class for animations, aptly named `Animation`.

Introducing the Explosion Program

The Explosion program creates an explosion animation in the middle of a graphics screen. The animation plays continuously so that you can get a good look at it. When you're done appreciating the cool effect, you can end the program by closing the graphics window. Figure 12.5 shows a snapshot of the program in action.

FIGURE 12.5

Although it's hard to tell from a still image, an explosion animates at the center of the graphics window.

Examining the Explosion Images

An animation is a sequence of images (also called *frames*) displayed in succession. I created a sequence of nine images that, when displayed in succession, resembles a fiery explosion. Figure 12.6 displays all nine images.

You can find the code for the program on the companion website (www.courseptr.com/downloads) in the Chapter 12 folder; the file name is explosion.py.

FIGURE 12.6

Shown in rapid
succession, these
nine frames look
like an explosion.

Setting Up the Program

As always, the initial code imports the modules I need and calls the initialization method:

```
# Explosion
# Demonstrates creating an animation

from livewires import games

games.init(screen_width = 640, screen_height = 480, fps = 50)
```

Then, I set the background of the graphics screen:

```
nebula_image = games.load_image("nebula.jpg", transparent = 0)
games.screen.background = nebula_image
```

Creating a List of Image Files

The constructor of the Animation class takes a list of image file names or a list of image objects for the sequence of images to display. So, next, I create a list of image file names, which corresponds to the images shown in Figure 12.6:

```
explosion_files = ["explosion1.bmp",
                   "explosion2.bmp",
                   "explosion3.bmp",
                   "explosion4.bmp",
                   "explosion5.bmp",
                   "explosion6.bmp",
                   "explosion7.bmp",
                   "explosion8.bmp",
                   "explosion9.bmp"]
```

Creating an Animation Object

Finally, I create an `Animation` object and add it to the screen:

```
explosion = games.Animation(images = explosion_files,
                            x = games.screen.width/2,
                            y = games.screen.height/2,
                            n_repeats = 0,
                            repeat_interval = 5)
games.screen.add(explosion)
```

The `Animation` class is derived from `Sprite`, so it inherits all of `Sprite`'s attributes, properties, and methods. Like all sprites, you can supply x- and y-coordinates to define where an animation will be located. In the previous code, I supply coordinates to the class constructor so that the animation is created at the center of the screen.

An animation is different from a sprite in that it has a list of images that it cycles through. So, you must supply a list of image file names as strings or a list of image objects for the images to be displayed. I supply a list of strings for the image file names, `explosion_files`, to `images`.

An object's `n_repeats` attribute represents how many times the animation (as a sequence of all of its images) is displayed. A value of 0 means that the animation will loop forever. The default value of `n_repeats` is 0. Since I pass 0 to `n_repeats`, the explosion animation will cycle forever (or at least until you close the graphics window).

An object's `repeat_interval` attribute represents the delay between successive images. A higher number means a longer delay between frames, resulting in a slower animation. A lower number represents a shorter delay, producing a faster animation. I pass `repeat_interval` the value 5 to get the speed I think is right for a convincing explosion.

Last but not least, I kick off the program by invoking the `screen` object's `mainloop()` method:

```
games.screen.mainloop()
```

WORKING WITH SOUND AND MUSIC

Sound and music add another sensory dimension to your programs. Loading, playing, looping, and stopping sound and music are easy to do with the `games` module. While people might argue about the difference between sound and music, there's no such argument when it comes to `livewires`, where there's a clear distinction between the two.

Introducing the Sound and Music Program

The Sound and Music program allows the user to play, loop, and stop the missile sound effect and the theme music from the Astrocrash game. The user can even play both at the same time. Figure 12.7 shows the program running (but, unfortunately, doesn't make a sound).

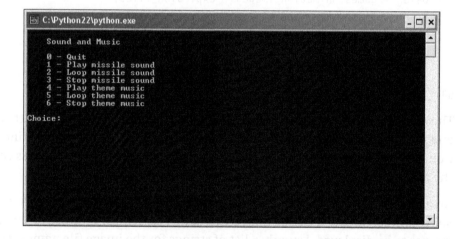

FIGURE 12.7

The program lets the user play a sound and some music.

 When you run the program, you'll want to interact with the console window. You should position the console window so that it's not hidden by the graphics window. You can ignore or even minimize the graphics window created by the program.

You can find the code for the program on the companion website (www.courseptr.com/downloads) in the Chapter 12 folder; the file name is sound_and_music.py.

Working with Sounds

You can create a sound object for use in a program by loading a WAV file. The WAV format is great for sound effects because it can be used to encode whatever you record with a microphone.

Loading a Sound

First, I set up the program as always:

```
# Sound and Music
# Demonstrates playing sound and music files

from livewires import games

games.init(screen_width = 640, screen_height = 480, fps = 50)
```

Then, I load a WAV file by using the games function load_sound().

```
# load a sound file
missile_sound = games.load_sound("missile.wav")
```

The function takes a string for the name of the sound file to be loaded. I load the file missile.wav and assign the resulting sound object to missile.

TRAP   You can only load WAV files with the load_sound() function.

Next, I load the music file:

```
# load the music file
games.music.load("theme.mid")
```

I'll save the music discussion until after I finish demonstrating sounds.

Playing a Sound

Next, I write the menu system that you first saw in Chapter 5:

```
choice = None
while choice != "0":

    print(
```

```
"""
Sound and Music

0 - Quit
1 - Play missile sound
2 - Loop missile sound
3 - Stop missile sound
4 - Play theme music
5 - Loop theme music
6 - Stop theme music
"""
)

choice = input("Choice: ")
print()

# exit
if choice == "0":
    print("Good-bye.")
```

If the user enters 0, the program says good-bye and then exits.

The following code handles the case where a user enters 1:

```
# play missile sound
elif choice == "1":
    missile_sound.play()
    print("Playing missile sound.")
```

To play the sound once, I invoke the sound object's play() method. When a sound plays, it takes up one of the eight available sound channels. To play a sound, you need at least one open sound channel. Once all eight sound channels are in use, invoking a sound object's play() method has no effect.

If you invoke the play() method of a sound object that's already playing, the sound will start playing on another sound channel, if one is available.

Looping a Sound

You can loop a sound by passing the number of additional times you want the sound played to the object's play() method. For example, if you pass 3 to play(), the corresponding sound will play four times (its initial playing plus three additional times). You can loop a sound forever by passing -1 to play().

The following code handles the case when a user enters 2:

```
# loop missile sound
elif choice == "2":
    loop = int(input("Loop how many extra times? (-1 = forever): "))
    missile_sound.play(loop)
    print("Looping missile sound.")
```

In this section of code, I get the number of additional times the user wants to hear the missile sound and then I pass that value to the sound object's play() method.

Stopping a Sound

You stop a sound object from playing by invoking its stop() method. This stops the particular sound on all channels that it's playing. If you invoke the stop() method of a sound object that's not currently playing, you'll find livewires is forgiving and won't complain with an error.

If the user enters 3, the following code stops the missile sound (if it's playing):

```
# stop missile sound
elif choice == "3":
    missile_sound.stop()
    print("Stopping missile sound.")
```

Working with Music

In livewires, music is handled somewhat differently than sound. First, there is only one music channel, so only one file can be designated as the current music file at any given time. However, the music channel is more flexible than the sound channels. The music channel accepts many different types of sound files, including WAV, MP3, OGG, and MIDI. Finally, since there is only one music channel, you don't create a new object for each music file. Instead, you access a set of functions to load, play, and stop music.

Loading Music

You saw the code for loading the music file in the section "Loading a Sound." The code accesses music from games. It's through music that you're able to load, play, and stop the single music track.

The code I used to load the music track, games.music.load("theme.mid"), sets the current music to the MIDI file theme.mid. You load a music file by calling the games.music.load() function and passing it the music file name as a string.

You have only one available music track. So, if you load a new music file, it replaces the current one.

Playing Music

The following code handles the case where the user enters 4:

```
# play theme music
elif choice == "4":
    games.music.play()
    print("Playing theme music.")
```

As a result, the computer plays the music file that I loaded, theme.mid. If you don't pass any values to games.music.play(), the music plays once.

Looping Music

You can loop the music by passing the number of additional times you want the music played to play(). For example, if you pass 3 to games.music.play(), the music will play four times (its initial playing plus an additional three times). You can loop a music file forever by passing -1 to the function.

The following code handles the case when a user enters 5:

```
# loop theme music
elif choice == "5":
    loop = int(input("Loop how many extra times? (-1 = forever): "))
    games.music.play(loop)
    print("Looping theme music.")
```

In this section of code, I get the number of additional times the user wants to hear the theme music and then I pass that value to play().

Stopping Music

If the user enters 6, the following code stops the music (if it's playing):

```
# stop theme music
elif choice == "6":
    games.music.stop()
    print("Stopping theme music.")
```

You can stop the current music from playing by calling games.music.stop(), which is what I do here. If you call the function while there is no music playing, livewires is forgiving and won't complain with an error.

Wrapping Up the Program

Finally, I wrap up the program by handling an invalid choice and waiting for the user:

```
# some unknown choice
else:
    print("\nSorry, but", choice, "isn't a valid choice.")

input("\n\nPress the enter key to exit.")
```

PLANNING THE ASTROCRASH GAME

It's time to return to the chapter project: the Astrocrash game. I plan to write progressively more complete versions of the game until it's done, but I still feel I need to list a few details of the program, including the game's major features, a few necessary classes, and the multimedia assets required.

Game Features

Although my game is based on a classic video game that I know well (and learned about the hard way, one quarter at a time), it's still a good idea to write out a list of features:

- The ship should rotate and thrust forward based on keystrokes from the player.
- The ship should fire missiles based on a keystroke from the player.
- Asteroids should float at different velocities on the screen. Smaller asteroids should generally have higher velocities than larger ones.
- The ship, any missiles, and any asteroids should "wrap around" the screen—if they move beyond a screen boundary, they should appear at the opposite boundary.
- If a missile hits another object on the screen, it should destroy the other object and itself in a nice, fiery explosion.
- If the ship hits any other object on the screen, it should destroy the other object and itself in a nice, fiery explosion.
- If the ship is destroyed, the game is over.
- If a large asteroid is destroyed, two new medium-sized asteroids should be produced. If a medium-sized asteroid is destroyed, two new small asteroids should be produced. If a small asteroid is destroyed, no new asteroids should be produced.
- Every time a player destroys an asteroid, his or her score should increase. Smaller asteroids should be worth more points than larger ones.
- The player's score should be displayed in the upper-right corner of the screen.
- Once all of the asteroids have been destroyed, a new, larger wave of asteroids should be created.

I leave out a few features of the original to keep the game simple.

Game Classes

Next, I make a list of the classes that I think I need:

- `Ship`
- `Missile`
- `Asteroid`
- `Explosion`

I know a few things about these classes already. `Ship`, `Missile`, and `Asteroid` will be derived from `games.Sprite`, while `Explosion` will be derived from `games.Animation`. I also know that this list could change as I put theory into practice and code the game.

Game Assets

Since the game includes sound, music, sprites, and animation, I know I need to create some multimedia files. Here's the list I came up with:

- An image file for the ship
- An image file for the missiles
- Three image files, one for each size of asteroid
- A series of image files for an explosion
- A sound file for the thrusting of the ship
- A sound file for the firing of a missile
- A sound file for the explosion of an object
- A music file for the theme

CREATING ASTEROIDS

Since the game involves deadly asteroids, I thought I'd start with them. Although this seems like the best first step to me, it may not to another programmer—and that's fine. You could certainly start with a different first step, such as getting the player's ship on the screen. There's no one right first step. The important thing to do is define and complete "bite-sized" programs that build on each other, working your way toward the completed project.

The Astrocrash01 Program

The Astrocrash01 program creates a graphics window, sets the nebula background, and spawns eight asteroids at random locations. The velocity of each asteroid is also randomly calculated, but smaller asteroids have the potential to move faster than larger ones. Figure 12.8 shows the program in action.

FIGURE 12.8

A field of moving asteroids is the foundation of the game.

You can find the code for the program on the companion website (www.courseptr.com/ downloads) in the Chapter 12 folder; the file name is astrocrash01.py.

Setting Up the Program

The program starts like most others:

```
# Astrocrash01
# Get asteroids moving on the screen

import random
from livewires import games

games.init(screen_width = 640, screen_height = 480, fps = 50)
```

I import the `random` module to generate random x- and y-coordinates for the asteroids.

The Asteroid Class

The Asteroid class is used for creating moving asteroids:

```
class Asteroid(games.Sprite):
    """ An asteroid which floats across the screen. """
    SMALL = 1
    MEDIUM = 2
    LARGE = 3
    images = {SMALL  : games.load_image("asteroid_small.bmp"),
              MEDIUM : games.load_image("asteroid_med.bmp"),
              LARGE  : games.load_image("asteroid_big.bmp") }


    SPEED = 2
```

The first thing I do is define class constants for the three different asteroid sizes: SMALL, MEDIUM, and LARGE. Then I create a dictionary with the sizes and corresponding asteroid image objects. This way, I can use a size constant to look up the corresponding image object. Finally, I create a class constant, SPEED, that I'll use as a base to calculate the random speed of each asteroid.

The _init()_ Method

Next, I tackle the constructor method:

```
    def __init__(self, x, y, size):
        """ Initialize asteroid sprite. """
        super(Asteroid, self).__init__(
            image = Asteroid.images[size],
            x = x, y = y,
            dx = random.choice([1, -1]) * Asteroid.SPEED * random.random()/size,
            dy = random.choice([1, -1]) * Asteroid.SPEED * random.random()/size)

        self.size = size
```

The value passed to size represents the size of the asteroid and should be one of the size constants: Asteroid.SMALL, Asteroid.MEDIUM, or Asteroid.LARGE. Based on size, the correct image for the new asteroid is retrieved and then passed along to Sprite's constructor (since Sprite is the superclass of Asteroid). The x and y values passed to Asteroid for the location of the new space rock are also passed on to Sprite's constructor.

The Asteroid constructor generates random values for the new object's velocity components and passes those off to Sprite's constructor. The velocity components are random, but smaller asteroids have the potential to move faster than larger ones. Finally, the Asteroid constructor creates and initializes the object's size attribute.

The update() Method

The update() method keeps an asteroid in play by wrapping it around the screen:

```
def update(self):
    """ Wrap around screen. """
    if self.top > games.screen.height:
        self.bottom = 0

    if self.bottom < 0:
        self.top = games.screen.height

    if self.left > games.screen.width:
        self.right = 0

    if self.right < 0:
        self.left = games.screen.width
```

The main() Function

Finally, the main() function sets the nebula background and creates eight asteroids at random screen locations:

```
def main():
    # establish background
    nebula_image = games.load_image("nebula.jpg")
    games.screen.background = nebula_image

    # create 8 asteroids
    for i in range(8):
        x = random.randrange(games.screen.width)
        y = random.randrange(games.screen.height)
        size = random.choice([Asteroid.SMALL, Asteroid.MEDIUM, Asteroid.LARGE])
        new_asteroid = Asteroid(x = x, y = y, size = size)
        games.screen.add(new_asteroid)

    games.screen.mainloop()
```

```
# kick it off!
main()
```

ROTATING THE SHIP

For my next task, I introduce the player's ship. My modest goal is to allow a user to rotate the ship with the arrow keys. I plan to attack the other ship functions later.

The Astrocrash02 Program

The Astrocrash02 program extends Astrocrash01. In the new version, I create a ship at the center of the screen that the player can rotate. If the player presses the right arrow key, the ship rotates clockwise. If the player presses the left arrow key, the ship rotates counterclockwise. Figure 12.9 shows the program in action.

FIGURE 12.9

The player's ship is now part of the action.

You can find the code for the program on the companion website (www.courseptr.com/downloads) in the Chapter 12 folder; the file name is astrocrash02.py.

The Ship Class

The main thing I have to do is write a Ship class for the player's ship:

```
class Ship(games.Sprite):
    """ The player's ship. """
    image = games.load_image("ship.bmp")
    ROTATION_STEP = 3

    def update(self):
        """ Rotate based on keys pressed. """
        if games.keyboard.is_pressed(games.K_LEFT):
            self.angle -= Ship.ROTATION_STEP
        if games.keyboard.is_pressed(games.K_RIGHT):
            self.angle += Ship.ROTATION_STEP
```

This class is similar to the Rotate Sprite program from earlier in this chapter, but there are some differences. First, I load the image of the ship and assign the resulting image object to the class variable image. Second, I use the class constant ROTATION_STEP for the number of degrees by which the ship rotates.

Instantiating a Ship Object

The last thing I do in this new version of the game is instantiate a Ship object and add it to the screen. I create the new ship in main():

```
# create the ship
the_ship = Ship(image = Ship.image,
                x = games.screen.width/2,
                y = games.screen.height/2)
games.screen.add(the_ship)
```

MOVING THE SHIP

In the next version of the program, I get the ship moving. The player can press the up arrow key to engage the ship's engine. This applies thrust to the ship in the direction the ship is facing. Since there's no friction, the ship keeps moving based on all of the thrust the player applies to it.

The Astrocrash03 Program

When the player engages the ship's engine, the Astrocrash03 program changes the velocity of the ship based on the ship's angle (and produces an appropriate sound effect, too). Figure 12.10 illustrates the program.

You can find the code for the program on the companion website (www.courseptr.com/downloads) in the Chapter 12 folder; the file name is astrocrash03.py.

Importing the math Module

The first thing I do is import a new module at the top of the program:

```
import math, random
```

The math module contains a bunch of mathematical functions and constants, but don't let that scare you. I use only a few in this program.

Adding Ship Class Variable and Constant

I create a class constant, VELOCITY_STEP, for altering the ship's velocity:

```
VELOCITY_STEP = .03
```

A higher number would make the ship accelerate faster, while a lower number would make the ship accelerate more slowly.

I also add a new class variable, sound, for the thrusting sound of the ship:

```
sound = games.load_sound("thrust.wav")
```

Modifying Ship's update() Method

Next, I add code to the end of Ship's update() method to get the ship moving. I check to see if the player is pressing the up arrow key. If so, I play the thrusting sound:

```
# apply thrust based on up arrow key
if games.keyboard.is_pressed(games.K_UP):
    Ship.sound.play()
```

Now, when the player presses the up arrow key, I need to alter the ship's velocity components (the Ship object's dx and dy). So, given the angle of the ship, how can I figure out how much to change each velocity component? Well, the answer is trigonometry. Wait, don't slam this book shut and run as fast as your legs can carry you, screaming incoherently. As promised, I use only two mathematical functions in a few lines of code to figure this out.

To start the process, I get the angle of the ship, converted to radians:

```
# change velocity components based on ship's angle
angle = self.angle * math.pi / 180  # convert to radians
```

A radian is just a measure of rotation, like a degree. Python's math module expects angles in radians (while livewires works with degrees) so that's why I need to make the conversion. In the calculation, I use the math module constant pi, which represents the number pi.

Now that I've got the ship's angle in radians, I can figure out how much to change each velocity component using the math module's sin() and cos() functions, which calculate an angle's sine and cosine. The following lines calculate the object's new dx and dy values:

```
self.dx += Ship.VELOCITY_STEP * math.sin(angle)
self.dy += Ship.VELOCITY_STEP * -math.cos(angle)
```

Basically, math.sin(angle) represents the percent of the thrust that should be applied to the ship's velocity in the x direction, while the -math.cos(angle) represents the percent of the thrust that should be applied to the ship's velocity in the y direction.

All that's left to do is handle the screen boundaries. I use the same strategy as I did with the asteroids: The ship should wrap around the screen. In fact, I copy and paste the code from Asteroid's update() method to the end of Ship's update() method:

```
# wrap the ship around screen
if self.top > games.screen.height:
    self.bottom = 0

if self.bottom < 0:
```

```
        self.top = games.screen.height

    if self.left > games.screen.width:
        self.right = 0

    if self.right < 0:
        self.left = games.screen.width
```

Although this works, copying and pasting large portions of code is usually a sign of poor design. I'll revisit this code later and find a more elegant solution.

Repeated chunks of code bloat programs and make them harder to maintain. When you see repeated code, it's often time for a new function or class. Think about how you might consolidate the code into one place and call or invoke it from the parts of your program where the repeated code currently lives.

Firing Missiles

Next, I enable the ship to fire missiles. When the player presses the spacebar, a missile fires from the ship's cannon and flies off in the direction the ship is facing. The missile should destroy anything it hits—but to keep things simple, I save the fun of destruction for another version of the program.

The Astrocrash04 Program

The Astrocrash04 program allows the player to fire missiles by pressing the spacebar, but there's a problem. If the player holds down the spacebar, a stream of missiles pours out of the ship at a rate of about 50 per second. I need to limit the missile fire rate, but I leave that issue for the next version of the game. Figure 12.11 shows off the Astrocrash04 program, warts and all.

You can find the code for the program on the companion website (www.courseptr.com/downloads) in the Chapter 12 folder; the file name is astrocrash04.py.

Stream of missiles

FIGURE 12.11

The missile fire
rate is too high.

Modifying Ship's update() Method

I modify Ship's update() method by adding code so that a ship can fire missiles. If the player presses the spacebar, a new missile is created:

```
# fire missile if spacebar pressed
if games.keyboard.is_pressed(games.K_SPACE):
    new_missile = Missile(self.x, self.y, self.angle)
    games.screen.add(new_missile)
```

Of course, in order to instantiate a new object from Missile(self.x, self.y, self.angle), I need to write a little something...like a Missile class.

The Missile Class

I write the Missile class for the missiles that the ship fires. I start by creating class variables and class constants:

```
class Missile(games.Sprite):
    """ A missile launched by the player's ship. """
    image = games.load_image("missile.bmp")
    sound = games.load_sound("missile.wav")
```

```
BUFFER = 40
VELOCITY_FACTOR = 7
LIFETIME = 40
```

image is for the image of a missile—a solid, red circle. sound is for the sound effect of a missile launching. BUFFER represents the distance from the ship that a new missile is created (so that the missile isn't created on top of the ship). VELOCITY_FACTOR affects how fast the missile travels. Finally, LIFETIME represents how long the missile exists before it disappears (so that a missile won't float around the screen forever).

The __init__() Method

I start the class constructor with the following lines:

```
def __init__(self, ship_x, ship_y, ship_angle):
    """ Initialize missile sprite. """
```

It may surprise you that the constructor for a missile requires values for the ship's x- and y-coordinates and the ship's angle, which are accepted into the ship_x, ship_y, and ship_angle parameters. The method needs these values so that it can determine two things: exactly where the missile first appears and its velocity components. Where the missile is created depends upon where the ship is located, and how the missile travels depends upon the angle of the ship.

Next, I play the missile-firing sound effect:

```
        Missile.sound.play()
```

Then, I perform some calculations to figure out the new missile's starting location:

```
        # convert to radians
        angle = ship_angle * math.pi / 180

        # calculate missile's starting position
        buffer_x = Missile.BUFFER * math.sin(angle)
        buffer_y = Missile.BUFFER * -math.cos(angle)
        x = ship_x + buffer_x
        y = ship_y + buffer_y
```

I get the angle of the ship, converted to radians. Then, I calculate the missile's starting x- and y- coordinates, based on the angle of the ship and the Missile.BUFFER. The resulting x and y values place the missile right in front of the ship's cannon.

Next, I calculate the missile's velocity components. I use the same type of calculations as I did in the `Ship` class:

```
# calculate missile's velocity components
dx = Missile.VELOCITY_FACTOR * math.sin(angle)
dy = Missile.VELOCITY_FACTOR * -math.cos(angle)
```

I invoke the `Sprite` constructor for the object:

```
# create the missile
super(Missile, self).__init__(image = Missile.image,
                              x = x, y = y,
                              dx = dx, dy = dy)
```

Finally, I give the `Missile` object a `lifetime` attribute so that the object won't be around forever.

```
self.lifetime = Missile.LIFETIME
```

The update() Method

Next, I write the `update()` method. Here's the first part:

```
def update(self):
    """ Move the missile. """
    # if lifetime is up, destroy the missile
    self.lifetime -= 1
    if self.lifetime == 0:
        self.destroy()
```

This code just counts down the life of the missile. `lifetime` is decremented. When it reaches 0, the `Missile` object destroys itself.

In the second part of `update()`, I include the familiar code to wrap the missile around the screen:

```
# wrap the missile around screen
if self.top > games.screen.height:
    self.bottom = 0

if self.bottom < 0:
    self.top = games.screen.height

if self.left > games.screen.width:
```

```
        self.right = 0

    if self.right < 0:
        self.left = games.screen.width
```

I see that the preceding code is now repeated three different times in my program. I'll defi-nitely be consolidating it later.

CONTROLLING THE MISSILE FIRE RATE

As you saw in the last program, the ship can fire about 50 missiles per second. Even for a player who wants to win, this is a bit much. So in this next version, I put a limit on the missile fire rate.

The Astrocrash05 Program

The Astrocrash05 program limits the missile fire rate by creating a countdown that forces a delay between missile firings. Once the countdown ends, the player is able to fire another missile. Figure 12.12 illustrates the program.

FIGURE 12.12

Now the ship fires missiles at a more reasonable rate.

You can find the code for the program on the companion website (www.courseptr.com/downloads) in the Chapter 12 folder; the file name is astrocrash05.py.

Adding a Ship Class Constant

My first step in forcing a delay between missile firings is to add a class constant to `Ship`:

```
MISSILE_DELAY = 25
```

`MISSILE_DELAY` represents the delay a player must wait between missile firings. I'll use it to reset a countdown that forces the player to wait.

Creating Ship's Constructor Method

Next, I create a constructor method for the class:

```
def __init__(self, x, y):
    """ Initialize ship sprite. """
    super(Ship, self).__init__(image = Ship.image, x = x, y = y)
    self.missile_wait = 0
```

The method accepts values for the x- and y-coordinates of the new ship and passes those off to the superclass of `Ship`, `games.Sprite`. The next line gives the new object an attribute named `missile_wait`. I use `missile_wait` to count down the delay until the player can fire the next missile.

Modifying Ship's update() Method

I add some code to `Ship`'s `update()` method that decrements an object's `missile_wait`, counting it down to 0.

```
# if waiting until the ship can fire next, decrease wait
if self.missile_wait > 0:
    self.missile_wait -= 1
```

Then I change the missile firing code from the last version of the game to the following lines:

```
# fire missile if spacebar pressed and missile wait is over
if games.keyboard.is_pressed(games.K_SPACE) and self.missile_wait == 0:
    new_missile = Missile(self.x, self.y, self.angle)
    games.screen.add(new_missile)
    self.missile_wait = Ship.MISSILE_DELAY
```

Now, when the player presses the spacebar, the countdown must be complete (`missile_wait` must be 0) before the ship will fire a new missile. Once a missile is fired, I reset `missile_wait` to `MISSILE_DELAY` to begin the countdown again.

HANDLING COLLISIONS

So far, the player can move the ship around the field of asteroids and even fire missiles, but none of the objects interact. I change all of that in this next version of the game. When a missile collides with any other object, it destroys that other object and itself. When the ship collides with any other object, it destroys the other object and itself. Asteroids will be passive in this system, since I don't want overlapping asteroids to destroy each other.

The Astrocrash06 Program

The Astrocrash06 program achieves all of the necessary collision detection with the `Sprite` `overlapping_sprites` property. I also have to handle the destruction of asteroids in a special way because, when large- and medium-sized asteroids are destroyed, two new but smaller asteroids are created.

 Because the asteroids are initially generated at random locations, it's possible for one to be created on top of the player's ship, destroying the ship just as the program begins. I can live with this inconvenience for now, but I'll have to solve this issue in the final game.

Figure 12.13 shows the program in action.

You can find the code for the program on the companion website (www.courseptr.com/downloads) in the Chapter 12 folder; the file name is astrocrash06.py.

FIGURE 12.13

The ship's missiles now destroy asteroids, but be careful—asteroids destroy the ship.

Modifying Missile's update() Method

I add the following code to the end of Missile's update() method:

```
# check if missile overlaps any other object
if self.overlapping_sprites:
    for sprite in self.overlapping_sprites:
        sprite.die()
    self.die()
```

If a missile overlaps any other objects, the other objects and the missile all have their die() methods called. die() is a new method I'll be adding to Asteroid, Ship, and Missile.

Adding Missile's die() Method

Missile, like any class in this version of the game, needs a die() method. The method is about as simple as it gets:

```
def die(self):
    """ Destroy the missile. """
    self.destroy()
```

When a Missile object's die() method is invoked, the object destroys itself.

Modifying Ship's update() Method

I add the following code to the end of the Ship's update() method:

```
# check if ship overlaps any other object
if self.overlapping_sprites:
    for sprite in self.overlapping_sprites:
        sprite.die()
    self.die()
```

If the ship overlaps any other objects, the other objects and the ship all have their die() method called. Notice that this exact code also appears in Missile's update() method. Again, when you see duplicate code, you should think about how to consolidate it. In the next version of the game, I'll get rid of this and other redundant code.

Adding Ship's die() Method

This method is the same as Missile's die() method:

```
def die(self):
    """ Destroy ship. """
    self.destroy()
```

When a Ship object's die() method is invoked, the object destroys itself.

Adding an Asteroid Class Constant

I add one class constant to Asteroid:

```
SPAWN = 2
```

SPAWN is the number of new asteroids that an asteroid spawns when it's destroyed.

Adding Asteroid's die() Method

Asteroid's die() method is more involved than the others:

```
def die(self):
    """ Destroy asteroid. """
    # if asteroid isn't small, replace with two smaller asteroids
    if self.size != Asteroid.SMALL:
        for i in range(Asteroid.SPAWN):
            new_asteroid = Asteroid(x = self.x,
                                    y = self.y,
                                    size = self.size - 1)
```

```
        games.screen.add(new_asteroid)
    self.destroy()
```

The wrinkle I add is that the `Asteroid.SPAWN` method has the potential to create new `Asteroid` objects. The method checks to see if the asteroid being destroyed isn't small. If it's not, two new asteroids, one size smaller, are created at the current asteroid's location. Whether or not new asteroids are created, the current asteroid destroys itself and the method ends.

ADDING EXPLOSIONS

In the previous version of the game, the player can destroy asteroids by firing missiles at them, but the destruction feels a bit hollow. So next, I add explosions to the game.

The Astrocrash07 Program

In the Astrocrash07 program, I write a new class for animated explosions based on `games.Animation`. I also do some work behind the scenes, consolidating redundant code. Even though the player won't appreciate these additional changes, they're important nonetheless. Figure 12.14 shows the new program in action.

FIGURE 12.14

All of the destruction in the game is now accompanied by fiery explosions.

You can find the code for the program on the companion website (www.courseptr.com/downloads) in the Chapter 12 folder; the file name is astrocrash07.py.

The Wrapper Class

I start with the behind-the-scenes work. I create a new class, Wrapper, based on games.Sprite.

The update() Method

Wrapper has an update() method that automatically wraps an object around the screen:

```
class Wrapper(games.Sprite):
    """ A sprite that wraps around the screen. """
    def update(self):
        """ Wrap sprite around screen. """
        if self.top > games.screen.height:
            self.bottom = 0

        if self.bottom < 0:
            self.top = games.screen.height

        if self.left > games.screen.width:
            self.right = 0

        if self.right < 0:
            self.left = games.screen.width
```

You've seen this code several times already. It wraps a sprite around the screen. Now, if I base the other classes in the game on Wrapper, its update() method can keep instances of those other classes on the screen—and the code only has to exist in one place!

The die() Method

I finish the class up with a die() method that destroys the object:

```
    def die(self):
        """ Destroy self. """
        self.destroy()
```

The Collider Class

Next, I take on more redundant code. I notice that both Ship and Missile share the same collision handling instructions, so I create a new class, Collider (based on Wrapper), for objects that wrap around the screen and that can collide with other objects.

The update() Method

Here's the update() method that handles collisions:

```
class Collider(Wrapper):
    """ A Wrapper that can collide with another object. """
    def update(self):
        """ Check for overlapping sprites. """
        super(Collider, self).update()

        if self.overlapping_sprites:
            for sprite in self.overlapping_sprites:
                sprite.die()
            self.die()
```

The first thing I do in Collider's update() method is invoke its superclass's update() method (which is Wrapper's update() method) to keep the object on the screen. Then I check for collisions. If the object overlaps any others, I call the die() method for the other objects and then the object's own die() method.

The die() Method

Next, I have a die() method for the class, since all Collider objects will do the same thing when they die—create an explosion and destroy themselves:

```
    def die(self):
        """ Destroy self and leave explosion behind. """
        new_explosion = Explosion(x = self.x, y = self.y)
        games.screen.add(new_explosion)
        self.destroy()
```

In this method, I create an Explosion object. Explosion is a new class whose objects are explosion animations. You'll see the class in its full glory soon.

Modifying the Asteroid Class

I modify Asteroid so that the class is based on Wrapper:

```
class Asteroid(Wrapper):
```

Asteroid now inherits update() from Wrapper, so I cut Asteroid's own update() method. The redundant code is starting to disappear!

The only other thing I do in this class is change the last line of Asteroid's die() method. I replace self.die() with the line

```
super(Asteroid, self).die()
```

Now, if I ever change Wrapper's die() method, Asteroid will automatically reap the benefits.

Modifying the Ship Class

I modify Ship so that the class is based on Collider:

```
class Ship(Collider):
```

In Ship's update() method, I add the line

```
super(Ship, self).update()
```

I can now cut several more pieces of redundant code. Since Collider's update() method handles collisions, I cut the collision detection code from Ship's update() method. Since Collider's update() method invokes Wrapper's update() method, I cut the screen wrapping code from Ship's update() method, too. I also cut Ship's die() method, as the class inherits Collider's version.

Modifying the Missile Class

In modifying the Missile class, I change its class header so that the class is based on Collider:

```
class Missile(Collider):
```

In Missile's update() method, I add the line

```
super(Missile, self).update()
```

Just as with Ship, I can now cut redundant code from Missile. Since Collider's update() method handles collisions, I cut the collision detection code from Missile's update() method. Since Collider's update() method invokes Wrapper's update() method, I cut the screen wrapping code from Missile's update() method, too. I also cut Missile's die() method, as the class inherits Collider's version.

 To help you understand the changes I describe, feel free to check out the complete code for all versions of Astrocrash on the book's companion website, www.courseptr.com/downloads.

The Explosion Class

Since I want to create animated explosions, I write an Explosion class based on games.Animation.

```
class Explosion(games.Animation):
    """ Explosion animation. """
    sound = games.load_sound("explosion.wav")
    images = ["explosion1.bmp",
              "explosion2.bmp",
              "explosion3.bmp",
              "explosion4.bmp",
              "explosion5.bmp",
              "explosion6.bmp",
              "explosion7.bmp",
              "explosion8.bmp",
              "explosion9.bmp"]
```

I define the class variable, sound, for the sound effect of an explosion. I define a class variable, images, for the list of image file names for the nine frames of the explosion animation.

Next, I write the Explosion constructor.

```
    def __init__(self, x, y):
        super(Explosion, self).__init__(images = Explosion.images,
                                        x = x, y = y,
                                        repeat_interval = 4, n_repeats = 1,
                                        is_collideable = False)
        Explosion.sound.play()
```

In the Explosion constructor, I accept values into the x and y parameters, which represent the screen coordinates for the explosion. When I invoke a superclass constructor (the games.Animation constructor), I pass these values to x and y so that the animation is created right where I want it. To the superclass constructor, I also pass images the list of image file names, Explosion.images. I pass to n_repeats the value 1 so that the animation plays just once. I pass to repeat_interval the value 4 so that the speed of the animation looks right. I pass is_collideable the value False so that the explosion animation doesn't count as a collision for other sprites that might happen to overlap it.

Finally, I play the explosion sound effect with Explosion.sound.play().

TRICK   Remember, you can pass the `games.Animation` constructor either a list of file names or a list of image objects for the frames of animation.

ADDING LEVELS, SCOREKEEPING, AND THEME MUSIC

The game needs just a few more things to feel complete. For my final pass, I add levels—meaning that when a player destroys all of the asteroids on the screen, a new, more plentiful batch appears. I also add scorekeeping functionality and tense theme music to round out the game experience.

The Astrocrash08 Program

In addition to levels, scorekeeping, and theme music, I add some code that may be less obvious to the player but is still important to complete the program. Figure 12.15 shows off my final version of the game.

FIGURE 12.15

The final touches let the game continue as long as the player's Astrocrash skills allow.

You can find the code for the program on the companion website (www.courseptr.com/downloads) in the Chapter 12 folder; the file name is astrocrash08.py.

Importing the color Module

The first addition is simple enough. Along with `games`, I import `color` from `livewires`:

```
from livewires import games, color
```

I need the `color` module so that the "Game Over" message can be displayed in a nice, bright red color.

The Game Class

Toward the end of the program, I add the `Game` class—a new class for an object that represents the game itself. Now, creating an object to represent the game may seem like an odd idea at first, but it makes sense the more you think about it. The game itself could certainly be an object with methods like `play()` to start the game, `advance()` to move the game to the next level, and `end()` to end the game.

The design decision to represent the game as an object makes it easy for other objects to send the game messages. For example, as the last remaining asteroid in a level is destroyed, the asteroid could send the game a message to advance to the next level. Or, just as the ship is destroyed, it could send the game a message to end.

As I go through the class, you'll notice that much of the code that was in `main()` has been incorporated into `Game`.

The __init__() Method

The first thing I do in the `Game` class is define a constructor:

```
class Game(object):
    """ The game itself. """
    def __init__(self):
        """ Initialize Game object. """
        # set level
        self.level = 0

        # load sound for level advance
        self.sound = games.load_sound("level.wav")

        # create score
        self.score = games.Text(value = 0,
                                size = 30,
                                color = color.white,
                                top = 5,
```

```
                               right = games.screen.width - 10,
                               is_collideable = False)
        games.screen.add(self.score)

        # create player's ship
        self.ship = Ship(game = self,
                         x = games.screen.width/2,
                         y = games.screen.height/2)
        games.screen.add(self.ship)
```

level is an attribute for the current game level number. sound is an attribute for the level-advance sound effect. score is an attribute for the game score—it's a Text object that appears in the upper-right corner of the screen. The object's is_collideable property is False, which means that the score won't register in any collisions—so the player's ship won't "crash into" the score and explode! Finally, ship is an attribute for the player's ship.

The play() Method

Next, I define the play() method, which starts up the game.

```
    def play(self):
        """ Play the game. """
        # begin theme music
        games.music.load("theme.mid")
        games.music.play(-1)

        # load and set background
        nebula_image = games.load_image("nebula.jpg")
        games.screen.background = nebula_image

        # advance to level 1
        self.advance()

        # start play
        games.screen.mainloop()
```

The method loads the theme music and plays it so that it will loop forever. It loads the nebula image and sets it as the background. Then the method calls the Game object's own advance() method, which advances the game to the next level. (You'll see what the advance() method is all about next.) Finally, play() invokes games.screen.mainloop() to kick off the whole game!

The advance() Method

The advance() method advances the game to the next level. It increments the level number, creates a new wave of asteroids, displays the level number briefly on the screen, and plays the level-advance sound.

The first thing I do in the method is simple enough—I increase the level number:

```
def advance(self):
    """ Advance to the next game level. """
    self.level += 1
```

The meat of the method is next: creating the new wave of asteroids. Each level starts with the number of asteroids equal to the level number. So, the first level starts with only one asteroid, the second with two, and so on. Now, creating a bunch of asteroids is easy, but I need to make sure that no new asteroid is created right on top of the ship. Otherwise, the ship will explode just as the new level begins.

```
# amount of space around ship to preserve when creating asteroids
BUFFER = 150

# create new asteroids
for i in range(self.level):
    # calculate an x and y at least BUFFER distance from the ship

    # choose minimum distance along x-axis and y-axis
    x_min = random.randrange(BUFFER)
    y_min = BUFFER - x_min

    # choose distance along x-axis and y-axis based on minimum distance
    x_distance = random.randrange(x_min, games.screen.width - x_min)
    y_distance = random.randrange(y_min, games.screen.height - y_min)

    # calculate location based on distance
    x = self.ship.x + x_distance
    y = self.ship.y + y_distance

    # wrap around screen, if necessary
    x %= games.screen.width
    y %= games.screen.height
```

```
# create the asteroid
new_asteroid = Asteroid(game = self,
                        x = x, y = y,
                        size = Asteroid.LARGE)
games.screen.add(new_asteroid)
```

BUFFER is a constant for the amount of safe space I want around the ship.

Next, I start a loop. In each iteration, I create one new asteroid at a safe distance from the ship.

x_min is the minimum distance the new asteroid should be from the ship along the x-axis, while y_min is the minimum distance that the new asteroid should be from the ship along the y-axis. I add variation by using the random module, but x_min and y_min will always total BUFFER.

x_distance is the distance from the ship for the new asteroid along the x-axis. It is a randomly selected number that ensures that the new asteroid will be at least x_min distance from the ship. y_distance is the distance from the ship for the new asteroid along the y-axis. It is a randomly selected number that ensures that the new asteroid will be at least y_min distance from the ship.

x is the x-coordinate for the new asteroid. I calculate it by adding the value of the x-coordinate of the ship to x_distance. Then I make sure x won't put the asteroid off the screen by "wrapping it around" the screen with the modulus operator. y is the y-coordinate for the new asteroid. I calculate it by adding the value of the y-coordinate of the ship to y_distance. Next, I make sure y won't put the asteroid off the screen by "wrapping it around" the screen with the modulus operator. Then, I use x and y to create the brand-new asteroid.

Notice that there's a new parameter in the Asteroid constructor, game. Remember, since each asteroid needs to be able to call a method of the Game object, each Asteroid object needs a reference to the Game object. So, I pass self to the parameter game, which the Asteroid constructor will use as an attribute for the game.

The last thing I do in advance() is display the new level number and play the level-advance sound:

```
# display level number
level_message = games.Message(value = "Level " + str(self.level),
                              size = 40,
                              color = color.yellow,
                              x = games.screen.width/2,
```

```
                        y = games.screen.width/10,
                        lifetime = 3 * games.screen.fps,
                        is_collideable = False)
        games.screen.add(level_message)

        # play new level sound (except at first level)
        if self.level > 1:
            self.sound.play()
```

The end() Method

The `end()` method displays the message "Game Over" in the middle of the screen in big, red letters for about five seconds. After that, the game ends and the graphics screen closes.

```
def end(self):
    """ End the game. """
    # show 'Game Over' for 5 seconds
    end_message = games.Message(value = "Game Over",
                                size = 90,
                                color = color.red,
                                x = games.screen.width/2,
                                y = games.screen.height/2,
                                lifetime = 5 * games.screen.fps,
                                after_death = games.screen.quit,
                                is_collideable = False)
    games.screen.add(end_message)
```

Adding an Asteroid Class Variable and Constant

I make a few changes in the Asteroid class, related to adding levels and keeping score. I add a class constant, POINTS:

```
POINTS = 30
```

The constant will act as a base value for the number of points an asteroid is worth. The actual point value will be modified according to the size of the asteroid—smaller asteroids will be worth more than larger ones.

In order to change levels, the program needs to know when all of the asteroids on the current level are destroyed. So, I keep track of the total number of asteroids with a new class variable, total, which I define toward the beginning of the class:

```
total = 0
```

Modifying Asteroid's Constructor Method

In the constructor, I add a line to increment `Asteroid.total`:

```
Asteroid.total += 1
```

Now, I want any asteroid to be able to send the `Game` object a message, so I give each `Asteroid` object a reference to the `Game` object. I accept the `Game` object in the `Asteroid` constructor by creating a new parameter:

```
def __init__(self, game, x, y, size):
```

The `game` parameter accepts the `Game` object, which I then use to create an attribute for the new `Asteroid` object:

```
self.game = game
```

So, each new `Asteroid` object has an attribute `game` that is a reference to the game itself. Through `game`, an `Asteroid` object can call a method of the `Game` object, such as `advance()`.

Modifying Asteroid's die() Method

I make a few additions to `Asteroid`'s `die()` method. First, I decrement `Asteroid.total`:

```
Asteroid.total -= 1
```

Next, I increase the score based on `Asteroid.POINTS` and the size of the asteroid (smaller asteroids are worth more than larger ones). I also make sure the score is always flush right, so I reset the `score`'s `right` property to be 10 pixels from the right edge of the screen.

```
self.game.score.value += int(Asteroid.POINTS / self.size)
self.game.score.right = games.screen.width - 10
```

When I create each of the two new asteroids, I need to pass a reference to the `Game` object, which I do by modifying the first line of the call to the `Asteroid` constructor:

```
new_asteroid = Asteroid(game = self.game,
```

Toward the end of `Asteroid`'s `die()` method, I test `Asteroid.total` to see if all the asteroids have been destroyed. If so, the final asteroid invokes the `Game` object's `advance()` method, which advances the game to the next level and creates a new group of asteroids.

```
# if all asteroids are gone, advance to next level
if Asteroid.total == 0:
    self.game.advance()
```

Adding a Ship Class Constant

I make several additions to the Ship class. I create a class constant, VELOCITY_MAX, which I use to limit the maximum velocity of the player's ship:

```
VELOCITY_MAX = 3
```

Modifying Ship's Constructor Method

Like an Asteroid object, a Ship object needs to have access to the Game object so it can invoke a Game object method. Just as I did with Asteroid, I modify the Ship's constructor:

```
def __init__(self, game, x, y):
```

The new parameter, game, accepts the Game object, which I then use to create an attribute for the Ship object:

```
self.game = game
```

So, each Ship object has an attribute game that is a reference to the game itself. Through game, a Ship object can call a method of the Game object, like end().

Modifying Ship's update() Method

In Ship's update() method, I cap the individual velocity components of a Ship object, dx and dy, using the class constant MAX_VELOCITY:

```
# cap velocity in each direction
self.dx = min(max(self.dx, -Ship.VELOCITY_MAX), Ship.VELOCITY_MAX)
self.dy = min(max(self.dy, -Ship.VELOCITY_MAX), Ship.VELOCITY_MAX)
```

The code ensures that dx and dy will never be less than - Ship.VELOCITY_MAX and never greater than Ship.VELOCITY_MAX. I use the min() and max() functions to accomplish this. min() returns the minimum of two numbers, while max() returns the maximum of two numbers. I cap the ship's speed to avoid several potential problems, including the ship running into its own missiles.

Adding Ship's die() Method

When the player's ship is destroyed, the game is over. I add a die() method to Ship that invokes the Game object's end() method to end the game.

```
def die(self):
    """ Destroy ship and end the game. """
    self.game.end()
    super(Ship, self).die()
```

The main() Function

Now that I have a Game class, the main() function becomes quite short. All I do in this function is create a Game object and invoke the object's play() method to put the game in action.

```
def main():
    astrocrash = Game()
    astrocrash.play()

# kick it off!
main()
```

SUMMARY

In this chapter, you extended your knowledge of multimedia programming to include sound, music, and animation. You learned how to load, play, and stop both sound and music files, and you saw how to create animations. You also learned a technique for creating large programs by writing increasingly more complete, working versions of the final product. You saw how to tackle one new objective at a time, building your way to the full program. Finally, you saw all of this new information and these new techniques put to use in the creation of a fast-paced action game with sound effects, animation, and its own musical score.

CHALLENGES

1. Improve the Astrocrash game by creating a new kind of deadly space debris. Give this new type of debris some quality that differentiates it from the asteroids. For example, maybe the debris requires two missile strikes to be destroyed.
2. Write a version of the Simon Says game where a player has to repeat an ever-growing, random sequence of colors and sounds using the keyboard.
3. Write your own version of another classic video game such as Space Invaders or Pac-Man.
4. Create your own programming challenge, but, most importantly, never stop challenging yourself to learn.

APPENDIX A

THE COMPANION WEBSITE

The companion website for this book is available at www.courseptr.com/
downloads. From the website, you can download all of the source code,
supporting files, and software packages described in this text.

THE ARCHIVE FILES

There are two files available for download:

- **py3e_source.zip**—contains the source code and supporting files for every
  complete program presented in this book
- **py3e_software**—contains files for all of the software packages described in
  this book, including the Python 3.1.1 Windows installer

Table A.1 describes the contents of py3e_source.zip while Table A.2 details the
contents of py3e_software.zip.

TABLE A.1 PY3E_SOURCE.ZIP CONTENTS	
Folder Name	**Description**
chapter01	Chapter 1 source code.
chapter02	Chapter 2 source code.
chapter03	Chapter 3 source code.
chapter04	Chapter 4 source code.
chapter05	Chapter 5 source code.
chapter06	Chapter 6 source code.
chapter07	Chapter 7 source code and data files.
chapter08	Chapter 8 source code.
chapter09	Chapter 9 source code.
chapter10	Chapter 10 source code and corresponding Windows batch files.
chapter11	Chapter 11 source code, corresponding Windows batch files, and multimedia files.
chapter12	Chapter 12 source code, corresponding Windows batch files, and multimedia files.

TABLE A.2 PY3E_SOFTWARE.ZIP CONTENTS	
Folder Name	**Description**
python	Python 3.1.1 Windows installer.
pygame	pygame 1.9.1 for Python 3.1.x Windows installer.
livewires	livewires game engine package.

HINT The pygame Windows installer in the py3e_software.zip file is compatible with Python 3.1.x, which means any iteration of Python 3.1 (so Python 3.1.0 through Python 3.1.9).

LIVEWIRES REFERENCE

This appendix includes almost everything you ever wanted to know about the modified version of the livewires package but were afraid to ask. I do leave out some portions for simplicity—if you want the ultimate "documentation," you can always check out the source code of the livewires modules themselves.

THE LIVEWIRES PACKAGE

The livewires package is a set of modules for writing games with graphics, sound, and animation. Table B.1 lists two modules. The livewires package requires the pygame multimedia package.

TABLE B.1	LIVEWIRES MODULES
Module	**Description**
games	Defines functions and classes that make writing games easier.
color	Stores a set of color constants.

GAMES CLASSES

games contains a group of classes and functions for game programming. Table B.2 describes the classes.

	TABLE B.2 GAMES CLASSES
Class	**Description**
Screen	An object of this class represents a graphics screen.
Sprite	An object of this class has an image and can be displayed on a graphics screen.
Text	An object of this class represents text on the graphics screen. Text is a subclass of Sprite.
Message	An object of this class represents a message, which disappears after a set period of time, on the graphics screen. Message is a subclass of Text.
Animation	An object of this class represents a series of images shown in succession on a graphics screen. Animation is a subclass of Sprite.
Mouse	An object of this class provides access to the mouse.
Keyboard	An object of this class provides access to the keyboard.
Music	An object of this class provides access to the music channel.

The Screen Class

A Screen object represents the graphics screen. The games.init() function creates a Screen object, screen, that represents the graphics screen. Generally, you should use screen instead of instantiating your own object from Screen. Table B.3 describes Screen properties, while Table B.4 details Screen methods.

	TABLE B.3 SCREEN PROPERTIES
Property	**Description**
width	Width of screen.
height	Height of screen.
fps	Number of times per second screen is updated.
background	Background image of screen.
all objects	List of all sprites on the screen.
event_grab	Boolean that determines if input is grabbed to screen. True for input grabbed to screen. False for input not grabbed to screen.

TABLE B.4	**SCREEN METHODS**

Method	Description
get_width()	Returns width of screen.
get_height()	Returns height of screen.
get_fps()	Returns the number of times per second screen is updated.
get_background()	Returns the background image of screen.
set_background(*new_background*)	Sets the background image of screen to *new_background*.
get_all_objects()	Returns list of all the sprites on the screen.
get_event_grab()	Returns the status of the input being grabbed to screen. True for input grabbed to screen. False for input not grabbed to screen.
set_event_grab(*new_status*)	Sets the status of input being grabbed to screen to new_status. True for input grabbed to screen. False for input not grabbed to screen.
add(*sprite*)	Adds *sprite*, a Sprite object (or an object of a Sprite subclass), to the graphics screen.
remove(*sprite*)	Removes *sprite*, a Sprite object (or an object of a Sprite subclass), from the graphics screen.
clear()	Removes all sprites from the graphics screen.
mainloop()	Starts the graphics screen's main loop.
quit()	Closes the graphics window.

The Sprite Class

A Sprite object has an image and can be displayed on a graphics screen. Table B.5 describes Sprite properties, while Table B.6 details Sprite methods.

TABLE B.5	**SPRITE PROPERTIES**

Property	Description
image	Image object of sprite.
width	Width of sprite image.
height	Height of sprite image.
angle	Facing in degrees.
x	x-coordinate.
y	y-coordinate.

position	Position of sprite. A two-element tuple that contains the x-coordinate and the y-coordinate of the object.
top	y-coordinate of top sprite edge.
bottom	y-coordinate of bottom sprite edge.
left	x-coordinate of left sprite edge.
right	x-coordinate of right sprite edge.
dx	x velocity.
dy	y velocity.
velocity	Velocity of sprite. A two-element tuple that contains the x velocity and the y velocity of the object.
overlapping_sprites	List of other objects that overlap sprite.
is_collideable	Whether or not sprite is collideable. True means sprite will register in collisions. False means sprite will not show up in collisions.
interval	Determines the object's tick() interval.

TABLE B.6   SPRITE METHODS

Method	Description
__init__(*image* [, *angle*] [, *x*] [, *y*] [, *top*] [, *bottom*] [, *left*] [, *right*] [, *dx*] [, *dy*] [, *interval*] [, *is_collideable*])	Initializes new sprite. *image* has no default value, so one must be passed to it. *angle, x, y, dx,* and *dy* all have the default value of 0. *top, bottom, left,* and *right* have the default value of None. If no value is passed to these parameters, the corresponding properties are not assigned a value upon initialization. *interval* has a default value of 1. *is_collideable* has a default value of True.
get_image()	Returns the sprite's image object.
set_image(*new_image*)	Sets the sprite's image object to *new_image*.
get_height()	Returns the height of the sprite's image.
get_width()	Returns the width of the sprite's image.
get_angle()	Returns the sprite's current angle in degrees.
set_angle(*new_angle*)	Sets the sprite's angle to *new_angle*.
get_x()	Returns sprite's x-coordinate.
set_x(*new_x*)	Sets sprite's x-coordinate to *new_x*.
get_y()	Returns the object's y-coordinate.
set_y(*new_y*)	Sets sprite's y-coordinate to *new_y*.
get_position()	Returns the sprite's x- and y-coordinates as a two-element tuple.

set_position(***new_position***)	Sets the sprite's x- and y-coordinates to the two-element tuple ***new_position***.
get_top()	Returns the y-coordinate of the sprite's top edge.
set_top(***new_top***)	Sets the y-coordinate of sprite's top edge to ***new_top***.
get_bottom()	Returns the y-coordinate of the sprite's bottom edge.
set_bottom(***new_bottom***)	Sets the y-coordinate of sprite's bottom edge to ***new_bottom***.
get_left()	Returns the x-coordinate of the object's left edge.
set_left(***new_left***)	Sets the x-coordinate of sprite's left edge to ***new_left***.
get_right()	Returns the x-coordinate of the object's right edge.
set_right(***new_right***)	Sets the x-coordinate of sprite's right edge to ***new_right***.
get_dx()	Returns the sprite's x velocity.
set_dx(***new_dx***)	Sets the sprite's x velocity to ***new_dx***.
get_dy()	Returns the sprite's y velocity.
set_dy(***new_dy***)	Sets the sprite's y velocity to ***new_dy***.
get_velocity()	Returns the sprite's x velocity and the y velocity as a two-element tuple.
set_velocity(***new_velocity***)	Sets the sprite's x velocity and the y velocity to the two-element tuple ***new_velocity***.
get_overlapping_sprites()	Returns a list of all collideable sprites that overlap with the object.
overlaps(***other***)	Returns True if object overlaps with ***other*** and False otherwise. Returns False if either object's is_collideable attribute is False.
get_is_collideable()	Returns the status of whether or not sprite is collideable. True means sprite registers in collisions. False means sprite does not show up in collisions.
set_is_collideable(***new_status***)	Sets the status of whether or not sprite is collideable to ***new_status***. True means sprite registers in collisions. False means sprite does not show up in collisions.
get_interval()	Returns the sprite's tick() interval.
set_interval(***new_interval***)	Sets the sprite's tick() interval to ***new_interval***.
update()	Updates sprite. Does nothing by default. Automatically called every mainloop() cycle. You might override this method in a subclass of Sprite.
tick()	Executes every interval mainloop() cycles. It does nothing by default. You might override this method in a subclass of Sprite.
destroy()	Removes sprite from the screen.

The Text Class

Text is a subclass of Sprite. A Text object represents text on the graphics screen. Text of course inherits Sprite's attributes, properties, and methods. Table B.7 describes additional Text properties, while Table B.8 details additional Text methods.

TABLE B.7	TEXT PROPERTIES
Property	**Description**
value	Value displayed as text.
size	Size of text.
color	Color of text. Can be set with a value from color module.

The Text class uses *text*, *size*, and *color* to create an image object that represents the text that is displayed.

TABLE B.8	TEXT METHODS

Method	Description
__init__(*value, size, color* [, *angle*] [, *x*] [, *y*] [, *top*] [, *bottom*] [, *left*] [, *right*] [, *dx*] [, *dy*] [, *interval*] [, *is_collideable*])	Initializes new object. *value* is the value to be displayed as text. *size* is the size of the text. *color* is the color of the text. *angle*, *x*, *y*, *dx*, and *dy* all have the default value of 0. *top*, *bottom*, *left*, and *right* have the default value of None. If no value is passed to these parameters, the corresponding properties are not assigned a value upon initialization. *interval* has a default value of 1. *is_collideable* has a default value of True.
get_value()	Returns the value displayed as text.
set_value(*new_value*)	Sets the value displayed as text to *new_value*.
get_size()	Returns the size of the text.
set_size(*new_size*)	Sets the size of the text to *new_size*.
get_color()	Returns the color of the text.
set_color(*new_color*)	Sets the color of the text to *new_color*. Can be set with a value from color module.

The Message Class

Message is a subclass of Text. A Message object represents a message on the graphics screen that disappears after a set period of time. A Message object can also specify an event to occur after it disappears.

Message inherits Text's attributes, properties, and methods. A Message object, however, has a new attribute, *after_death*—code to be executed after the object disappears, such as a function or method name. The default value is None.

Message defines a new __init__() method: __init__(*value, size, color* [, *angle*] [, *x*] [, *y*] [, *top*] [, *bottom*] [, *left*] [, *right*] [, *dx*] [, *dy*] [, *lifetime*] [, *is_collideable*] [, *after_death*]). The method initializes a new object. *value* is the value to be displayed as text. *size* is the size of the text. *color* is the color of the text. *angle*, *x*, *y*, *dx*, and *dy* all have the default value of 0. *top*, *bottom*, *left*, and *right* have the default value of None. If no value is passed to these parameters, the corresponding properties are not assigned a value upon initialization. *lifetime* represents how long the message appears on the screen in mainloop() cycles before it destroys itself. If it is given a value of 0, then the object is not set to destroy itself. *lifetime* has a default value of 0. *is_collideable* has a default value of True. *after_death* has a default value of None.

 The value of the *lifetime* parameter is simply assigned to the Message object's *interval* property. A Message object has no *lifetime* attribute or property.

The Animation Class

The Animation class is a subclass of Sprite. An Animation object represents a series of images shown in succession. Animation inherits Sprite's attributes, properties, and methods. Animation defines additional attributes, described in Table B.9.

TABLE B.9	ANIMATION ATTRIBUTES
Attribute	**Description**
images	List of image objects.
n_repeats	Number of times the complete animation cycle should repeat. A value of 0 means repeat forever. The default value is 0.

`Animation` defines a new __init__() method: __init__(*images* [, *angle*] [, *x*] [, *y*] [, *top*] [, *bottom*] [, *left*] [, *right*] [, *dx*] [, *dy*] [, *repeat_interval*] [, *n_repeats*] [, *is_collideable*]). The method initializes a new object. *images* can be passed either image objects or file names as strings from which to create image objects. *angle*, *x*, *y*, *dx*, and *dy* all have the default value of 0. *top*, *bottom*, *left*, and *right* have the default value of None. If no value is passed to these parameters, the corresponding properties are not assigned a value upon initialization. *repeat_interval* determines the object's tick() interval and therefore the speed of the animation. The default value is 1. *n_repeats* has a default value of 0. *is_collideable* has a default value of True.

HINT The value of the *repeat_interval* parameter is simply assigned to the Animation object's *interval* property. An Animation object has no *repeat_interval* attribute or property.

The Mouse Class

A Mouse object provides access to the mouse. The games.init() function creates a Mouse object, mouse, for use in reading the mouse position and testing for button presses. Generally, you should use mouse instead of instantiating your own object from Mouse. Table B.10 describes Mouse properties, while Table B.11 details Mouse methods.

TABLE B.10 MOUSE PROPERTIES

Property	Description
x	x-coordinate of mouse pointer.
y	y-coordinate of mouse pointer.
position	Position of the mouse pointer. A two-element tuple that contains the x-coordinate and the y-coordinate of mouse pointer.
is_visible	Boolean value for visibility of mouse pointer. True is visible, while False is not visible. Default value is True.

TABLE B.11 MOUSE METHODS

Method	Description
get_x()	Returns the x-coordinate of mouse pointer.
set_x(*new_x*)	Sets the x-coordinate of the mouse pointer to *new_x*.
get_y()	Returns the y-coordinate of mouse pointer.

set_y(*new_y*)	Sets the x-coordinate of the mouse pointer to *new_y*.
get_position()	Returns the mouse pointer's x- and y-coordinates as a two-element tuple.
set_position(*new_position*)	Sets the mouse pointer's x- and y-coordinates to the two-element tuple *new_position*.
set_is_visible(*new_visibility*)	Sets the visibility of the mouse pointer. If *new_visibility* is True, pointer is visible; if *new_visibility* is False, the pointer is not visible.
is_pressed(*button_number*)	Tests for a button press. Returns True if mouse button button_number is pressed; otherwise, returns False.

The Keyboard Class

A Keyboard object provides access to the keyboard. The games.init() function creates a Keyboard object, keyboard, for use in testing for keypresses. Generally, you should use keyboard instead of instantiating your own object from Keyboard.

The class has a single method, is_pressed(*key*), which returns True if the key being tested for, *key*, is pressed, and False, if not. The games module defines constants that represent keys that you can use as an argument for this method. The constants are listed in this appendix, in the section "games Constants."

The Music Class

A Music object provides access to the single music channel, allowing you to load, play, and stop a music file. Generally, you should use music instead of instantiating your own object from Music.

The music channel accepts many different types of files, including WAV, MP3, OGG, and MIDI. Table B.12 lists Music's methods.

TABLE B.12 MUSIC METHODS

Method	Description
load(*filename*)	Loads the file *filename* into the music channel, replacing any currently loaded music file.
play([*loop*])	Plays the music loaded in the music channel *loop* number of times in addition to its initial playing. A value of -1 means loop forever. The default value of *loop* is 0.
fadeout(*millisec*)	Fades out the currently playing music in *millisec* milliseconds.
stop()	Stops the music playing on the music channel.

GAMES FUNCTIONS

The games module defines functions for working with images and sound. They are described in Table B.13.

TABLE B.13	GAMES FUNCTIONS
Function	**Description**
init([*screen_width*,] [*screen_height*,] [*fps*])	Initializes the graphics screen with width *screen_width*, height *screen_height* that updates itself *fps* times per second. Creates the object screen from games.Screen, which provides access to the game screen. Creates the object mouse from games.Mouse, which provides access to the player's mouse. Creates the object keyboard from games.Keyboard, which provides access to the player's keyboard. Creates music from games.Music, which provides access to the single music channel.
load_image(*filename* [, *transparent*])	Returns an image object loaded from the file named in the string *filename* and sets transparency if *transparent* is True. The default value of *transparent* is True.
scale_image(*image*, *x_scale* [, *y_scale*])	Returns a new image object scaled in the x direction by a factor of *x_scale* and in the y direction by a factor of *y_scale*. If no value is passed to *y_scale*, then the image is scaled by a factor of *x_scale* in both directions. The original image *image* is unchanged.
load_sound(*filename*)	Returns a sound object from a WAV file named in the string *filename*.

The sound object returned by load_sound() has several methods available to it, which are listed in Table B.14.

TABLE B.14   SOUND OBJECT METHODS

Method	Description
play([*loop*])	Plays the sound *loop* number of times in addition to its initial playing. A value of -1 means loop forever. The default value of *loop* is 0.
fadeout(*millisec*)	Fades out the sound in *millisec* milliseconds.
stop()	Stops the sound on all channels.

GAMES CONSTANTS

The games module defines a list of constants for keyboard keys. The complete list is in Table B.15.

TABLE B.15   GAMES KEY CONSTANTS

Constant	Key	Constant	Key
K_BACKSPACE	Backspace	K_2	2
K_TAB	Tab	K_3	3
K_RETURN	Return	K_4	4
K_PAUSE	Pause	K_5	5
K_ESCAPE	Escape	K_6	6
K_SPACE	Spacebar	K_7	7
K_EXCLAIM	Exclamation Point	K_8	8
K_QUOTEDBL	Double Quote	K_9	9
K_HASH	Hash Mark	K_COLON	Colon
K_DOLLAR	Dollar Sign	K_SEMICOLON	Semicolon
K_AMPERSAND	Ampersand	K_LESS	Less-than Sign
K_QUOTE	Single Quote	K_EQUALS	Equals Sign
K_LEFTPAREN	Left Parenthesis	K_GREATER	Greater-than Sign
K_RIGHTPAREN	Right Parenthesis	K_QUESTION	Question Mark
K_ASTERISK	Asterisk	K_AT	At Symbol
K_PLUS	Plus Sign	K_LEFTBRACKET	Left Bracket
K_COMMA	Comma	K_BACKSLASH	Backslash
K_MINUS	Minus Sign	K_RIGHTBRACKET	Right Bracket
K_PERIOD	Period	K_CARET	Caret
K_SLASH	Forward Slash	K_UNDERSCORE	Underscore
K_0	0	K_a	A
K_1	I	K_b	B

K_c	C	K_KP_PLUS	Keypad Plus
K_d	D	K_KP_ENTER	Keypad Enter
K_e	E	K_KP_EQUALS	Keypad Equals
K_f	F	K_UP	Up Arrow
K_g	G	K_DOWN	Down Arrow
K_h	H	K_RIGHT	Right Arrow
K_i	I	K_LEFT	Left Arrow
K_j	J	K_INSERT	Insert
K_k	K	K_HOME	Home
K_l	L	K_END	End
K_m	M	K_PAGEUP	Page Up
K_n	N	K_PAGEDOWN	Page Down
K_o	O	K_F1	F1
K_p	P	K_F2	F2
K_q	Q	K_F3	F3
K_r	R	K_F4	F4
K_s	S	K_F5	F5
K_t	T	K_F6	F6
K_u	U	K_F7	F7
K_v	V	K_F8	F8
K_w	W	K_F9	F9
K_x	X	K_F10	F10
K_y	Y	K_F11	F11
K_z	Z	K_F12	F12
K_DELETE	Delete	K_NUMLOCK	Num Lock
K_KP0	Keypad 0	K_CAPSLOCK	Caps Lock
K_KP1	Keypad 1	K_SCROLLOCK	Scroll Lock
K_KP2	Keypad 2	K_RSHIFT	Right Shift
K_KP3	Keypad 3	K_LSHIFT	Left Shift
K_KP4	Keypad 4	K_RCTRL	Right Ctrl
K_KP5	Keypad 5	K_LCTRL	Left Ctrl
K_KP6	Keypad 6	K_RALT	Right Alt
K_KP7	Keypad 7	K_LALT	Left Alt
K_KP8	Keypad 8	K_LSUPER	Left Windows
K_KP9	Keypad 9	K_RSUPER	Right Windows
K_KP_PERIOD	Keypad Period	K_HELP	Help
K_KP_DIVIDE	Keypad Divide	K_PRINT	Print Screen
K_KP_MULTIPLY	Keypad Multiply	K_BREAK	Break
K_KP_MINUS	Keypad Minus		

color Module Constants

The color module provides some constants that you can use anywhere the games module wants a color. The constants are as follows:

- red
- green
- blue
- black
- white
- dark_red
- dark_green
- dark_blue
- dark_gray
- gray
- light_gray
- yellow
- brown
- pink
- purple

INDEX

Note: Page number followed by a "t" or "f" indicate that the entry is included in a table or figure.

SPECIAL CHARACTERS

A